Advance Praise for

Transforming Identities:
How an EdD Program Develops Practitioners into Scholar-Practitioners

A distinguishing factor for the Education Doctorate is the development of a scholarly prac-titioner. Transforming Identities: How an EdD Program Develops Practitioners into Scholar-Practitioners *illustrates the transformational evolution of professionals shifting from an expert practitioner to a scholar-practitioner through engagement in an innovative EdD online program. The authors have carefully crafted an overview of this program, high-lighting the intentional critical reflection experiences that led to an identity transformation for the professionals earning this EdD. The powerful stories of recent graduates serve as a reflection of how this EdD program shaped their professional identities as scholarly practi-tioners leading impact in their professional practice.*

—Dr. Sandi Cooper, Professor, Baylor University,
Founding Director, EdD in Learning and Organizational Change,
(CPED Program of the Year, 2022)

FINALLY! . . . A book on practitioner scholarship that showcases the real experts on the subject—scholar-practitioners themselves! The fourteen beautifully written self-told stories of identity transformation provided by EdD graduates in Transforming Identities: How an EdD Program Develops Practitioners into Scholar-Practitioners *are sure to inspire, enrich and encourage current EdD students on their own transformational journeys. A thought-provoking text for all involved in any capacity with an EdD program that is sure to stimulate lively discussion on what it means to be a scholar-practitioner.*

—Nancy Fichtman Dana, Professor and Distinguished
Teaching Scholar, University of Florida

This book represents a beautiful journey into and through the CPED-affiliated EdD program at Johns Hopkins University. The faculty authors describe how the program's components are intentionally woven together in a tapestry that gently but securely supports each student's journey from "experienced practitioner-aspiring scholar" to "scholar practitioner." But it is the alumni and their very personal and powerful stories of identity development who give the tapestry its bold colors and rich textures and invite us all to embrace the change that they have become. This book is a must-read for anyone interested in what the EdD is meant to be.

—Deanna Hill, PhD, JD., EdD Program Director, Drexel University

For institutions committed to advancing knowledge while simultaneously addressing complex, community-based dilemmas, the education doctorate is perhaps one of our strongest leverage points. Transforming Identities: How an EdD Program Develops Practitioners into Scholar-Practitioners *reminds us of the primacy of the evolution of the EdD candidate in this work. By foregrounding identity construction, Pape, Bryant, JohnBull, and Karp have illustrated for us all a salient way of building, analyzing, and refining our EdD programs while simultaneously serving as a model for how we center those we serve in our collective work.*

—Thomas E. Hodges, Dean and Professor,
College of Education, University of South Carolina

Already a world-renowned research university, Johns Hopkins University is home to a relatively recent addition to its advanced graduate degree offerings. Established in 2012, Johns Hopkins University's online EdD Program in Education seeks to address complex problems that education-practitioners face by preparing them to think critically about these problems and use research to develop meaningful, practical, and sustainable solutions within their educational institutions. The editors and contributing authors of Transforming Identities: How an EdD Program Develops Practitioners into Scholar-Practitioners *skillfully tell the story of their EdD program's development, its structure, and how graduates seek to keep research off the shelf. This edited volume highlights the potential of a thoughtfully structured EdD program, guided by an improvement science framework and CPED design principles, for generating meaningful research and facilitating the development of scholar-practitioners who will continue to affect change in educational organizations in the US and abroad.*

—W. Kyle Ingle, Professor, University of Louisville

Having navigated through the JHU EdD program personally, I find this book to be authentic! Many of the stories by fellow students resonate with me as I entered the JHU program as a business leader of 32 years at a fortune 500 company—wanting to make the transformation to higher education leadership. This book clearly illustrates the growth model I went through from an "Experienced Practitioner—Aspiring Scholar" as a pre-doctoral student to a "Scholar-Practitioner" post-graduation. A must read to get a glimpse of the journey and the transformation!

—John Porter, EdD, President, Lindenwood University

There was a time when an EdD program looked pretty much the same as a PhD, with both culminating in dissertations that would have been hard to accurately sort into one category or the other. Each might have been focused on a problem of practice, but not in any practical way, an approach that compromised both the PhD and the EdD. Then came the Carnegie Project on the Education Doctorate. As a representative of one of the founding institutions to redesign doctoral preparation for professional practitioners, I'm excited to see the work that has come from this initiative. As this book demonstrates, the field has grown from interesting, but professionally disconnected, doctoral research to projects that move practice forward while enriching and expanding the professional capabilities and perspectives of those who enter these programs. While we have evidence of the usefulness of the outcomes of dissertations in practice (sometimes called capstones, and at JHU Applied Dissertations), there has been much less documentation about how these programs grow the student in addition to the field. The transformations of the JHU students, now graduates, in their own words are inspiring, as is the program that they undertook. This publication is both a guidebook and a motivator for higher education.

—Dr. Charol Shakeshaft, Professor, Virginia Commonwealth University

Transforming Identities

Dr. Jill Alexa Perry

The mission of The Coming of Age of the Education Doctorate series is to present volumes of research and work focused on the improvement of the Education Doctorate (EdD) and, over the course of the past 14 years, that faculty and schools of education around the US and the world have made to professionalize this degree for the advanced preparation of educational practitioners. Specifically, this series will highlight efforts to improve the purpose, curriculum, and milestone experiences of the degree, in addition to highlighting the work of those who have graduated from redesigned EdD programs. The series will consist of print books, e-books, and fractional digital content for faculty, pre-service teachers, practitioners, and libraries.

Upcoming Titles in the Series

Challenges in (Re)designing EdD Programs: Supporting Change with Learning Cases
edited by Jill A. Perry (pub. 2023)
Reclaiming the Education Doctorate: A Guidebook for Preparing Scholarly Practitioners
by Jill A. Perry (2023)
Teaching Critical Inquiry and Applied Research in Ed.D. Programs:
Moving beyond Traditional Methods
by Christopher Benedetti and Amanda Covarrubias (2023)
Transforming Identities: How EdD Programs Develop Practitioners into Scholar-Practitioners
Edited By Stephen J. Pape, Camille L. Bryant, Ranjini Mahinda JohnBull,
and Karen S. Karp (2023)
Innovation and Impact: The Origins and Elements of Ed.D. Program Excellence
Edited by W. Kyle Ingle and Harriette Thurber Rasmussen (2024)
The IMPACT of the Scholarly Practitioner Doctorate:
Exercising Socially Just Leadership and Making Equitable Change
Edited by Stephanie Smith Budhai and Deanna Hill (2024)
The Importance of the Dissertation in Practice (DiP):
A Resource Guide for EdD Students, Their Committee Members and Advisors,
and Departmental and University Leaders Involved with EdD Programs
by Kimberlee Everson, Kelly M. Torres, Lynn Hemmer, Suha Tamim (2024)
The Disquisition: An Equity-Driven Capstone for Leadership Preparation Programs
(Working title)
by Jess Weiler and Emily Virtue (2024)
Social Justice Praxis in Ed.D Programs
by Ignacio Hernández and Alexia Theresa Pimentel (2024)

Dr. Jill Alexa Perry is the Executive Director of the Carnegie Project on the Educational Doctorate (CPED) and an Associate Professor of Practice in the Educational Foundations, Organizations and Policy at the University of Pittsburgh. Her research focuses on professional doctorate preparation in education, organizational change in higher education, and faculty leadership roles. Currently she is researching the ways EdD programs teach practitioners to utilize research evidence. She teaches and coaches how to teach Improvement Science in EdD programs. Her books include *The Improvement Science Dissertation in Practice, The EdD and the Scholarly Practitioner,* and *In Their Own Words: A Journey to the Stewardship of the Practice in Education.* Dr. Perry is a graduate of the University of Maryland, where she received her PhD in International Education Policy. She holds an MA in Higher Education Administration and a BA in Spanish and International Studies from Boston College. She has more than 25 years of experience in leadership and program development in education and teaching experience at the elementary, secondary, undergraduate, and graduate levels in the US and abroad. She is a Fulbright Scholar (Germany) and a returned Peace Corps Volunteer (Paraguay).

Transforming Identities

How an EdD Program Develops Practitioners
into Scholar-Practitioners

EDITED BY *Stephen J. Pape, Camille L. Bryant,*
Ranjini Mahinda Johnbull,
and Karen S. Karp

Gorham, Maine

Myers
Education
Press

WE DEDICATE THIS book to all our courageous doctoral scholar-practitioners who took on this journey of identity transformation to improve education for others. Their work benefits so many as they spread their expertise and enact changes within their professional organizations. We especially appreciate the 14 authors in this volume who took the next step to unpack their experiences with us. Many of you indicated that this was a cathartic experience, and we are grateful for your reflection on your experience, your willingness to open your lives to inform others of the potential of a doctoral journey, and the courage with which you told your stories. Thank you for your words in this volume. Your stories are enlightening and informative for students and faculty as they improve their programs!

Contents

Jill Alexa Perry

THE MISSION OF *The Coming of Age of the Education Doctorate* series is to present volumes of research and work focused on the redesign of the Education Doctorate (EdD). I created the book series to showcase the past 16 years of efforts that faculty from schools of education around the United States and the world have undertaken to professionalize this degree for the advanced preparation of educational practitioners. Specifically, this series will highlight efforts to enhance and enrich the purpose, curriculum, and milestone experiences in the EdD in addition to spotlighting the work of those who have graduated from (re)designed EdD programs. I chose this volume, *Transforming Identities: From Practitioner to Scholar-Practitioner*, to be a part of the series because it uniquely centralizes the experiences of EdD graduates. Through firsthand accounts, the authors offer the reader stories of how one EdD program has shaped the identities of highly qualified professionals to become a scholarly practitioner. This offering is of particular use to doctoral candidates who have much to learn from the stories of these alumni.

As the Executive Director of Carnegie Project on the Education Doctorate (CPED), I have worked alongside my faculty colleagues to distinguish the intricacies of doctoral learning opportunities in professional education. This work has taken me down roads of curriculum development, traditional and alternative dissertation designs, assessment and experiential learning activities, and more. Much of this work has been shaped by the CPED definition of the scholarly practitioner, or one who:

- blends practical wisdom with professional skills and knowledge to name, frame, and solve problems of practice;
- uses practical research and applied theories as tools for change;

- understands the importance of equity and social justice;
- disseminates their work in multiple ways; and
- resolves problems of practice by collaborating with key stakeholders, including the university, the educational institution, the community, and individuals (CPED, 2010)

Yet, despite the numerous discussions of how these program components contribute to the development of a scholarly practitioner, little has been discussed about the identity of a scholarly practitioner or how one transforms into that identity because of their program experiences. This book does just that.

The lead authors of this book, who are faculty of the Johns Hopkins University (JHU) EdD program, are exceptionally suited to present this book, having been the designers and teachers of the program and advisers and mentors to the graduates who share their stories. They seek to help the reader see how the intersection of identities of their students—professional and personal—can be transformed through transformational learning theory to bring about the scholarly practitioner identity that aligns with the definition of an EdD graduate. Often, we forget the necessary attention that must be paid, across the components and mechanisms of an EdD program, to the development of the student into a "new" identity because of their learning and experiences. That is, in addition to course work and assessment milestones, such as comprehensive exams or dissertations in practice, the teaching faculty must consider how these exercises and experiences form the professional practitioner into a scholarly practitioner. They must consider how their program uniquely shapes this new identity and how this identity will grow and flourish in the students' field of practice long after they have graduated.

The alumni authors are equally suited to present this book as they offer the reader a detailed journey of how their individual identity transformation happened because of their participation in the JHU program. From a student/graduate perspective, we see that becoming a scholarly practitioner is not simply an act of participating in courses in a doctoral program, achieving good grades, and graduating with the title of "doctor." Rather, the authors demonstrate that becoming a scholarly practitioner means actively learning new knowledge, new skills, and new ways of problem solving while incorporating this new knowledge, skills, and problem solving as part of their own identities.

The alumni authors demonstrate how they learned to apply inquiry to practice (understanding of extant literature, research skills, and inquiry skills), how they approach their work by using a theoretical lens, and how their own process of change became a model for improving practice.

Together, the authors provide the reader with a comprehensive understanding of why focusing on identity transformation is an essential part of an EdD program, how this change is carried out through the incorporation of identity theory into all aspects of the doctoral program, and what it looks like from the perspective of the students who undergo this transformation. In the ongoing quest to distinguish the Education Doctorate as the professional practice doctorate in education, this volume in the series is a major contribution because it helps the reader to see why identity development is an important part of nurturing scholar practitioners and how individuals are transformed through doctoral study. To this end, the examples in this book provide concrete examples that demonstrate the design concept of scholarly practitioner and pushes our understanding of what the role of identity plays in the distinction of the EdD from the PhD.

Jill A. Perry
Carnegie Project on the Education Doctorate, University of Pittsburgh

The JHU EdD Program: Designed to Transform Local Contexts Through Shifting Student Identities

Stephen J. Pape, Camille L. Bryant,
Ranjini Mahinda JohnBull, and Karen S. Karp

Never doubt that a small group of thoughtful, committed citizens can change the world; indeed, it's the only thing that ever has.

—MARGARET MEAD

Introduction

MARGARET MEAD'S WORDS describe the vision of the EdD crafters at Johns Hopkins University (JHU)—to build a cadre of scholarly problem solvers by providing powerful experiences to transform expert practitioners' professional and personal identities to those of scholar-practitioners. In this volume, we draw upon literature that closely links personal identity and professional identity (Trede et al., 2012), calling on the notion of personal epistemology as central to professional identity development (Baxter Magolda, 2004). Further, we hold that reflection may be the mediator between an individual's experience and their developing professional identity (De Weerdt et al., 2006). Finally, critical to professional identity formation is the social cognitive construct of self-efficacy (Bandura, 1977). The evolution of one's identity from an expert practitioner to a scholar-practitioner necessarily requires the development of self-efficacy within this new role (McBrayer et al., 2021) and knowledge to function in one's professional context as the scholar-practitioner (Zambo et al., 2015). By scholar-practitioner, we mean individuals who rely on and value research at the forefront of thinking about and changing their practice in conjunction with knowledge and traditions built from years of practice. We recognize that in some contexts, the term scholarly practitioner is used to reflect the ways of being of our graduates. We choose the moniker scholar-practitioner to precisely describe the identities of our graduates regardless of their position, to elevate their role within their organization, and to honor the deep work of our graduates in transforming their identities. They engaged in this transformation through the deep immersion into research and theory in order to grapple with how to do research and how to use research in practice. We hold that our graduates function in their professional practice differently. They are both practitioners and scholars.

The JHU Doctor of Education (EdD) online doctoral program was created in 2012 with the goal of developing global leaders working in a variety of fields in education to use specialized knowledge, skills, and dispositions to rigorously and systematically examine an educational Problem of Practice (POP) they encounter daily rigorously and systematically. We intended that this program would transform not only individuals but also the specific ways in which our students operate within their professions after the program. As scholar-practitioners, we envisioned they would ultimately become change agents who would work in partnership with their organizations to see the system in which educational POPs exist and to generate positive organizational improvement. Further, it was intended that they would value garnering the support and insight of professional partners to carry out this exploration and intervention work as they engaged and focused a social justice lens. We believed that this goal of developing scholar-practitioners within our EdD program would be achieved through personal and professional identity shifts that, for example, give voice to the classroom teacher on their grade-level planning team, build a strong foundation for the assistant principal to take a place at the table among district-level decision-makers, elevate a district professional's capacity to direct district-level policy or state-level standards revisions, or augment the research acumen of the professional development provider to join the research team within their education organization.

The JHU EdD program was designed using an improvement science framework and founded on the Carnegie Project on the EdD principles (Carnegie Project on the Education Doctorate [CPED], 2009). From the beginning, the JHU School of Education (SOE) set out to develop a unique set of experiences for practitioners that would engage them differently in their work, equipped with new knowledge and frameworks to view their experiences. We developed this online doctoral program to reach a diverse, broad, national, and international student population, enabling them to elevate the learning and growth of one another. In the first three chapters of this book, we provide insight into the mechanisms we embedded within the JHU EdD program that we believed at the outset would support this identity transformation. In Chapter 1, we provide an overview of the EdD program components, highlighting how we used Bryk et al.'s (2015) improvement science principles as a structure for the Applied Dissertation process and a framework for building scholarly knowledge and skills. We use the term Applied Dissertation in lieu of the CPED term Dissertation in Practice (DiP) (CPED, 2009) to make clear that the JHU SOE dissertation was conceived as a culminating project that is similar to a typical dissertation but is different in its focus on application. In Chapter 2, we describe the processes of transformation, highlighting theoretical and practical considerations gleaned from research literature, and explicate the mechanisms embedded within our program beyond the Applied Dissertation to support identity transformation. In Chapter 3, we delve deeply into a central component of these mechanisms for identity transformation, the research methods sequence. These descriptions of our EdD program frame the stories of our graduates as they each reflect upon and depict their identity transformation across the program; these are presented in the subsequent chapters (Chapters 4–17). Our graduates tell compelling stories of their dramatic transformation from practitioner to scholar-practitioner, the components of the EdD that supported their transformation, and the effects of this transformation within their professional context. These inspiring stories represent the triumphs of students from seven U.S. states, the District of Columbia, Egypt, and India. It is their stories that illuminate the potential of an EdD program to transform not only individuals, but also educational systems touched by these leaders.

Making the Dissertation Relevant: Improvement Science as a Frame for the Applied Dissertation

There are differences between the program goals and practices of a typical Doctor of Philosophy (PhD) program and those of an EdD. In a PhD program, students typically seek mentorship from faculty who are actively conducting research, often examining education phenomena within controlled studies. Research methodologies typically focus on parsing out the variance of components of a phenomenon that may contribute to a particular education problem or solution, but the phenomena are decontextualized from the doctoral student's everyday professional practice. These studies are typically conducted with large samples, sometimes from multiple sites, which allows the student researcher to engage in basic and often advanced inferential statistics that are important but often disconnected from practice and the individuals who may benefit. Some PhD dissertations may tell the story of individuals within educational contexts that reflect their lived experience, while others may describe the cluster of perspectives from groups without changing the context of their experience or outcomes.

To shift away from researching phenomena that are disconnected from professional practice, the JHU EdD Applied Dissertation situates students' work within their context of professional practice. This change in emphasis requires that EdD students conduct their research, including a needs assessment study and intervention, within their workplace and engage their professional partners to collaborate with them to understand a contextualized POP or opportunity for growth that their organization is grappling with as a wicked problem (Cabrera & Cabrera, 2015). This deep understanding of the system in which the opportunities or POPs exist is critical to our students' subsequent development of an intervention that aligns with the scholar-practitioner's understanding of the system, is successful in shifting the conditions that resulted in the POP, and allows the interpretation of findings from a systems perspective. This model supports a different way of performing their duties as practitioners (and researchers) by aligning this work with the CPED's distinguishing features of the Dissertation in Practice, "the major focus should be problems of practice, the research should be applied, and development of the product should be built throughout and across coursework" (Perry et al., 2020, p. 1). In the following sections, we present the overview of the JHU EdD program framed within Bryk and colleagues' (2015) principles of improvement.

Table 1.1 presents the EdD program components by year that we argue supported our students' identity transformation. In the top row, we present the required courses in which students engage across the program. In the second and third rows, we present selected program components and dissertation components completed by students during the program that we highlight across the first three chapters of this book. Finally, the improvement science principles are depicted at the bottom of the figure to indicate the ways in which the principles are enacted across the program and the process of the Applied Dissertation over time.

Applied Dissertation: Seeing the System of Problem-Specific and User-Centered Problems of Practice

The structure of our Applied Dissertation is unique (Pape et al., 2022). It is tailored to the needs of our advanced practitioners, who desire to become scholar-practitioners, in several ways. Aligned with the first principle of improvement science, which is to "make the work problem-specific and user-centered" (Bryk et al., 2015, p. 21), students focus on a POP they have observed within their context. The students spend approximately a year to better understand the POP through the research literature from educational contexts that are similar to their own. POPs previously explored include such topics as implementation of educational technology to support student-centered instructional practices, inclusion of students with special needs in Egyptian schools, and structural racism and access to educational opportunities within educational institutions.

A student's POP statement consists of an assertion of the problem within a broader context, at least three ways in which the problem manifests itself within education broadly with evidence from the research literature, and a statement that reveals the problem within their context. This problem statement is initially written within the student's application and further edited and refined during orientation sessions prior to the start of the program as well as in their first-year coursework assignments. During orientation, for example, students are engaged in an activity that encourages them to construct an initial conceptual framework for their POP by manipulating sticky notes on which they have represented their

Table 1.1

Building Scholar-Practitioner Self-Efficacy through Changing Practitioners' Frames of Reference

	Pre-doctoral	Year 1	Year 2	Transition between Years 2 & 3	Year 3
Coursework		1. Contemporary Approaches to Educational Problems 2. Disciplinary Approaches to Education 3. Research Methods and Systematic Inquiry I 4. Multiple Perspectives on Learning and Teaching	1. Specialization Courses 2. Multicultural Education 3. Research Methods and Systematic Inquiry II 4. Evaluation of Education Policies and Programs		1. Specialization Courses 2. Electives
Program Component	• Identification of POP in application • Program orientation	• Improvement science • Measurement • Systems thinking • Multiple perspectives on factors related to POP	• Multicultural education critical reflection experiences • Analyzing needs assessment data • Developing intervention	• Comprehensive examination • Proposal defense • Human subjects review process • Recruitment of study participants	• Final defense & dissemination
Dissertation Component	Identify the POP	Examine the POP and potential contributing factors broadly from multiple perspectives: • Literature synthesis of factors • Needs assessment study	Based on understanding of POP and contributing factors in literature and within context: • Intervention literature synthesis • Methods for process and outcome evaluation	Applied Dissertation proposal – Chs. 1-4	Applied Dissertation – Chs. 1-5
Improvement Science Principles	Problem Focused & User Centered				
		See the System & Attend to Variability			
			Embrace Measurement; Learn Through Disciplined Inquiry		
	Organized Networks of EdD and Professional Colleagues				

current understanding of the factors that may contribute to their POP. During the first semester, they participate in a course, *Contemporary Approaches to Educational Problems*, that introduces students to topics such as improvement science (Bryk et al., 2015) and systems thinking approaches through such integrated lenses as Bronfenbrenner's (1994; Bronfenbrenner & Morris, 2006) ecological systems theory, Neal and Neal's (2013) networked ecological systems theory, and Cabrera and Cabrera's (2015) systems thinking approach. At the same time, students consider their POP through the multiple lenses of economics, history, anthropology, and sociology within the *Disciplinary Approaches to Education* course. Finally, during the second semester of their doctoral program, our students participate in a learning theories course, *Multiple Perspectives on Learning and Teaching*, which exposes them to various theories that help them see learning and teaching differently.

These various perspectives during the first two semesters of the program are intended to broaden the students' viewpoints related to their POP so that they might engage their professional colleagues within a process of what Bryk et al. (2015) called "focus[ing] on variation" (p. 35) and "seeing the system that produces the current outcomes" (p. 57), the second and third principles of improvement science, respectively. That is, our students remain with the problem for a year and refrain from moving too rapidly toward solutions, to avoid *solutionitis* (Bryk et al., 2015, p. 24), an impulsive jump that often plagues education organizations and results in "chronic failure of promising reform ideas" (p. 5). Instead, student researchers examine the factors associated with their POP through a literature review that is written across the first year of the program within various course assignments. This literature review leads to the construction of a conceptual framework (cf. Lester, 2005) that delineates the factors associated with the POP, and, importantly, considers the relationships between these factors as known through existing empirical research. This conceptual framework and reflection on students' sphere of influence within their professional context together serve as a roadmap for their needs assessment study. Specifically, in this empirical study they explore how the malleable factors that emerged from their exploration of existing research literature are operating within their context, which deepens their understanding of "the system that produces the current outcomes" (Bryk et al., 2015, p. 57).

During the second semester of the program, students begin their three-course research methodology sequence (see Chapter 3 for a description of student experiences in the research methods course sequence) with *Research Methods and Systematic Inquiry I*, which supports them to explore selected factors from their conceptual framework in their needs assessment study. This focus on measurement aligns with Bryk and colleagues' (2015) fourth and fifth principles, "we cannot improve at scale what we cannot measure" (p. 87) and "use disciplinary inquiry to drive improvement" (p. 113). Through this empirical study, our students develop a disciplined understanding of how these factors that emerged from the research literature are functioning within their context and potentially contributing to the processes and outcomes they wish to change.

For example, a scholar-practitioner who is a school principal might be considering a school-wide shift to a project-based learning (PBL) model of instruction. For their needs assessment study, they may explore their teachers' present practices that align with a PBL model, knowledge of research-informed PBL instructional strategies, and teachers' beliefs about PBL. Factors more distant from the school principal such as school funding and district policy may influence a decision to adopt a PBL model, but these factors are not considered for intervention or within the needs assessment study because they are not judged as malleable given the context and the scholar-practitioner's role and purview within the organization. Rather, the school principal may engage in continuous improvement activities focused on implementing PBL. Finally, they may engage in plan-do-study-act (Bryk et al., 2015) cycles either during or following the completion of their dissertation study as part of continuous improvement.

In Table 1.1, we depict these phases of the program. Prior to entering the program, students submit a POP within their application and begin to refine their understanding of the POP as well as factors that likely contribute to the problem through their initial engagements with the program. Through their initial courses, they work to see the system in which their POP is embedded as well as the variability in the factors that may be operating to produce the POP within their context. During these phases, our students engage in collaborative activities to form EdD program colleague networks with which many of them work across the program, especially as they study for their oral comprehensive examination.

Applied Dissertation: Exploring, Proposing, Delivering, and Evaluating the Intervention

The first four chapters of the JHU EdD Applied Dissertation comprise the student's dissertation proposal and are completed across the first 2 years of the program. The first chapter is a literature review of the factors that potentially contribute to the POP, which is often framed using the levels of the ecological systems theory (Bronfenbrenner, 1994; Bronfenbrenner & Morris, 2006) and focused by their conceptual framework. The second chapter is the needs assessment study, which includes methods for examining potential contributing factors related to their POP and understanding how these factors are functioning in their context. These chapters are written as a story of their exploration of the POP leading to literature related to potential interventions that match both the research-based and site-centered findings. Based on these findings from the field and from their context, they then explore the intervention research literature targeted toward a small number of contributing factors that emerged from the needs assessment study as potentially contributing to their POP.

Students synthesize the intervention literature across the second year of the program within their discipline-focused specialization courses. These unique specialization areas include *Mind, Brain, and Teaching*; *Entrepreneurial Leadership in Education*; *Urban Leadership*; *Instructional Design and Online Teaching and Learning*; and *Technology Integration in K–16 Education*. The intent of specializing in an area of interest is to bolster our graduates' disciplinary knowledge to continue to deepen their understanding of their POP and to provide a theoretical and empirical foundation for their intervention. The third chapter of their Applied Dissertation, therefore, focuses on a synthesis of the intervention literature related to multiple potential options for an intervention.

While pursuing their specialization courses, students participate in two additional research courses, *Research Methods and Systematic Inquiry II* and *Evaluation of Education Policies and Programs* (See Chapter 3 for further descriptions). These courses support students to develop the skills to analyze their needs assessment study data as well as to develop the research methods to rigorously evaluate the intervention they enact within their Applied Dissertation, which aligns with Bryk and colleagues' (2015) fourth (i.e., improvement through measurement) and fifth (i.e., disciplinary inquiry to make change) principles of improvement science. In the final research methods course, students write two assignments that become the foundation for their fourth chapter, which is a methodology chapter including research questions, method, and procedure to rigorously examine the process of implementing the intervention and proximal outcomes that may result from the intervention.

The focus of the process evaluation is to examine the intervention implementation fidelity and to capture the participant's experiences during the intervention in their own voice. Essentially, the student examines whether they delivered the intervention as planned and how it changed from the plan. Only in this way can the outcomes be accurately linked to the actual intervention. Further, the goal of the process evaluation is to capture the participants' experiences during the intervention because these individuals are typically professional partners within the student's professional context. The voice of the participant is critical to inform next steps for their organization and to inform our students relative to their future work within their workplace. By documenting any changes in methodology and resulting shifts in the factors that potentially contribute to the POP, our students are better able to establish meaningful recommendations for the field based on their experience implementing the intervention. Finally, during their final semesters in the program the student researchers implement their intervention and evaluate both the process of the intervention implementation and the associated proximal outcomes.

In Table 1.1, we see the continued focus on variability through year 2 of the program as students examine the data they collect from their professional partners to understand how the factors that emerged from the literature review in Chapter 1 of their dissertation are functioning within their context. They gain a perspective on the POP that is focused on the malleable factors that may be the focus for their intervention. They embrace measurement and learn about their contextualized POP through this disciplined inquiry. Finally, based on this understanding, they synthesize the intervention literature and develop the intervention for their Applied Dissertation.

Conclusion

The advantages and opportunities of the JHU EdD professional doctorate include a focus on directly improving practice; continuous collaboration with professional partners; development of solutions based on a strong, empirical understanding of the problem within a familiar context; synthesis of literature focused on intervention related to the needs assessment study findings; and research-informed improvement science principles as a frame for the study. It is this structure and these components that we believe hold potential for supporting powerful shifts in our students' identities in becoming scholar-practitioners who continue this work by practicing in situ what they will do in the future—all while mentored and guided by expert faculty. We anticipate that our graduates will systematically examine issues that arise in their professional context prior to reaching a solution as a result of completing the Applied Dissertation, engage their colleagues in understanding the problem and root causes as well as developing a solution, and evaluate the intervention rigorously by considering their professional partners' voices relative to the intervention as well as measuring outcomes that may stem from their intervention.

We believe our graduates are equipped with the knowledge and skills that allow them to be effective change agents within their educational organizations because they have established themselves as leaders in an area of need by their actions and displays of capacity to do so. Many of our graduates experience significant shifts in their identity and agency, and their stories in the chapters that follow provide rich and engaging evidence of these professional and personal transformations. Their stories illustrate how changing oneself in collaboration with professional partners and mentors can bring greater equity and community improvement, and ultimately allow them to live out Margaret Mead's vision for the potential for change. Prior to these stories from graduates (Chapters 4–17), in Chapter 2, we explore our understanding of identity transformation and the mechanisms we believe support this evolution for our students. Chapter 3 explores the experiences and pedagogies implemented in the research methods course sequence to support the development of our practitioners' self-efficacy for engaging in research, a critical component of developing a scholar-practitioner identity. We explore the research methods sequence in depth because of the importance these courses hold in doctoral students' identity transformations.

References

Bandura, A. (1977). Self-efficacy: Toward a unifying theory of behavioral change. *Psychological Review, 84*(2), 191–215. https://doi.org/10.1037/0033-295X.84.2.191

Baxter Magolda, M. B. (2004). Evolution of a constructivist conceptualization of epistemological reflection. *Educational Psychologist, 39*(1), 31–42. https://doi.org/10.1207/s15326985ep3901_4

Bronfenbrenner, U. (1994). Ecology models of human development. In T. N. Postlewaite & T. Husen, (Eds.), *International encyclopedia of education* (2nd ed., Vol. 3, pp. 1643–1647). Elsevier.

Bronfenbrenner, U., & Morris, P. A. (2006). The biological model of human development. In W. Damon & R. M. Lerner (Eds.), *Handbook of child psychology: Theoretical models of human development* (6th ed., Vol. 1, pp. 793–828). John Wiley & Sons. https://doi.org/10.1002/9780470147658.chpsy0114

Bryk, A., Gomez, L., Grunow, A., & LaMahieu, P. G. (2015). *Learning to improve: How America's schools can get better at getting better.* Harvard Education Press.

Cabrera, D., & Cabrera, L. (2015). *Systems thinking made simple: New hope for solving wicked problems* (2nd ed.). Plectica Publishing.

Carnegie Project on the Education Doctorate (CPED). (2009). *The CPED framework.* https://www.cpedinitiative.org/the-framework

De Weerdt, S., Bouwen, R. Corthouts, F., & Martens, H. (2006). Identity transformation as an intercontextual process. *Industry & Higher Education, 20*(5), 317–326. https://doi.org/10.5367/000000006778702373

Lester, F. K. (2005). On the theoretical, conceptual, and philosophical foundations for research in mathematics education. *ZDM, 37*(6), 457–467. https://doi.org/10.1007/BF02655854

McBrayer, J. S., Fallon, K., Tolman, S., Calhoun, D. W., Ballesteros, E., & Mathewson, T. (2021). Examining educational leadership doctoral students' self-efficacy as related to their role as a scholarly practitioner researcher. *International Journal of Doctoral Studies, 16*, 487–512. https://doi.org/10.28945/4811

Neal, J. W., & Neal, Z. P. (2013). Nested or networked? Future directions for ecological systems theory. *Social Development, 22*(4), 722–737. https://doi.org/10.1111/sode.12018

Pape, S. J., Bryant, C. L., JohnBull, R. M., & Karp, K. S. (2022). Improvement science as a frame for the dissertation in practice: The Johns Hopkins University experience. *Impacting Education, 7*(1), 59–66. https://doi.org/10.5195/ie.2022.241

Perry, J. A., Zambo, D., & Crow, R. (2020). *The improvement science dissertation in practice: A guide for committee members, and their students*. Myers Education Press.

Trede, F., Macklin, R., & Bridges, D. (2012). Professional identity development: A review of the higher education literature. *Studies in Higher Education, 37*(3), 365–384. https://doi.org/10.1080/03075079.2010.521237

Zambo, D., Buss, R. R., & Zambo, R. (2015). Uncovering the identities of students and graduates in a CPED-influenced EdD program. *Studies in Higher Education, 40*(2), 233–252. https://doi.org/10.1080/03075079.2013.823932

From Doctoral Students to Scholar-Practitioners: Mechanisms for Identity Transformation

Ranjini Mahinda JohnBull, Camille L. Bryant, Karen S. Karp, and Stephen J. Pape

> *To be the change you want to see in the world, you must see yourself differently.*
>
> —MAHATMA GANDHI

Introduction

DOCTORAL STUDENTS NEED to see themselves differently within their systems in order to think and behave differently in their professional contexts. In this chapter, we describe how our doctoral students come to know themselves and their contexts more deeply to grow into scholar-practitioners. To "know thyself" is to deeply understand how we see the world, label our realities, see ourselves within those realities, and interact in our professional organizations with this level of awareness and knowing. A doctoral student journey continues a lifelong transformation that is both personal and professional. We discuss the personal and professional identity transformation mechanisms of the Johns Hopkins University (JHU) Doctor of Education (EdD) program through the lenses of transformational learning theory (Mezirow, 1997) and social cognitive theory's construct of self-efficacy (Bandura, 1977).

Education doctoral students join the JHU EdD program as practitioners who are typically highly specialized and effective in their professions. Most of them enter with high levels of professional self-efficacy, or positive beliefs in their capabilities as professionals (Bandura, 1977; see Figure 2.1). Students often seek doctoral programs with instrumental goals, such as to attain a degree that seems like an endpoint, improve their salary, improve their knowledge and skills within their profession, become an expert, advance in their career, or change professional directions, to name a few. We hold that as students go through the doctoral journey process, other, more nuanced reasons for this degree attainment emerge for them. These reasons are illustrated throughout this book in our graduates' reflections on their journey toward realizing a scholar-practitioner identity.

Through the program experiences, we help them build upon their knowledge, skills, dispositions, and practical expertise to grow their professional self-efficacy to higher levels, while we simultaneously help them grow their scholarly self-efficacy beliefs. In Figure 2.1, we depict this convergence of practitioner self-efficacy (PSE) and scholar self-efficacy (SSE) as students traverse the EdD program experiences leading to the intersectional identity of scholar-practitioner and strong scholar-practitioner self-efficacy (SPSE). Prior to entering the doctoral program, our students do not consider themselves to be scholars or scholar-practitioners. To help them transform and merge their views of themselves into this new kind of professional, a scholar-practitioner, we carefully crafted experiences over the course of the program to help them adjust their frames of references through critical reflection experiences that develop new habits of mind and new points of view, two critical components of identity transformation described by Mezirow (1997).

This chapter describes our conceptualization of personal and professional identities and mechanisms for identity shifts. We explore several aspects of the JHU EdD program as mechanisms for shifts in our students' identity to elaborate the structure of the program provided in Chapter 1. Specifically, we illuminate how identity development was facilitated in and throughout the program through the required program components and the advising and mentoring relationships that were fostered and that flourish today. As depicted in Figure 2.1, we hold that the program supports the development of students' SSE, which enables their identity transformation to that of a scholar-practitioner.

Figure 2.1

Scholar-Practitioner Self-Efficacy and Identity Growth Model

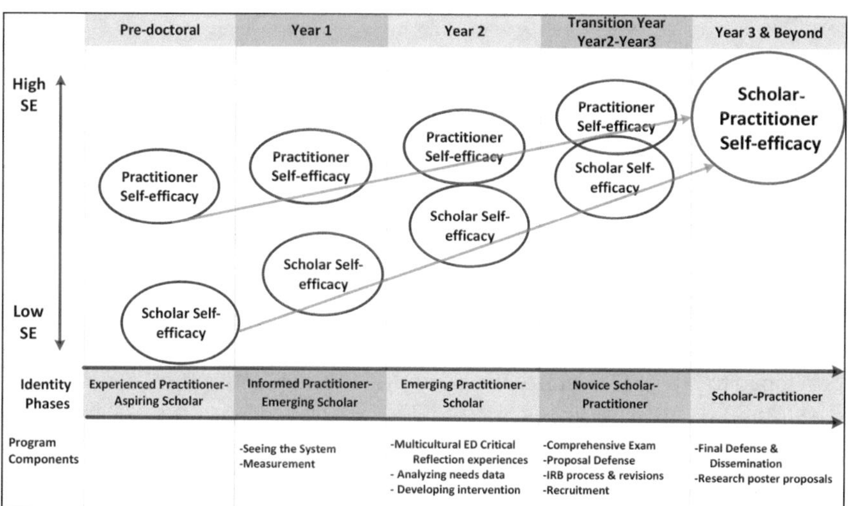

Identity and Identity Transformation

Although the EdD journey primarily involves the development of an individual's professional identities, we assert that it is impossible to divorce one's professional identities from one's intersectional personal identities. Therefore, in the following sections, we delineate the intersectionality of personal identity and professional identity. We then define and describe identity transformation as the process that occurs from transformational learning experiences (Mezirow, 1997) and entails the transition and evolution from thinking about oneself and viewing oneself in one's current state, to thinking about oneself and behaving in ways that align with a new conception of oneself in a particular context and role. Further, we describe the essential nature of self-efficacy as a mechanism for identity transformation. In the chapters throughout this book, our graduates tell their integrated stories of their intersectional personal and professional identity journeys by reflecting on who they thought they were, realizing their personal identities in new frames, and building upon their professional identities with their new layers of scholarly knowledge, skills, insights, and dispositions. Specifically, the doctoral students' transformations are transitions into individuals who are deeply aware of their intersectional personal and professional identities as scholar-practitioners working within systems of advantage and oppression.

Personal Identity

The optimal theory applied to identity development (OTAID; Myers et al., 1991) describes personal identity as a sense of self and being, which is already a holistic and complete human. Thus, identity development is a spiraled discovery process of self-knowledge through expanding one's understanding of oneself in relation to others, to one's ancestors, and to one's historical and present systems in which one lives to realize this positive holistic sense of self. This theory was developed to provide an intersectional multicultural identity theory to integrate the individual identity theories that capture only one part of an individual's identity (i.e., race, ethnicity, sex, gender, ability). It provides a counterbalanced narrative to oppressive contexts, like the United States, where the "ideal" identity is one of "White" race and "male" gender and has systems of power and oppression that advantage this type of identity. This identity development theory describes the process of individuals moving through phases starting with a phase of unawareness of their self as distinct from others, dissonance related to their positions within systems, understanding their individual intersectional identities, understanding their identities in relation to others and systems of power, and, finally, seeing their identities as interconnected to all communities and living things. Specifically, this theory affirms that this identity development process allows an individual to understand their intersectional identity more deeply and expansively in order to better comprehend their holistic and inherently good self in relation to the world around them.

As a very intentional design of the JHU EdD program, we explicitly provide experiences for students to help them see the systems in which they live and work. We want them to see themselves as important actors in these systems. As overviewed in Chapter 1, during the first 2 years of the program, students learn about different systems theories, including the ecological systems theory (EST; e.g., Bronfenbrenner, 1994) and networked EST (Neal & Neal, 2013); and they learn about systems of power, policy, culture, and history, to better understand their Problem of Practice (POP) and the factors that influence their

POP in these systems. During the second year of the program, they also engage in learning about their own intersectional identities to better understand their own personal identities and how their intersectional identities operate within these systems of power. For example, students engage in deep reflection on their intersectional identities through the required *Multicultural Education* course. Our diverse students are given opportunities to make their personal intersectional identities explicit through conversations and discussions. They then engage in reflections together and begin to realize and see others' intersectional identities clearer as they see their own. Thus, our students progress through the program both better understanding themselves and seeing the people they work with (i.e., adults, students, communities, families) as interconnected individuals who are influenced by and who influence their communities and different levels of the systems within which they live.

Professional Identity

Professional identity is not well-defined in the literature (Trede et al., 2012), but the literature on scholar-practitioner identity is even more varied and disparate based upon the types of scholar identities in different fields of study (De Weerdt et al., 2006). Trede and colleagues' (2012) review of 20 articles on professional identity in undergraduate programs found definitions that coalesced around the idea of "a way of being and a lens to evaluate, learn and make sense of practice" (p. 374). Most other researchers who have discussed scholar-practitioner identity development have focused primarily on the development of identities as researchers, academics, and scholars and transitioning their identities from the practitioner experts to this new role (Caskey et al., 2020; Hall & Burns, 2009; Lesham, 2020; Rigler et al., 2021). Specifically, in most other studies, identities of doctoral students have been explored in reference to their development of their researcher identities and agency (Foot et al., 2014), not their intersectional identities as scholar-practitioners where both identities are operating in their professional contexts in conjunction with their intersectional personal identities. Zambo et al.'s (2015) qualitative study of 35 EdD students' identities defined the scholarly practitioner through the metaphor of layered identities. That is, they are viewed as adding layers to their current identities of a learner, a leader, and an action researcher. While we agree with this characterization of these identities to some degree, we also assert that these identities transform more than are they augmented. A doctoral student's identity should become deeper and more nuanced as they better understand their intersectional personal identities in relation to their intersectional scholar-practitioner identities and the responsibilities that result from their deeper levels of knowledge of self, disciplinary knowledge, research methodologies appropriate for contextualized research, and the systems in which they operate. We expect and hope that our graduates will act within their professional contexts with a new identity and new tool kits and skill sets that allow them to engage with their professional communities in a more systematic way.

Merging Intersectional Identities

In the JHU EdD, most students come from an *educational* professional context, but this is not true for all students. Thus, we will refer to this identity transformation more generally because our students represent teachers, education specialists, education leaders, entrepreneurs, business professionals, higher education faculty, organizational consultants, education technologists, superintendents, and many more. Specifically, we assert that our EdD students experience an identity transformation from that of a practitioner or an expert practitioner to viewing themselves as a scholar-practitioner and behaving in their profession in ways that align with those new integrated identities. These identities manifest in nuanced ways in their individual professional contexts that each have different systems of power, oppression, and advantage. Further, we define a scholar-practitioner as an individual who relies on the combination of their professional experience, their knowledge of research literature to inform their approach to their work in their profession, and their personal identity awareness. They integrate their knowledge from extant empirical research, their own research from the Applied Dissertation in the EdD program, and their practice-based expertise to guide and inform their menu of options for how they operate and behave in their professional roles.

We contend that the scholar-practitioner identity is an integrated sense of self that is a transformed version of the experienced practitioner. EdD students do not relinquish their practitioner identities. Rather, their practitioner identities evolve into scholar-practitioners who add and weave this new scholar identity into a new sense of their practitioner selves. They develop into research-oriented systems thinkers who see their positionality in this system, who persist in their fields of practice as research-practice partners and persist as matters of personal and professional responsibility. As their identities evolve into these new types of professionals, their organizations and communities of practice also change around them because of the ways they use their new knowledge, skills, and insider roles within their organizations. In the following sections, we explore two theoretical frameworks related to our perspective on identity transformation, Mezirow's (1997) transformational leaning theory and Bandura's (1986) social cognitive theory, in particular the construct of self-efficacy.

Transformational learning theory.

To build students' self-efficacy as scholar-practitioners and to help them see themselves in these new professional identities, we created critical reflection activities for them to experience transformational learning throughout the program. Selected reflection activities are depicted within Figure 2.1 in the program components section. Transformational learning theory (Mezirow, 1997) describes how certain types of critical reflection experiences help people change their *frames of reference,* which involves changing *habits of mind* and *points of view.* Our frames of reference guide how we behave and help us to think about how to integrate new knowledge and insights into our current knowledge frameworks. Mezirow (1997) stated:

> Frames of reference are the structures of assumptions through which we understand our experiences. They selectively shape and delimit expectations, perceptions, cognition, and feelings. They set our "line of action." Once set, we automatically move from one specific activity (mental or behavior) to another. . . . When circumstances permit, transformative learners move toward a frame of reference that is more inclusive, discriminating, self-reflective, and integrative of experience. (p. 5)

Mezirow (1997) described four different learning mechanisms, the last two of which shift individuals' frames of reference. First, *elaboration* on an existing point of view means finding information that affirms this point of view. The second learning mechanism, establishing *new similar* points of view, allows the learner to continue to affirm their original point of view and, therefore, does not shift the learner's frame of reference. A third learning process is to *transform the point of view* through an encounter that provides a disorienting dilemma, which involves an experience that results in an individual who can no longer move forward with the same biases or frames of reference because an experience or set of experiences disconfirms the ideas in their frames of reference. A final learning process involves *fully transforming our habits of mind* through deep critical reflections on our frames of references. Mezirow described this process as atypical in most learning environments because it requires deep analysis of one's beliefs in the face of contradictory evidence or experiences. Further, Mezirow described discourse and critical reflection as key components in transforming these frames of reference, which ultimately lead to changes in how one conceptualizes identity.

For example, some White American educators may believe the cultural notion that in the United States, you can "pull yourself up by the bootstraps" if you "work hard enough." They may strongly believe this platitude because it aligns with how they have viewed the world and their own personal experiences of working hard and succeeding in school and in their professions. For example, if school principals hold this frame of reference about students, they may fail to see how structural systems influence students' experiences with teachers and school systems. These disparate experiences influence the variability in learning outcomes, especially for outcomes of students of color. Their attribution for the disparities may only be centered in their frames of reference that students are not trying hard enough. Principals who engage in numerous disorienting dilemmas and critical reflection experiences through discourse may come to learn that "working hard" is not the only factor that influences student learning and outcomes. They may realize that their own intersectional identities as White Americans may have helped them succeed and achieve the principalship because they benefited from the positive stereotypes and assumptions about White Americans being "hard workers." This type of identity awareness may transform these White American school principals' understanding of themselves and their understanding of the factors that play different supportive and debilitating roles in educational experiences and outcomes. These critical reflections serve to transform their views of themselves and their views of others' identities and their situated experiences within systems of advantage and op-pression. In the sections that follow, we delineate several disorienting events and critical reflections that serve to shift our doctoral students' frames of refer-ence leading to their identity transformation. Next, we discuss the importance of self-efficacy in our students' transformation from experienced practitioner to scholar-practitioner.

Building self-efficacy for scholar-practitioner identities.

Self-efficacy is important to identity transformation because one is rarely effective in a new role without higher levels of self-efficacy. Moreover, self-effi-cacy is inherently a judgment about how one sees oneself and one's abilities to be effective in a specific role given one's competencies, knowledge, and skills. Bandura's (1977) social cognitive theory described human motivation and behavior as a process that involves the interaction between cognition, social interactions with others in their environment, and personal factors such as self-efficacy. Bandura named this phenomenon triadic reciprocal determinism to describe the interplay of these three components. Among these, the personal factor of self-efficacy is one of the most influential personal beliefs that directs an individual to take action (Bandura, 1977). This foundational construct of self-efficacy asserts that individuals behave in ways that align with their levels of self-efficacy. Self-efficacy beliefs are highly contextual, which means that one's self-efficacy beliefs vary based on different contexts and different tasks.

Bandura (1977) described four sources of information that people rely upon to make judgements about their own self-efficacy beliefs: mastery experiences, vicarious experiences, verbal persuasion, and physiological and emotional feedback. Within their professions, our doctoral students have mastered the basic functions of their jobs and experienced success in performing their roles as teachers, school and district leaders, and organizational entrepreneurs, to name a few. They have learned how to become more effective by watching their peers (vicarious experiences) and emulating what they've learned from those peers. They've heard positive encouragement from respected colleagues (verbal persuasion), and they have experienced the physiological and emotional effects of elation and joy when they have experienced success in their roles. Building upon their PSE, the JHU EdD program aims to facilitate the growth of their self-efficacy in their new roles as scholar-practitioners. Figure 2.1 depicts the convergence of students' PSE and SSE. As students traverse the program components, we hypothesize that students' PSE continues to grow as their SSE increases until the two are merged in a transformed SPSE.

To illustrate how self-efficacy beliefs play out in professional practice, consider the principal from Chapter 1, a student who has just entered the JHU EdD program. They may feel that they are highly effective at garnering family support for new initiatives such as project-based learning as an instructional model because the principal feels confident about their communication skills and their ability to develop relationships with families. This principal has high self-efficacy for achieving positive parent engagement in the school, especially from White American families. During Year 1 of the program, however, this principal may recognize that they do not have a strong record of garnering engagement from international families at the school, which make up approximately 30% of the population. The communication strategies and relationship development practices that the principal uses for domestic families do not result in increased attendance at school events, communication or responses in surveys, or participation in feedback from international families. For the context of international families, the principal has low self-efficacy for community engagement in terms of this international population. In terms of Figure 2.1, the principal may have high self-efficacy for many aspects of their position, but low self-efficacy related to communication with international families, which may reflect their early phase personal identity awareness and emerging SSE. This principal's development in Year 1 may align with the informed practitioner-emerging scholar identity phase where they feel efficacious in their job, and they are becoming more informed about their practices and the different social and cultural factors that influence their practice and their systems.

To develop self-efficacy through the EdD program, our students build skills and competencies in understanding research, implementing research methodologies through their studies, and working together in their profession to implement these research projects and the Applied Dissertation. They move from their role as solely an experienced practitioner to question certain assumptions they have had about their practice and the problems they encounter in their professional context to using different theories and research data to inform how they understand their contexts and possible solutions. Further, they learn to communicate and collaborate with their professional partners about how to tackle context-based problems differently using their research-informed knowledge, which strengthens their self-efficacy beliefs as scholar-practitioners (Greeley et al., 1989).

During and after students' matriculations through the program, their approach to their professional practice evolves as their scholar-practitioner identities emerge through program activities that support self-efficacy. In the case of the previously mentioned principal, for example, instead of relying *only* upon their expertise as a strong and efficacious school leader and communicator, the emerging scholar-practitioner principal would go to the research literature to explore how others have studied school-community relationships between international families and U.S. school communities to glean insights. They might also design a small focus group to interview parents and personally ask for help in understanding the communication methods and cultures of the families as a scholar-practitioner approach to this nuanced problem in their professional context. Engaging in these learning activities and community activities strengthens both their PSE and their SSE. As their scholar-practitioner identities and self-efficacy increase and become more apparent, they are more aware of the complexities of educational issues and opportunities. Further, scholar-practitioner graduates such as the aforementioned principal are no longer bound by traditional habits of mind, points of view, and patterns of being and acting in their roles that reflect their former frames of reference.

Critical Reflection Through Disorienting Dilemmas in the EDD Program Experiences

Earlier in this chapter, we described Mezirow's (1997) contention that changing one's frame of reference must involve critical reflection through discourse related to disorienting dilemmas. Then, we spoke about how PSE and SSE are instrumental constructs that we aim to buttress throughout the program (see Figure 2.1). The anecdote about the aforementioned principal illustrated what an emerging scholar-practitioner looks like while they are going through the EdD journey. In the following sections, we describe the mechanisms more deeply for how an emerging scholar-practitioner principal would come to this new identity.

We describe how different experiences within the EdD program create opportunities and affordances for students to engage in discourse around disorienting dilemmas and critical reflections related to their identities, their points of view, and their habits of mind. These experiences are the mechanisms that engender what we believe are instrumental changes in their frames of reference that allow them to see themselves as scholar-practitioners who view themselves as individuals with intersectional identities and interact with others in their profession in more nuanced ways through systems mindsets. These identity changes occur as consequences of very intentional milestones throughout the EdD student's doctoral journey. In the following sections, we highlight several components of the JHU EdD program that offer the students opportunities for critical reflection leading to identity transformation: discussion posts in the online courses, course-based assignments, oral comprehensive examinations, adviser doctoral mentorship, and the Applied Dissertation.

Critical Reflection and Discourse: Making Thinking Visible in Online Courses

In the online JHU EdD program, we intentionally structure the courses and course assignments in ways that require students to post their thoughts and reflections on research and theory, and by doing so, make their thinking visible, open to others, and malleable. These critical reflection discussion posts were created for several reasons. First, their written posts hone their skills as scholarly writers and expand their abilities to critique research and reflect upon how the research was or was not relevant for their professional context. That is, the discussion posts help students to develop as *conversant scholars* who can digest literature, discuss the merits of studies, and critique the strengths and limitations of the studies from multiple perspectives and lenses. Second, by engaging in this discourse in asynchronous and synchronous settings with their peers, they begin to build their self-efficacy as critical consumers of research literature. They begin to relinquish their frame of reference from which they view research from a broad perspective and take on new perspectives that allow them to see research articles as specific, context-based studies that might have deep flaws or might have generalizable findings.

Third, they are asked to describe and reflect on the systems identified or not identified in the studies and to describe their POP through these systems lenses in their discussions with peers. These ongoing cycles of iterating on the POP through the different lenses presented in their coursework (e.g., historical, cultural/anthropological, sociological, economic, and learning theories) allows them to identify their points of view, question and debate those personal points of view about the driving factors or root causes of the problem, and engage in examining new points of view for conceptualizing their POP. Engaging in this sense-making in these asynchronous collaborative spaces with their peers further deepens our students' empathic stances toward themselves and toward the people in their spheres of influence.

Course-Based Projects as Mechanisms for Merging Identities

Numerous course-based assignments and projects engage our doctoral students in activities that build their sense of self-efficacy as a scholar-practitioner while they are in the program. For example, students in a core leadership course are asked to perform a strengths, weaknesses, opportunities, and threats (SWOT) analysis and write a paper about the leadership actions they will take and how these actions align with their chosen theory of leadership. They must identify whether they see themselves as a transformational leader, a transactional leader, or an authentic leader, for example, to engage in this assignment. This critical reflection requires that they analyze their current practice in their professional context and imagine how they want to proceed as an educational leader. These reflections on their leadership allow the students to live out those ideals. These changes in their leadership become apparent to their professional colleagues as they see them learning and growing through the EdD program.

In some required courses, students are asked to write a policy brief to address a factor of their POP, and they are encouraged to share these papers with leaders in their context. In this exercise, students succinctly summarize the current policy or practice in their organization, describe the advantages and disadvantages of the current policy or practice, then outline three possible solutions for moving forward in a new direction to ameliorate the shortcomings of the current policy or practice. This writing and review of the research requires the doctoral students to communicate their argument in a balanced and concise format to demonstrate their knowledge of the literature and to demonstrate their ability to communicate their knowledge in a digestible way to an organizational leader or to a policy maker, a person who may not know the education jargon. Our students report that engaging in these policy papers helps them to hone their communication skills, their writing skills, and their research-practice partnership skills to better translate research to their professional partners. Many of the doctoral students ask for input on these assignments from their organizational leaders so that the documents will be helpful to the organization and for the doctoral student. Many students also report that these policy papers elicit positive change within their organizations because their leaders are presented with viable solutions. Through these exercises, our students' identities as scholar-practitioners become more solidified as their self-efficacy in their intersectional identities as both a scholar and an experienced practitioner expand.

In later courses, students develop research conference proposals and research posters for presenting their dissertation or needs assessment study findings to a professional conference audience. In this exercise, they engage in winnowing down their research story to the most salient pieces, packaging them in a brief conference proposal, and then developing the research poster for dissemination. This process involves several levels of feedback from their peers and instructors and several rounds of refinement. Most students submit these course-based proposals to conferences, and some of these presentations result in publications through these professional conferences. Through these preparation and presentation activities, students' scholar-practitioner identities are affirmed. They see themselves recognized as worthy scholar-practitioners not only in their professional contexts and by their professors, but they are also acknowledged by outside scholarly communities. Their SPSE is thereby increased.

Oral Comprehensive Exams to Confirm Scholar-Practitioner Competencies

Oral comprehensive exams are required of JHU EdD students to demonstrate their competence with numerous bodies of literature, abilities to synthesize the literature across their program, and application of this knowledge to practice. These 2-hour oral exams are held with their dissertation advisory committee. Because of the intense nature of this examination, we encourage students to prepare by forming communities of practice to discuss potential questions, review the literature together, conduct mock sessions with one another, and be in a scholarly community together (Coffman et al., 2016). Although we encourage group formation, we do not typically facilitate group membership, which the students report is better done organically through their social networks. These study groups provide a network of EdD colleagues (see Table 1.1 in Chapter 1) who embarked on similar professional journeys by joining the EdD community. They also provide safe spaces for students to test out their scholar-practitioner identities and to build their self-efficacy. In collaboration with peers in these comprehensive exam study groups, students develop enhanced empathy because they hear the different points of view that their peers brought to their responses to practice questions, especially social justice-oriented practice questions.

Students report that these practice sessions facilitate their perspective-taking to better understand problems from different lenses and viewpoints, particularly cultural, racial, and ethnic perspectives that they might not have considered before this EdD program. Their shifts in their points of view through these sessions and reflections with their peers allows the students to develop new habits of mind, ways of thinking, and using the research that become automatic because of their repeated rehearsals and regular review and practice sessions. Their deep immersion in and review of content to verbally address questions of translation and synthesis of research to practice and practice to research in these networks prepares our students for a broader role in their workplaces, one where they can share well-researched expertise using their newly developed agility with orally communicating research to practice. Finally, students' oral success in front of a panel of scholars demonstrates to both the panel and the student that they are indeed burgeoning scholar-practitioners. This milestone marks a major transition in students' identities to doctoral candidates who have demonstrated both mastery of the content and oral dexterity in addressing research-practice partnership questions from a panel of scholars. Their mastery in this culminating event solidifies their self-efficacy beliefs as scholar-practitioners who have experienced not only the excitement of the mastery experience during the oral comprehensive exam but also the verbal persuasion of the committee in confirming their doctoral candidacy as legitimate. They leave these momentous occasions with a new sense of self, more robust feelings of SSE, and a new boost in their motivations to implement and complete their Applied Dissertation studies in collaboration with their advisers and professional partners.

Advising as a Mentoring Partnership

In the JHU EdD program, students were matched with a faculty adviser during their first semester of the program after the student had refined their conception of their POP. Because of the embedded nature of the dissertation within the coursework, this mentoring partnership with the doctoral student serves as one of the signature pedagogies (Carnegie Project on the Education Doctorate, 2009; Shulman, 2005) whereby the adviser partners with the student for the duration of their doctoral studies. Through regular mentoring and advising sessions, the adviser builds upon the strengths of the student to co-construct pathways for understanding the POP from multiple lenses within the research literature. Advisers engage in a variety of skill-building and knowledge-building activities, such as kind critical consciousness building through the critiquing of the students' literature reviews as they scan for evidence of the doctoral student honoring all people in their writing and research and using asset-based, nondeficit discourse frameworks or labels. The advisers build upon students' strengths rather than focusing on what they lack or can't do well. Using this strengths-based approach, the advisers model ways to build upon the strengths of their professional partners in their dissertation research projects for their students. They also model the types of partnership with the student that we expect the student to enact with their professional partners in the field. Through this long-term mentoring relationship, advisers work to build students' self-efficacy as scholar-practitioners through their acknowledgement of mastery experiences, verbal persuasion, vicarious experiences, and critical reflection activities in helping students shape their dissertation research and providing tailored guidance for their partnership work in their contexts.

Applied Dissertation Process to Grow into the Novice Scholar-Practitioner

We provided an overview of the structure of the JHU EdD Applied Dissertation in Chapter 1 of this volume. This culminating experience, which is taken up across the program in various course assignments, is an important component in the identity development process and the doctoral student's organizational change process. Through the preparation and implementation of the dissertation intervention, students further develop their research-practice partnerships while they explore their POP, conduct the needs assessment study, and develop the intervention to study for the Applied Dissertation. The research-practice partnership runs counter to the "ivory tower" notion of researchers or consultants telling practitioners what to do with their organizations. Instead, the researcher is a practitioner, working as a partner within the organization, and gaining (and using) new knowledge and insights from the doctoral journey. Organizational change happens through many mechanisms, but many of those change mechanisms fail to produce lasting change. In this model, personal and professional identity change catalyzes organizational change.

The research-practice partnership process begins before the doctoral student is admitted with the development of the problem-focused and user-centered focus of their doctoral work. After conducting a needs assessment study in their professional context (e.g., school, district, or professional organization), the doctoral student comes together with their professional partners, including their professional colleagues, adviser, and EdD colleagues, to analyze the data and the implications of the findings. As students engage in this sense-making activity with their professional partners, they begin to move from a practitioner identity to a scholar-practitioner identity. The needs assessment study activities allow for the translation of knowledge within their contexts using their context-specific data and findings. The doctoral students bring the knowledge they are gaining from their courses and their own readings of empirical literature to share with their professional partners through informal conversations and formal professional development sessions. Instead of relying exclusively on their practice-based expertise, the doctoral students share their new nuanced understanding of the research about their practice and potential avenues for understanding the needs of their colleagues and stakeholders.

Through deep contemplation of literature and their context-specific factors, students then select a research design to honor both the participants and the intentions of the intervention or needs assessment. This deliberate research design that honors the integrity of the participants affords the opportunity for the students' partnerships with their colleagues to evolve into new collaborative relationships. This process allows the professional partners to see and interact with the doctoral student in a new role: the embedded research-practice partner, a novice scholar-practitioner. As the doctoral student engages with their colleagues with this new identity and experiences how their colleagues now view them and regard their knowledge and understanding, they also begin to shift how they view themselves. Being "seen" both literally and figuratively by their colleagues in a new light allows them to see themselves differently. It is the engagement of these professional scholarly experiences that facilitates this shift in identity.

Interacting with one's colleagues in relation to a POP and the data from a needs assessment study opens the door for collaborative conversations and sense-making with respect to the data. These conversations permits the doctoral student to shed light on the data by sharing their knowledge of other research from similar contexts that they have gained during their literature review related to the POP. Rather than looking for new programs to solve their context-based problems, they first investigate why that problem is happening within that context. Then, the doctoral student can bring context-focused ideas from the research to share with their partners to start brainstorming possible solutions and interventions that they might adapt from the literature on intervention studies. Specifically, our students report that this new knowledge and burgeoning scholar-practitioner identities allow them to have an elevated voice at their leadership tables in their professional contexts. They are being viewed as and are acting as a scholar-practitioner resource in their contexts.

Through this partnership work of collaborating on the dissertation, which includes the needs assessment and the intervention studies, students' identities as scholar-practitioners and research-practice partners help elevate practitioner voices in the research process and help elevate the importance of research findings within professional conversations. Further, this partnership allows new types of research to be communicated in the profession as the doctoral student works together with colleagues in a research-practice partnership to learn more deeply about their education problems, identify opportunities for growth, and develop potential solutions together, thereby catalyzing organizational change and growth from the inside out.

Scholar-Practitioners as Place-Based Research-Practice Partners for Social Justice

Without understanding personal positionality in terms of our personal and professional intersectional identities, it is difficult to see our own privileges and to recognize injustices and inequities in schools and organizations. In some ways, we have been conditioned to ignore these inequities (Tatum, 2017). Further, when one becomes aware of their multifaceted, intersectional identities and privileges, an individual can better leverage those privileges to disrupt systems of oppression in education and in educational organizations. Our intentions for the JHU EdD is to ensure that our graduates can no longer "not see" the systems-level inequities after they have moved into this level of knowing. They are scholar-practitioners who are insiders, no longer practitioner insiders. We assert that this level of knowing and identity phase is akin to the last phase in the OTAID model, the transformation phase, whereby people understand the interconnectedness between themselves, the people around them, and the systems in which they live. The scholar-practitioner at this level also understands their personal responsibility to partner in these spaces to facilitate more equitable and socially just organizations.

The JHU EdD faculty designed the program not only to provide professional advancement opportunities but also to facilitate this transformation of identities for our students. We aimed to help our students grow from highly successful practitioners into lifelong scholarly practitioners. We believed and still believe that evidence-based perspectives can improve and influence equity-oriented solutions for educational problems and opportunities. However, even more importantly, we assert that scholar-practitioners in the profession play an essential role in transforming education as they continue to serve, seek, research, and partner with diverse communities of practice. It is through this transformation of identities that they become agents of social justice change in education communities across the United States and around the world. They began their transformation of identities during their tenure with us in our program, and they continue expanding their spheres of influence as they carry on the good work that emerged and grew during their doctoral journey.

References

Bandura, A. (1977). Self-efficacy: Toward a unifying theory of behavioral change. *Psychological Review, 84*(2), 191–215. https://doi.org/10.1037/0033-295X.84.2.191

Bronfenbrenner, U. (1994). Ecology models of human development. In T. N. Postlewaite & T. Husen, (Eds.), *International encyclopedia of education* (2nd ed., Vol. 3, pp. 1643–1647). Elsevier.

Carnegie Project on the Education Doctorate. (2009). *The CPED framework.* https://cped.memberclicks.net/the-framework

Caskey, M. M., Stevens, D. D., & Yeo, M. (2020). Examining doctoral student development of a researcher identity: Using the Draw a Researcher Test. *Impacting Education: Journal on Transforming Professional Practice, 5*(1). https://doi.org/10.5195/ie.2020.92

Coffman, K., Putman, P., Adkisson, A., Kriner, B., & Monaghan, C. (2016). Waiting for the expert to arrive: Using a community of practice to develop the scholarly identity of doctoral students. *International Journal of Teaching and Learning in Higher Education, 28*(1), 30–37.

De Weerdt, S., Bouwen, R. Corthouts, F., & Martens, H. (2006). Identity transformation as an intercontextual process. *Industry & Higher Education, 20*(5), 317–326. https://doi.org/10.5367/000000006778702373

Foot, R., Crowe, A. R., Tollafield, K. A., & Allan, C. E. (2014). Exploring doctoral student identity development using a self-study approach. *Teaching and Learning Inquiry, 2*(1), 103–118. https://doi.org/10.20343/teachlearninqu.2.1.103

Greeley, A. T., Johnson, E., Seem, S., Braver, M., Dias, L., Evans, K., Kincade, E., & Pricken, P. (1989). *Research Self-Efficacy Scale.* [Unpublished scale presented at the conference of the Association for Women in Psychology, Bethesda, MD].

Hall, L., & Burns, L. (2009). Identity development and mentoring in doctoral education. *Harvard Educational Review, 79*(1), 49–70. https://doi.org/10.17763/haer.79.1.wr25486891279345

Leshem, S. (2020). Identity formations of doctoral students on the route to achieving their doctorate. *Issues in Educational Research, 30*(1), 169–186.

Mezirow, J. (1997). Transformative learning: Theory to practice. *New Directions for Adult and Continuing Education,* (74), 5–12. https://doi.org/10.1002/ace.7401

Myers, L. J., Speight, S. L., Highlen, P. S., Cox, C. I., Reynolds, A. L., Adams, E. M., & Hanley, C. P. (1991). Identity development and worldview: Toward an optimal conceptualization. *Journal of Counseling & Development, 70*(1), 54–63. https://doi.org/10.1002/j.1556-6676.1991.tb01561.x

Neal, J. W., & Neal, Z. P. (2013). Nested or networked? Future directions for ecological systems theory. *Social Development, 22*(4), 722–737. https://doi.org/10.1111/sode.12018

Rigler, K. L. Jr., Anastasia, C. M., El-Amin, A., & Throne, R. (2021). Scholarly voice and academic identity: A systematic review of doctoral student agency. In A. Zimmerman

(Ed.), *Handbook of research on developing students' scholarly dispositions in higher education* (pp. 63–89). IGI Global. https://doi.org/10.4018/978-1-7998-7267-2.ch004

Shulman, L. (2005). Signature pedagogies in the professions. *Daedalus, 134,* 52–59. https://doi.org/10.1162/0011526054622015

Tatum, B. D. (2017). *Why are all the Black kids sitting together in the cafeteria? And other conversations about race.* Hachette UK.

Trede, F., Macklin, R., & Bridges, D. (2012). Professional identity development: A review of the higher education literature. *Studies in Higher Education, 37*(3), 365–384. https://doi.org/10.1080/03075079.2010.521237

Zambo, D., Buss, R. R., & Zambo, R. (2015). Uncovering the identities of students and graduates in a CPED-influenced EdD program. *Studies in Higher Education, 40*(2), 233–252.

CHAPTER 3

The Role of Research Methods Courses in Transforming the Identities of Scholar-Practitioners

*Camille L. Bryant, Stephen J. Pape,
Ranjini Mahinda JohnBull, and Karen S. Karp*

> *These scholars must ensure … that younger scholars receive the training they need to develop core competence in education research.*
>
> —DEBORAH LOEWENBERG BALL AND FRANCESCA M. FORZANI

Introduction

RESEARCH METHODS COURSES in practitioner-oriented doctoral programs (as well as other types of doctoral programs) are central to the dissertation. They lay the foundation for rigorous studies that demonstrate students' competency to conduct research-informed empirical studies as a culminating experience of their doctoral journey and well-thought-out inquiry beyond the doctoral program. Within Doctor of Education (EdD) programs, research methods are central to the structured exploration of educational problems, practices, policies, behaviors, and interventions, to name a few. The research methods courses within the EdD program at Johns Hopkins University (JHU) aim to help students disentangle complex issues or wicked problems (Cabrera & Cabrera, 2018) within context-based research sites to propose and potentially implement a relevant and targeted solution. Determining how, why, and the extent to which a problem and associated contributing factors operate within a context relies on the strategic use of relevant research methods. Learning and applying concepts such as participatory research, variables, constructs, research question development, research paradigms, designs, sampling, data analysis, mitigating bias, identifying strengths and limitations, and the connection across these ideas is central to investigating problems deeply through empirical exploration such as the needs assessment study and making incremental change in context-based research as described by Bryk et al. (2015). The premise of this approach is guided by five of the six core principles of improvement science: problem-focused and user-centered, variation in performance, seeing the system, the role of measurement, and disciplined inquiry to support improvement (Bryk et al., 2015). The three research methods courses within the JHU program apply these core principles to support the Applied Dissertation, future scholarly practice within the doctoral students' professional context, and the critical examination of research studies they will encounter during and after the dissertation in the literature and in practical applications.

As was discussed in Chapter 1 of this book, central to our program's approach is the examination of Problems of Practice (POPs) from the beginning of the program. Instead of taking courses and then homing in on a topic of interest, our students propose their direction in their application to the program. In this way and through each course, students build on a known situation that stems from their "insider" perspective within their professional practice. However, as they better understand the problem and the system within which it operates, empirically examine contributing factors, and intervene in those problems, they must also take on the role of "outsider," to understand the problem from a different vantage point and minimize biases they bring as an insider.

As research methods are unveiled, students learn content for its utility in their study. Not only do students make connections between course content and their dissertation research, but they apply their knowledge in real time to complete portions of their dissertation chapters within their courses. The instructional approach of learning through application requires supports that aim to build and strengthen students' research competencies (Rockinson-Szapkiw, 2018), research self-efficacy (Bieschke et al., 1996; Greeley et al., 1989), relevant constructs for doctoral studies, and scholar-practitioner identity.

Research Methods and Systematic Inquiry I (RMI) is designed to support and encourage students' first shift in their identity transformation—from experienced practitioner-aspiring scholar to informed practitioner-emerging scholar (see Figure 3.1), through empirical exploration of the problem via a needs assessment study. In doing so, students are primed to explore factors from their literature review in the first chapter of their dissertation, which surveys potential contributing factors related to the POP, within their sphere of influence in their context of professional practice. RMI provides students with the empirical skills to examine how factors within and across levels of the system influence the problem and plan for improvement through disciplined inquiry that relies on sound measurement, which aligns with Bryk and colleagues' (2015) principles of improvement science.

Research Methods and Systematic Inquiry II (RMII) is a data analysis course created to fine-tune students' methodological decision-making primarily for their needs assessment study, while laying a foundation for empirical work throughout their doctoral studies. Students take a deep dive into quantitative, qualitative, and mixed methods research analyses to support the investigation of variation in the system and change in outcomes through the improvement cycles for their dissertation research. This course aims to produce the emerging scholar practitioner. The final course, *Evaluation of Educational Policies and Programs* (Eval), is designed to help students plan, execute, and evaluate an intervention that will address the salient factors from the initial needs assessment empirical investigation. As novice scholar-practitioners, students learn to make meaningful methodological decisions to examine the intervention process and outcomes to determine not just what works, "but what works for whom, where, when, and why" (Honig, 2006, p. 2). The next section explores each course more deeply, focusing on the content, connection to the applied dissertation, and role in fostering the skills and dispositions of a scholar-practitioner to support doctoral students' identity transformation.

Research Methods Courses

Improving students' research methods self-efficacy guides the approaches of the JHU research methods faculty. As described in Chapter 2 of this book, self-efficacy was defined by Bandura (1977) as "beliefs in one's capabilities to organize and execute the courses of action required to produce given attainments" (p. 3). Self-efficacy related to research methods is a mediating variable

Figure 3.1

Practices in Research Methods Courses that Support Research Methods Self-Efficacy and Identity Transformation

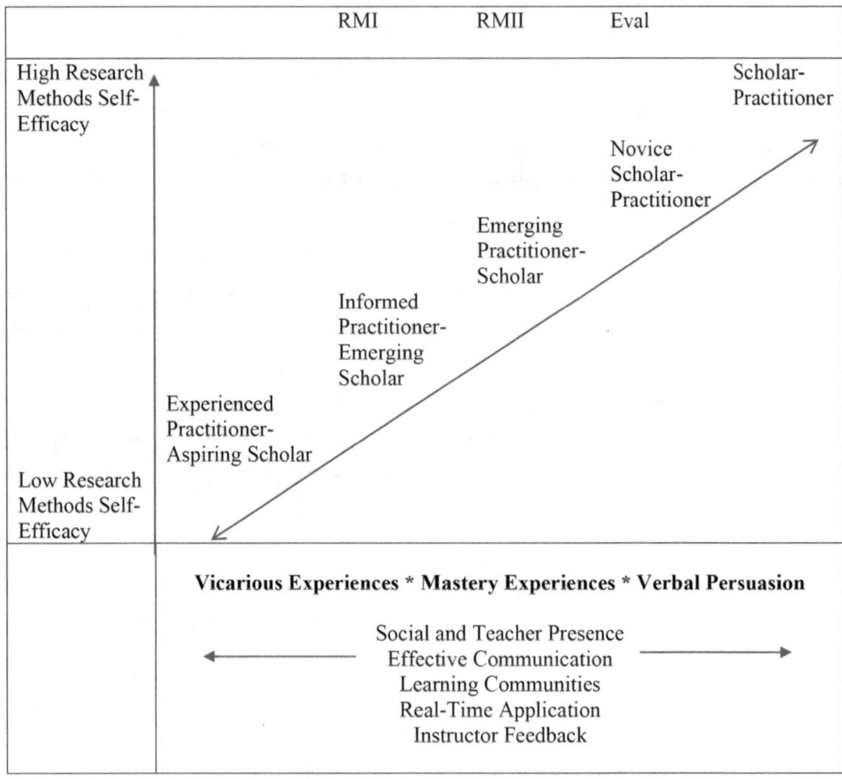

for achievement outcomes and influences students' persistence in a task (Zambo et al., 2015). The JHU EdD program aims to support and improve students' research methods self-efficacy primarily through vicarious experiences, mastery experiences, and verbal persuasion, which have been named as sources of efficacy information (Bandura, 1977), all supported by knowledgeable others.

Research Methods and Systematic Inquiry I

RMI is a foundational research methods course in the JHU EdD program. To encourage the informed practitioner-emerging scholar phase, students learn "introductory concepts in quantitative, qualitative, and mixed methods research" (Eith, 2023, p. 1) by applying this new knowledge to plan their needs assessment study during which they empirically examine potential contributing factors related to their POP. This approach to the course aligns with best practices for teaching research methods in which concepts are applied to a problem that is meaningful to students as identified by Remler and Van Ryzkin (Sage, 2014).

Students are exposed to three major research paradigms—quantitative, qualitative, and mixed methods—and embedded concepts such as identifying constructs; conducting literature analysis and synthesis; writing design-appropriate research questions; selecting purpose-driven instrumentation; critiquing validity, reliability, and trustworthiness; considerations for participant selection; data collection and management; and effective analysis. Instructional methods include student-centered approaches emphasizing practice-based opportunities. For example, when students learn about participatory research, they are assigned to observe and interview stakeholders within their diverse professional contexts as a preliminary approach to understanding the scope of their POP. These observations and conversations reveal potential contributing factors within their professional context of which they may not be aware. Although challenging to do two things at the same time, doing the work of research as they learn new concepts, this approach not only fortifies and solidifies prior and new knowledge but also reduces the stress the students may experience when eventually applying these skills independently. This blending of learning with action provides mental residue of learning that stays with them over time and increases their self-efficacy (Lane et al., 2004).

As with most online programs, discussions with peers offer students opportunities to refine their thinking and understanding of concepts within the lenses of multiple learners, cultures, thoughts, and experiential backgrounds. This practice not only encourages vicarious experiences where students naturally compare their performance with their peers', which is a significant source of information for efficacy judgments (Bandura, 1977), the discussions also allow students the opportunity to apply ideas prior to planning their study. Further, these experiences aim to support the role of the learning community in shaping the identity transformation for doctoral students (Coffman et al., 2016) while building their agency to bolster their efforts to accomplish the project successfully.

RMI is the course in which students begin to experience the iterative nature of the research process. Unlike assignments for other degrees, this work is not ultimately checked off and relegated to a computer file folder. Assignments and subsequent targeted instructor feedback to support verbal persuasion (Bandura, 1977) require revisiting, reflection, and the realization that research is dynamic and evolving as well as tied to the ultimate dissertation product. This course also helps students better understand the program's alignment with our university's deep commitment to contributing to the public discourse on improvement of education with attention to inclusion and policies and practices that reflect social justice. This commitment results in careful attention to looking at researchers' biases both explicit and implicit and both in reading others' studies and in planning for their own.

Research Methods and Systematic Inquiry II

The second course, RMII, engages students in trialing the analysis of quantitative data using inferential statistics, qualitative data using inductive and deductive approaches, and mixed methods to blend both designs for greater depth and breadth as described by Johnson et al. (2007). Students also explore the logic of using each approach given a research purpose and question. In this course, students use common data sets (i.e., survey and focus group data) related to online learning self-efficacy that were collected from their peers at a previous annual summer orientation and residency. Group activities allow them to practice prior to encountering independent assignments and encourages and increases dialogue as students tackle complex concepts, as characterized by Harris et al. (2007). During this group work, students create a question, explore techniques for organizing the data, develop an analysis plan, and carry it out. They must learn the cautionary approaches to preventing pursuing the wrong path when the evidence isn't substantive (e.g., choosing a parametric statistical test when the evidence points to a nonparametric test). In this way, the course is designed to support the emerging scholar practitioner by providing mastery experiences that allow students to safely practice approaches with their peers, an essential source of efficacy information (Bandura, 1977), which supports students' perceived quality of learning in online research methods courses (Lim et al., 2008) and their "sense of identity" as a doctoral student (Seyri & Rezaee 2022, p. 55).

In addition, students have opportunities to engage in vicarious experiences through faculty modeling that aim to support, build, and strengthen their research methods self-efficacy prior to engaging in independent analysis for the course and, ultimately, their dissertation research. Modeling through strong and relevant examples is a common approach by faculty in methods courses. Bransford et al. (1989) identified two key characteristics of a quality example: providing reasoning behind the solution and drawing attention to the most important characteristics of the concept. In methods courses, modeling through examples, while also explaining why one approach is more appropriate than another, is critical as students build their research knowledge and acumen (Chew, 2007).

There are three assignments in this course. The first assignment focuses on inferential statistical analysis in which students develop a research question using a common data set and conduct a statistical analysis to answer the question. They make decisions based on statistical evidence supporting either a parametric or a nonparametric inferential test. The second assignment focuses on qualitative analysis. Here, students apply their knowledge of inductive and deductive qualitative analysis approaches and methods to establish trustworthiness to mitigate bias as the research instrument. The third assignment ventures into mixed methods approaches, looking for cross-cutting themes using numbers and participants' words as data. This assignment allows students to integrate qualitative and quantitative data using systematic steps as described by Corrigan and Onwuegbuzie (2020) and Johnson and colleagues (2017) to make meta-inferences.

Evaluation of Education Policies and Programs

The final course in the trilogy centers on evaluation methods for program improvement, implementation fidelity, and successful program outcomes. As such, the research questions students learn to consider align with the purposes of (1) demonstrating that the intervention they delivered was implemented with fidelity in part by capturing the voices of their professional partners engaged in the intervention, and (2) investigating the degree to which proximal outcomes were met. The process of planning an evaluation requires students to identify and consider the role of key stakeholders (Bryk et al., 2015). In addition, structures such as logic models, theory of treatment plans (Leviton & Lipsey, 2007), and research summary matrices are developed to communicate their organized approach to justifying their decisions. Students also learn about threats to validity, models to examine causality (Shadish et al., 2001) for evaluating program outcomes, and how their role as an insider in the organization may influence the evaluation. Their plan is also developed taking into consideration plan-do-study-act cycles of improvement (Bryk et al., 2015; Christie et al., 2017).

Partnering not only with their course instructor but also with their dissertation adviser, the students embed these products within their dissertation methodology chapter. Importantly, they also complete a portion of the human subjects review process application to understand the protections their participants require, which supports building robust recruitment and retention plans, mitigating any issues of authority or privilege, and preparing them for developing their own human subjects review process application. This is particularly important since students are engaging in participatory research within their contexts of professional practice and may hold positions of power, which could have implications for participant autonomy.

Through the cycle of continuous improvement, students craft an intervention to make a difference in their context. The addition of the role of change maker necessitates they look at their considerations of power, culture, positionality, and the context-based language and practices that only an insider would know (Atkins & Duckworth, 2019). As such, while the insider role may be an advantage, it is critical that students balance this identity with an outsider perspective to mitigate bias. These more nuanced ways of thinking about research and their role, as well as building on knowledge gained from RMI and RMII, supports the transition from the emerging to the novice scholar-practitioner.

Throughout students' research methods courses, faculty have aimed to provide students with mastery and vicarious experiences to support their competencies in "the techniques and procedures that produce research evidence" (Remler & Van Ryzin, 2015, p. 3) and increased self-efficacy. Further, faculty provide extensive and prompt feedback, described by Harris et al. (2007) as important qualities for online methods courses. Feedback is intended to acknowledge students' strengths through verbal persuasion, an important source of information related to self-efficacy (Bandura, 1977), while encouraging growth within areas for improvement.

Supporting the Scholar-Practitioner Identity

"The process of doctoral study is as much about identity formation as it is about knowledge production" (Green, 2005, p. 153). Doctoral students enter programs with professional and research identities (Council of Graduate Schools, 2005). Although some students may begin as research novices with some levels of trepidation, anxiousness, and dread about research methods courses and others as more experienced and confident, our goal is that students' transformation leads to scholar-practitioners who are efficacious as producers, researchers, and consumers of scholarship. This is important as students meet and explore educational problems throughout their professional careers.

Research methods courses that include introductory concepts, analysis methods, and specialized approaches relevant to students' applied research (e.g., program evaluation) are essential in practitioner-oriented doctoral programs to support the development of the scholar-practitioner identity. Although the content of the courses in the JHU EdD program may share commonalities with other doctoral programs of study, the instructional approaches and real-time application of the content in a familiar context uniquely positions students to foster deeper understanding and maximizes student self-efficacy for research methods (Lane et al., 2004). This is important because research methods and statistics courses are often regarded as challenging, disconnected, boring (Dunn et al., 2007; Lane et al., 2004; Onwuegbuzie & Wilson, 2003), and/or anxiety inducing (Onwuegbuzie et al., 1997). Further, doctoral students in an online methods course are less motivated when they cannot "find meaning or value in their highly demanding coursework in the absence of a concrete idea about their dissertation research" (Lim et al., 2008, p. 229). The role of application is also important because our program is built on a level of efficiency that requires effective decision-making for timely program momentum.

Mitigating barriers to learning research methods in an online environment requires intentional guidance and approaches that aim to foster a scholar-practitioner identity so that students not only have the skills to complete their dissertation but can use their knowledge of research methods to explore and intervene in educational problems in their professional practice, initially as educational diagnosticians and ultimately as problem solvers. As diagnosticians, students have the methodological skills to identify and investigate a problem through the exploration of literature and an empirical needs assessment study. They do not rush to solutions that are based solely on their practice or history within the organization, and/or without considering the prevalence of variation across contexts (Bryk et al., 2015). Instead, they carefully explore why the problem occurs from a systems perspective, acknowledging the complexity of contributing forces acting on the problem, the multiple factors at play, and the interactions between factors within and across levels of the system, while also being aware of and minimizing a deficit perspective in this work. This understanding guides the empirical exploration by which they craft quality research questions and make sound methodological decisions (e.g., research design, sampling, and analysis). This approach to tackling a problem and using their acquired skills allows students to draw informed conclusions about the nature of the problem, which can then support targeted solutions that are implemented and evaluated through an iterative process. This iterative process of change allows for incremental modifications to practice that "accelerates" the learning and growth of an organization's improvement for long-standing problems (Bryk et al., 2015).

Two overarching program practices that encourage this disposition as scholar-practitioner are social and teacher presence grounded in effective communication between instructors and students (Harris et al., 2007; Lim et al., 2008) and structured and cohesive opportunities for engagement. These are needed to support advanced levels of critical reasoning and knowledge production in online learning environments (Aviv et al., 2003; Garrison & Cleveland-Innes, 2005; Thomas, 2002). Social presence is regarded as "interpersonal contact, communicational intimacy, and immediacy, perceived by students in a virtual learning environment" (Gunawadena, 2004 as cited in Lim et al., 2008, p. 225). More importantly, "teacher presence in the form of facilitation is crucial in the success of online learning" (Garrison & Cleveland-Innes, 2005, p. 136). Teacher presence encourages students to "explore, integrate, and test concepts and solutions," which are necessary for students' cognitive presence (Garrison & Cleveland-Innes, 2005, p. 135) and ultimately deep learning (Biggs & Tang, 2011) where concepts are "embraced and digested in [a] search for meaning" (Garrison & Cleveland-Innes, 2005, p. 137).

In our program, providing synchronous and asynchronous opportunities to interact with instructors through planned sessions, office hours, group meetings, discussion summaries, weekly announcements (written, video, and audio), "prompt correspondence" via e-mail (Lim et al., 2008, p. 232), and detailed assignment feedback (Harris et al., 2007), to name a few, are ways in which the research methods faculty aim to foster a robust social presence and provide multiple opportunities for personal contact with students. Further, deeper meaning-making is supported by teacher presence where discourse and quality interaction meet.

The methods courses aim to improve students' research methods self-efficacy within a virtual environment that provides "a unique . . . opportunity to build up a quality learning community" where "active engagement in learning and their identity transformation are all possible" (De Bryun, 2004; Francescato, et al. 2006 as cited in Lim et al., 2008, p. 225). Consistent teacher and social presence facilitated by personalized and varied faculty-student communication plays a critical role as students apply and engage in learning activities within an online setting.

Conclusion

The sequence of research methods courses within the JHU EdD program are designed to support students' research methods self-efficacy and competencies needed as scholar-practitioners. We rely on an applied approach, in which students learn by doing. As such, students complete portions of their dissertation research as they learn and gain knowledge of the three research paradigms embedded within each course.

In RMI, students prepare for the examination of factors related to their POP as they learn introductory research methods concepts. In RMII, students apply analysis approaches to refine their empirical needs assessment study from RMI and think ahead to a potential intervention study. Finally, they apply their knowledge in the evaluation course to plan the process and outcome evaluations for examining their proposed intervention. Application alongside instructional strategies (e.g., learning communities) with consistent and varied communication aim to provide experiences that improve students' self-efficacy and competencies in research methods and support the transformation of students' identities from practitioner-scholar to scholar-practitioner.

References

Atkins, L., & Duckworth, V. (2019). *Research methods for social justice and equity in education.* Bloomsbury Academic.

Aviv, R., Erlich, Z., Ravid, G., & Geva, A. (2003). Network analysis of knowledge construction in asynchronous learning networks. *Journal of Asynchronous Learning Networks, 7*(3), 1–20. https://doi.org/10.24059/olj.v7i3.1842

Ball, D. L., & Forzani, F. M. (2007). 2007 Wallace Foundation Distinguished Lecture—what makes education research "educational"? *Educational Researcher, 36*(9), 529–540. https://doi.org/10.3102/0013189x07312896

Bandura, A. (1977). Self-efficacy: Toward a unifying theory of behavior change. *Psychological Review, 84*(2), 191–215. https://doi:10.1037/0033-295X.84.2.191

Bieschke, K. J., Bishop, R. M., & Garcia, V. L. (1996). The utility of the research self-efficacy scale. *Journal of Career Assessment, 4*(1), 59–75. https://doi.org/10.1177/106907279600400104

Biggs, J., & Tang, C. (2011). *Teaching for quality learning at university.* McGraw-Hill.

Bransford, J.D., Franks, J.J., Vye, N.J., & Sherwood, R.D. (1989). New approaches to instruction: Because wisdom can't be told. In S. Vosniadou & A. Ortony (Eds.), *Similarity and analogical reasoning* (pp. 470–497). NY: Cambridge University Press.

Bryk, A. S., Gomez, L. M., Grunow, A., & LeMahieu, P. G. (2015). *Learning to improve: How America's schools can get better at getting better.* Harvard Education Press.

Cabrera, D., & Cabrera, L. (2018). *Systems thinking made simple: New hope for solving wicked problems.* Plectica Publishing.

Chew, S. L. (2007). Designing effective examples and problems for teaching statistics. In D. Dunn, R. A. A. Smith, & B. Beins (Eds.), *Best practices for teaching statistics and research methods in the behavioral sciences* (pp. 73–92). Lawrence Erlbaum.

Christie, C. A., Inkelas, M., & Lemire, S. (2017). *Improvement science in evaluation: Methods and uses.* Wiley & Sons.

Coffman, K., Putman, P., Adkisson, A., Kriner, B., & Monaghan, C. (2016). Waiting for the expert to arrive: Using a community of practice to develop the scholarly identity of doctoral students. *International Journal of Teaching and Learning in Higher Education, 28*(1), 30–37.

Corrigan, J., & Onwuegbuzie, A. (2020). Toward a meta-framework for conducting mixed methods representation analyses to optimize meta-inferences. *The Qualitative Report.* https://doi.org/10.46743/2160-3715/2020.3579

Council of Graduate Schools in the U.S. (2005). *The doctor of philosophy degree: A policy statement.* U.S. Department of Education. https://files.eric.ed.gov/fulltext/ED331420.pdf

De Bruyn, L. L. (2004). Monitoring online communication: Can the development of convergence and social presence indicate an interactive learning environment? *Distance Education, 25*(1), 67–81. https://doi.org/10.1080/0158791042000212468

Dunn, D., Smith, R. A., & Beins, B. (2007). *Best practices for teaching statistics and research methods in the behavioral sciences.* Lawrence Erlbaum.

Eith, C. A. (2023). *Research methods and systematic inquiry I* [Syllabus]. School of Education, Johns Hopkins University.

Francescato, D., Porcelli, R., Mebane, M., Cuddetta, M., Klobas, J., & Renzi, P. (2006). Evaluation of the efficacy of collaborative learning in face-to-face and computer-supported university contexts. *Computers in Human Behavior, 22*(1), 163–176. https://doi.org/10.1016/j.chb.2005.03.001

Garrison, D. R., & Cleveland-Innes, M. (2005). Facilitating cognitive presence in online learning: Interaction is not enough. *American Journal of Distance Education, 19*(3), 133–148. https://doi.org/10.1207/s15389286ajde1903_2

Greeley, A. T., Johnson, E., Seem, S., Braver, M., Dias, L., Evans, K., Kincade, E., & Pricken, P. (1989). *Research Self-Efficacy Scale.* [Unpublished scale presented at the conference of the Association for Women in Psychology, Bethesda, MD].

Green, B. (2005). Unfinished business: Subjectivity and supervision. *Higher Education Research and Development, 24*(2), 151–163. https://doi.org/10.1080/07294360500062953

Gunawadena, C. (2004). Designing the social environment for online learning: The role of social presence. In D. Murphy, R. Carr, J. Taylor, & T. Wong (Eds.), *Distance education and technology: Issues and practices* (pp. 255–270). Open University Press.

Harris, C. M., Mazoué, J. G., Hamdan, H., & Casiple., A. R. (2007). Designing an online introductory statistics course. In D. Dunn, R. A. A. Smith, & B. Beins (Eds.), *Best practices for teaching statistics and research methods in the behavioral sciences* (pp. 93–108). Lawrence Erlbaum.

Honig, M. (2006). Complexity and policy implementation: Challenges and opportunities for the field. In M. I. Honig (Ed.), *New directions in education policy implementation: Confronting complexity* (pp. 1–24). State University of New York Press.

Johnson, R. B., Onwuegbuzie, A. J., & Turner, L. A. (2007). Toward a definition of mixed methods research. *Journal of Mixed Methods Research, 1*(2), 112–133. https://doi.org/10.1177/1558689806298224

Johnson, R. E., Grove, A. L., & Clarke, A. (2017). Pillar Integration Process: A joint display technique to integrate data in mixed methods research. *Journal of Mixed Methods Research, 13*(3), 301–320. https://doi.org/10.1177/1558689817743108

Lane, A. M., Davenport, T. J., & Horrell, A. (2004). Self-efficacy and research methods. *Journal of Leisure, Hospitality, Sport and Tourism Education, 3*(2), 25–38. https://doi.org/10.3794/johlste.32.59

Leviton, L. C., & Lipsey, M. W. (2007). A big chapter about small theories: Theory as method: Small theories of treatments. *New Directions for Evaluation,* (114), 27–62. https://doi.org/10.1002/ev.224

Lim, J. H., Dannels, S. A., & Watkins, R. (2008). Qualitative investigation of doctoral students' learning experiences in online research methods courses. *The Quarterly Review of Distance Education, 9*(3), 223–236.

Onwuegbuzie, A. J., & Wilson, V. A. (2003). Statistics anxiety: Nature, etiology, antecedents, effects, and treatments—a comprehensive review of the literature. *Teaching in Higher Education, 8*(2), 195–209. https://doi.org/10.1080/1356251032000052447

Onwuegbuzie, A. J., Da Ros, D., & Ryan, J. M. (1997). The components of statistics anxiety: A phenomenological study. *Focus on Learning Problems in Mathematics, 19* (4),11–35.

Remler, D. K., & Van Ryzin, G. G. (2015). *Research methods in practice: Strategies for description and causation.* Sage Publications.

Rockinson-Szapkiw, A. (2018). The development and validation of the scholar–practitioner research development scale for students enrolled in professional doctoral programs. *Journal of Applied Research in Higher Education, 10*(4), 478–492. https://doi.org/10.1108/jarhe-01-2018-0011

Sage. (2014). *Teaching research methods: How to make it meaningful to students* [Video]. YouTube. https://www.youtube.com/watch?v=bgoQ_63z-ZU

Seyri, H., & Rezaee, A. A. (2022). PhD students' identity construction in face-to-face and online contexts. *Research in Post-Compulsory Education, 27*(1), 48–65. https://doi: 10.1080/13596748.2021.2011507

Shadish, W. R., Cook, T. D., & Campbell, D. T. (2001). *Experimental and quasi-experimental designs for generalized causal inference* (2nd ed.). Wadsworth Cengage Learning.

Thomas, M. J. W. (2002). Learning within incoherent structures: The space of online discussion forums. *Journal of Computer Assisted Learning, 18*(3), 351–366. https://doi.org/10.1046/j.0266-4909.2002.03800.x

Zambo, D., Buss, R. R., & Zambo, R. (2015). Uncovering the identities of students and graduates in a CPED-influenced EdD program. *Studies in Higher Education, 40*(2), 233–252. https://doi.org/10.1080/03075079.2013.823932

CHAPTER 4

Trees and Transformation: From Seed to Forest

Amanda L. Palmer

WANGARI MAATHAI, THE renowned Kenyan political activist, said, "A tree has roots in the soil yet reaches to the sky. It tells us that in order to aspire, we need to be grounded, and that no matter how high we go, it is from our roots that we draw sustenance." She was right.

A Seed: Nothing Will Grow Without Those Who Plant and Nurture

A seed does nothing without water, nutrients, and sunlight. As I reflect on my journey in the program from practitioner-scholar to scholar-practitioner, I recognize my roots and the parts of me that haven't changed: a devoted commitment to student sense of belonging and a fierce dedication to social justice. I also recognize the parts that have shifted and adapted as I've grown from those roots: an ever-increasing self-awareness of my Whiteness within this work and an ability to support my real-world classroom experiences with empirical data. However, without others, I was just a seed. A motivated seed eager to continue sprouting, but a seed nonetheless.

My professional growth would be nothing without the thought leaders and civil rights activists who cultivate a soil filled with nutrients. Social reformers, colleagues, professors, and my students provide water and sunlight to encourage my continued development. As a White woman writing about the change I have brought to institutions and the broader educational landscape, I must first intentionally hold space, in print, to recognize those who have been working toward these shared goals long before I began this journey. Not only do I stand on the shoulders of giants, but I've also been able to grow, further root, adapt, and spread my branches because of and in concert with other members of this ecosystem—too many to name—subsequently contributing additional nutrients to support the soil.

A Sapling: Where It All Began

Teaching, of any sort and in any context, nourished me long before my transformative doctoral journey. Helping others see their own potential is the water and sunlight that sustains me. That sustenance is second only to the feeling of my own continued education—through conversations, experiences, and professional learning. When viewed in sum, my path has always pointed me toward a lifetime of teaching and learning, culminating (at least for now...) in the transformation I experienced in my Doctor of Education (EdD) program at Johns Hopkins University (JHU).

During my third year teaching, from across an inclusion classroom, I heard a new student say, "Which teacher do I give the paper to?" One of my first graders responded, distinguishing between another teacher and myself, "Oh, the White one." I then heard a third voice join the conversation, shouting, "Don't you call my teacher White! It's not her fault! She's just light-skinned!" As I sat in the stairwell debriefing that moment with my learner, his cries echoing in the stairwell around us, it hit me. Though I saw myself as someone who developed a sense of belonging and community in my learning spaces, I hadn't really flipped the narrative; I hadn't reflected on my students' true understanding of me.

Three years later, in a different context, a student ran up to me in the hallway and exasperatedly said, "Ms. Palmer, can you translate for me?" He'd pushed past his stutter to self-advocate for something he needed, but another White teacher wouldn't acknowledge his need until he spoke "grammatically correctly." I replayed this moment for months, stuck on its many layers, but especially his use of the word "translate."

For years prior to and between both of these moments, I'd recognized patterns in my classes. I'd known my students enjoyed learning in my classroom and felt they could be their full, unapologetic selves in my learning spaces. I knew this helped them push through challenges, retain content, and navigate social dynamics. These moments sparked curiosities in my predoctoral identity that wouldn't go away and to which I couldn't find answers. My mind was running and it wouldn't stop. I reflected on culture, pedagogy, and identity—what was it about me, especially in comparison to other White teachers, that contributed to the authenticity and joy I saw in my learners? For years I'd been told I had "something special" in my praxis, but I now felt unable to brush that off as a nice compliment from grateful families or qualifiers from administrators sandwiched between requests. What about my relationship with students contributed to these special moments and helped me create communities of trust? In addition to persistent systemic inequities, what were the implications of inequities at the classroom level? Could I help mitigate unjust experiences for students in classrooms beyond my own? How might I create change while avoiding a White savior approach? Questions abounded.

Those questions, and the resulting curiosities, served as new nourishment. The injustices and inequities I observed in my environment, and that I knew existed elsewhere, further catalyzed my desire to fight for change. My passive engagement in issues of social justice would no longer suffice; I could no longer be a seed simply waiting for some rain. I'd started to sprout and was craving the nourishment to grow tall enough to alter the landscape. The persistence of these questions and a desire to create change in the educational forest, not just a tree here or there, fueled my commitment to learn from experts in the field.

Strengthening Roots and Growing Taller: Nurturing the Tree With Self-Discovery

I first felt myself shifting identities from a practitioner to a scholar-practitioner while writing my application for the EdD program. The application requirement to identify a specific, contextualized Problem of Practice (POP) in my field enabled me to pinpoint the root of my discontent, curiosity, and drive for change. Specifically, in my predominantly White institution, my students of color were experiencing a different sense of belonging as they moved from one classroom to the next. Was it the identity makeup of peers or adults, or the broader school environment? Was it a presence, or a lack, of windows to see the perspectives of others and mirrors to see themselves (Style, 1996)? Was it the teacher's pedagogy, personality, or both? What, if any, of those variables could be targeted and changed in support of learners? Questions outweighed answers and I was ready to problem-solve.

During the first gathering of our doctoral cohort at an orientation residency, professors and program alums echoed the same narrative: First you must understand the problem. At the time, I thought I did understand the problem because I saw it impact my students in real time. I knew that the world favors those with power and privilege. My students described the authenticity they could bring to my classroom, and I saw them assimilate in other spaces; I watched those experiences influence their learning. However, I soon learned the naivety behind my solution-oriented eagerness. I began to recognize just how much water, soil, and sunlight I needed to truly understand my POP—and myself.

Memorably, at that residency, professors modeled the creation of logic models and conceptual frameworks. We sat at large round tables manipulating sticky notes and examining factors that might contribute to our POPs. We were prompted to think beyond what was obvious and clear, as professors asked, "But why?" and more questions filled my mind.

My identity change continued as I moved through early classes in the program. *Disciplinary Approaches to Education, Contemporary Approaches to Educational Problems, Multiple Perspectives on Learning and Teaching,* and *Multicultural Education* helped me build a robust conceptual framework, evaluate my POP from all angles, and more critically begin to shift the way I saw the world. I evaluated my own practice through a more complete lens, noticed the presence of other POPs in my context and elsewhere, and developed a depth of understanding that I hadn't before experienced. Bronfenbrenner's (1979) ecological systems theory (EST), Spencer's (2008) phenomenological variant of the EST (PVEST), and their applicability to nearly every interaction I witnessed or experienced shed additional light on my observations and experiences. Through discussions, conversations with professors, and engagement with our texts, I began to understand why my own tree had grown the way it did and the significance of each ring inside its trunk.

Learning from these early courses helped me develop the tools and resources to examine my own context. My data supported the literature; participants influenced student sense of belonging not only through their teaching, their cultural competency, or the posters on the wall, but also the culture they cultivated in learning spaces.

Adaptations: Shifting in Response to the Environment Around Me

Building on my years of experience, I knew the only way to survive in a changing environment was to adapt. Armed with my ability to synthesize years of coursework, research, and the program's collaborative learning experiences, I continued to grow more branches. As I felt *myself* change, I felt my praxis and my dissertation change in tandem. While my depth of understanding grew more branches, I pruned factors out of my POP based on my needs assessment data and research results. My work was exclusively about neither teachers' implicit bias nor students' sense of belonging; it was every element of the teaching and learning environment that mattered. Building on the concept of culturally responsive teaching (Gay, 2000), I began to use the phrase *culturally responsive teaching practices* (CRTP) to inclusively describe what had previously felt nebulous.

My research for my Applied Dissertation demonstrated that a teacher's ability (or lack thereof) to recognize their own culture and identity, and those of their students, influenced their ability to create inclusive learning spaces. My experiences told me that I create those spaces by building authentic, caring relationships with my learners. My well-established tree was adapting to the environment around it. My POP's manifestations and contributing factors were becoming clear. I synthesized my tree's growth and adaptations, designing contextualized research focused on practitioners' development of students' sense of belonging. However, as I transitioned into this new identity as a doctoral candidate, I wondered if all of this was teachable. My tree had adapted. I'd been nourished by my classmates, my professors, and my readings—watered by my experiences and research discoveries. However, could I nourish others with just the right nutrients? Could I teach others to adapt their praxis, prune what wasn't working for their learners, and cultivate culturally responsive spaces?

My intervention focused on increasing teachers' abilities to cultivate a space of belonging for each and every learner. I committed to using CRTP (Gay, 2000; Palmer, 2022) to encompass not only culturally responsive teaching but also a comprehensive understanding of the relationships, environment, and pedagogy present in a learning space that influence students' sense of belonging.

While leveraging my roots in classroom experiences, leaning on my trunk of self-discovery and learning, and with all of my developmental adaptations as a result of my education in the EdD program, I successfully implemented my intervention focused on developing practitioners' CRTP knowledge and self-efficacy. My tree had grown significantly, and propagation was in the near future. My resulting professional learning series for my colleagues yielded incredible results. After the intervention, across multiple measures, participants significantly increased their CRTP knowledge and self-efficacy. My study's results were inarguably robust and invigorating and demonstrated new growth. The promise of other possibilities gave me the strength to dig my roots deeper and grow taller as I emerged as a scholar-practitioner.

Stature and Strength: Strengthening My Roots and Spreading My Branches

The combined components of my EdD program gave me the confidence, language, and empirically based results to support what I knew was effective practice. I had data to support my experiences and the language to explain them. I knew if I left the classroom, I would be one step removed from the quickly changing environmental culture our students experience. I'd be closing myself off from sunlight, ultimately doing a disservice to those I wanted to support. My EdD program gave me the confidence and capacity to say, "I'm staying put," while also pursuing change outside of my classroom. My roots were firmly planted *while* my branches continued to grow. Those in positions of power began to listen.

I cited research during curriculum discussions, conducted cultural identity self-reflection exercises (Hammond, 2015; Hollie, 2012) during new teacher orientations, and introduced PVEST (Spencer, 2008) during student support meetings. With the skills learned in doctoral coursework and program experiences I had the leverage to formalize my role as an Instructional Coach, bringing CRTP into classrooms across my institution. Using my newfound ability to evaluate systems through an improvement science lens as described by Bryk and colleagues (2015), I discovered significant discrepancies between my institution's strategic plan and student outcomes. Leveraging those findings, I supported the development of culturally responsive environments and culturally diverse partnerships as described by Lim and Renshaw (2001). Collaborative work with professors and advisers refining my theoretical framework helped me evaluate systems within and beyond my context. I used data analysis skills acquired during research methods coursework to collect and analyze data for my school's strategic planning. Work with my committee every step of the way taught me the importance of iterative processes and the inextricable connection between securing stakeholders' support and creating systemic change. I had the tools and language to describe the process of creating culturally responsive spaces to stakeholders in my context, invigorating them to push for more growth. I *became* that needed change agent. And I did it all while saying, "In my classroom, we . . ." and "You're welcome to come visit my space anytime."

A Tree, Firmly Rooted Where It Began, Can Support Other Growth

In my identity post degree, I feel my branches soaring. I'm firmly rooted, and those roots continue to be nourished by students in my learning spaces. My doctoral journey, in particular the focus on an ability to synthesize content and engage as a scholar-practitioner, has positioned me for growth within and beyond my personal and professional experiences.

In the same way that I synthesized and utilized nutrients acquired through the program's mechanisms for personal growth, I professionally synthesized my lessons, experiences, and now formalized expertise into Palmer Educational Services, LLC. What had before been tutoring services and teacher mentorship became formalized educational consulting, wherein I began to support teachers and families outside of my own context. I turned those "Can I pick your brain?" conversations into consulting, and the "What do I do next?" moments into teacher coaching. This work is inherently valuable to me; in our sociopolitical climate, professionalization of my work also indicates its importance to certain stakeholders. My research and work now branch outside of my context to contextually support other leaders, educators, learners, and learning environments.

My identity transformed from being an invited "teacher's voice" on panels to instead being a critical sought-out advocate catalyzing systemic change. I was promoted to be a Diversity, Equity, Inclusion, and Belonging Coordinator, a public-facing role at my school, where I support students as they navigate a system not reliably designed for them. I also create a school environment that invites and supports all community members. As an instructional coach, I diversify curriculum through modeling and collaboration, increase the use of CRTPs, and create inclusive spaces wherein teachers and students can bring their authentic selves to the learning process. While maintaining my roots in the classroom, I provide an open door to other educational advocates, teacher-learners, and families as I recognize and name my teaching moves as described by Hammond (2015). My experiences in the EdD program, especially those in which I practiced synthesizing and sharing content with others in meaningful ways, cultivated a knowledge base and self-confidence that made it possible for me to stand up for what is right *and* to do so in a way that makes others listen and act. I point out the sunlight, water, and soil needed to grow, and I outline a path toward sustainable growth and change. Other people listen, then follow that path.

Of all the professional transformations I've experienced as a result of this program, maintaining my roots is perhaps the most critical element of my growth. My roots connect me to my predoctoral form as a seed, support my growth, and keep me strong enough to reach for more. My branches are strong enough for people to take cuttings and propagate; my firmly rooted tree's offshoots are turning into trees of their own. Professionally, I have watched my context transform, in part as a result of my participants' knowledge acquisition and implementation. Without leaving my soil, I'm actively developing a full forest that continues to expand and impact the landscape.

Forests provide oxygen. They provide shelter. They sustain biodiversity and fuel recreation and education. Forests provide the resources we need to function and grow as a society. As the EdD program taught me, nothing exists in a vacuum. My work is not complete nor fully operationalized if it is merely one tree. It's not about me; it's not about one tree's ability to grow, survive, thrive, and propagate. It's about the bigger picture; how can we solidify our roots and expand our reach to provide a supportive forest for all? Although I won't ever have all the answers, the transformation I experienced through this program gave me the scholar-practitioner tools to keep searching for them in my postdoctoral journey.

It takes desire and drive to become a teacher. It takes persistence, curiosity, resilience, and reflection to *stay* a teacher. Though I embodied many of those characteristics prior to my EdD program, it was impossible to anticipate the professional and personal identity transformation that resulted from my JHU experience. The program fueled my passions, fanned my curiosity, and illuminated my understanding of systems and my existence within them—all while

I remained an insider (Banks, 2015) as an active practitioner in my context, supporting an ever-expanding forest.

References

Banks, J. A. (2015). Researching race, culture, and difference. In J. A. Banks (Ed.), *Cultural diversity and education: Foundations, curriculum, and teaching* (6th ed; pp. 137-159). Upper Saddle River, NJ: Pearson.

Bronfenbrenner, U. (1979). *The ecology of human development: Experiments by nature and design*. Harvard University Press.

Bryk, A. S., Gomez, L. M., Grunow, A., & LeMahieu, P. G. (2015). *Learning to improve: How America's schools can get better at getting better*. Harvard Education Press.

Gay, G. (2000). *Culturally responsive teaching: Theory, research, and practice*. New York, NY: Teachers College Press.

Hammond, Z. (2015). *Culturally responsive teaching and the brain: Promoting authentic engagement and rigor among culturally and linguistically diverse students*. Corwin.

Hollie, S. (2012). *Culturally and linguistically responsive teaching and learning: Classroom practices for student success*. Shell Publishing.

Lim, L., & Renshaw, P. (2001). The relevance of sociocultural theory to culturally diverse partnerships and communities. *Journal of Child and Family Studies, 10*, 9–21. https://doi:10.1023/A:1016625432567

Palmer, A. L. (2022). *Increasing teachers' culturally responsive teaching practices knowledge and self-efficacy: An intervention* [Doctoral dissertation, Johns Hopkins University]. JScholarship. https://jscholarship.library.jhu.edu/handle/1774.2/66987

Spencer, M. B. (2008). Phenomenology and ecological systems theory: Development of diverse groups. In W. Damon, R. M. Lerner, D. Kuhn, R. S. Siegler, & N. Eisenberg (Eds.), *Child and adolescent development: An advanced course* (pp. 696–740). John Wiley & Sons.

Style, E. (1996). Curriculum as window and mirror. *Social Science Record, 33*(2), 21–28.

CHAPTER 5

My Doctoral Journey:
See Them With Your Heart

Soha R. Elzalabany

Predoctoral Identity: You Were Practically Born an Educator

I SMILED AND agreed with the interviewer's insightful observation as they looked at my resume. The school principal made me think about my past career choices, saying "You always work as a teacher, you were practically born an educator." At that moment, I realized that I have been identified as an educator from the time I was young, teaching my dolls or working as a teaching assistant at my neighborhood nursery over summer vacations in Egypt. When I got married, I stayed home to teach and care for my two sons during their first 5 precious years. Once they attended formal schooling, I started to feel an urge of wanting more in life; I wanted to learn to support vulnerable children. Therefore, I applied for a special education teaching program at one of our Egyptian universities in 2004. After graduating with high grades, I started my first teaching position as a special education teacher in 2006. At that time, my identity has evolved to be an advocate for children with diverse learning needs in Egypt.

Promoting social justice, equity, and fair learning opportunities for my students—whom I deliberately call my children—was my passion and a central driver behind my professional decisions. At that time, I realized that the Egyptian policies and procedures governing special education were fragile and needed to be translated into a system to protect children's rights for equitable education. Throughout the academic year, the interdisciplinary team of specialists, teachers, and I were devoted to accommodating our children's social and academic needs at school, leaving no stone unturned. The school year usually ended with us celebrating our children and their families' successes; then the summer wind would come. During summer vacations, the school leaders, with limited knowledge about special education, solely made the decision to demote or expel some students based on their low grades. Year after year, I realized that my hard work and goodwill were never enough. Although I systematically reported my students' performances and abilities to the principal, I had little impact on the decisions the school administration made about my students' promotion.

My predoctoral role as an advocate was not effective. Feeling the urge to learn further, I decided to continue my education to better serve my students' learning journey. In 2008, I earned a scholarship for a master's degree in special education from the University of London in the United Kingdom. Applying my studies to my practices in Egypt, I was thrilled to observe the changes in my students as a result of the accommodations and modifications that I enacted based on their educational plans. My children started to be more confident and engaged in their school life, and their grades and behavior improved remarkably.

One semester before my master's degree graduation, I was afforded a transformational opportunity. It was the same year of the Arab Spring, in 2011, and Egypt's future was in turmoil. Regardless of the turbulence and chaos, Egypt launched the Science, Technology, Engineering, and Mathematics (STEM) Education Program. Eight Egyptian science teachers were chosen to travel to the United States to receive STEM training at the Center for Talented Youth at Johns Hopkins University (JHU). I was always interested in teaching students with unique profiles, whom I would call the polarized ends of the educational spectrum; that is, students with below-average abilities and those with above-average abilities. When I traveled, I was astounded by the amount and depth of academic research in gifted education, a deserted field in Egypt. Also, our JHU mentors' and professors' attitudes toward learning and learners were unprecedented in my experience, as they unconditionally cared about us. Supported by their encouragement and love for science, we wanted to excel and be the best version of ourselves.

The skillfully designed program raised our awareness and curiosity to be lifelong learners in gifted education. I noticed the gap in the Egyptian educational landscape and decided to introduce a gifted and talented program in my district. Although leading the school community out of their comfort zone was difficult, I had a clear plan. I scheduled a series of buy-in meetings with my supervisors to ask for their support, built the knowledge and capacity of a group of teachers and parents, and created the policy and procedures to govern my gifted students' right to quality learning opportunities. From that moment, my role as an educator changed forever as I started to be a game changer. I learned how to be a self-directed learner; I used my personality traits, knowledge, problem-solving skills, and passion to make a difference in the school community supporting academic diversity.

Your Laws Do Not Protect You!

Being told that the laws do not protect me, as this header conveys, awakened the same old feeling: A change must happen to support my children at school. I was in a meeting with my school principal, and I had prepared all the documents needed to plead for the promotion of a student with diverse learning needs. Again, the school principal denied the student's right to promotion. I passionately explained that based on the Egyptian legislative acts the student had the right to a set of test accommodations to succeed. The principal calmly pointed to the ineffectiveness of legislative acts and asked me to stop being emotional, as the student had no hope at our school due to his low grades. In this crystallizing moment, I decided that there must be a systematic change and the advocacy for my children must take a different turn. School policies and procedures must be based on Egyptian educational laws, and they must be implemented into the school handbook. To realize this dream of this systematic change, I decided to seek a career opportunity as a school leader and to apply to the doctoral program at the JHU School of Education.

Starting my dissertation's literature review, I developed a more confident lens through which to "see" and scrutinize the Egyptian educational landscape. During my first year of the JHU doctoral program, I examined my context and understood that educators typically know what outcomes they want, but often lack the knowledge of what they need to change to achieve them, as described by Bryk et al. (2015). As a researcher, I found that the school leaders exerted limited effort toward translating educational laws into effective practices, policies, and procedures (United Nations Educational, Scientific and Cultural Organization, 1994; United Nations International Children's Emergency Fund, 2020). Also, the school leaders who implemented the educational policies were not well-equipped to transform their schools to account for academic diversity (Organisation for Economic Co-operation and Development, 2015). Teachers' pedagogic practices were outmoded (Badran & Toprak, 2020; Hargreaves, 1997; Hargreaves, 2001; Sobhy, 2012), and standards and training to support diverse learners were absent from teachers' and principals' professional development (Elzalabany, 2021).

During my second year of the program, my needs assessment study for my dissertation included 100 teachers, two school principals, and two policy advisors who helped me to examine the three ecological layers of the school system (e.g., national policy, school leadership, and teachers' practices). As a result of the study, we learned of the absence of a school vision for academic diversity and implementation plan (Elzalabany, 2021). Despite teachers showing positive attitudes toward inclusive practices, I learned that they expressed a need for knowledge. Also, the school leaders' duties hindered their role as instructional transformational leaders for academic diversity (cf. DeMatthews, 2015; Galloway & Isimaru, 2015; Wallace Foundation, 2013). Feng (2016) defined authentic leaders as those who endorse a shared vision with their colleagues and teams, build school capacity, act as role models, engage in critical thinking and problem-solving skills, and adopt a collaborative reflective culture at school. Thus, authentic leaders for academic diversity contribute to an effective inclusive educational program for learners with diverse learning needs through a shared vision with their team and collaborative decision-making (Crippen, 2012).

The JHU Doctor of Education program required that we specialize in an area of focus. From my specialization in entrepreneurial leadership in education, I saw opportunities for successful ventures and competitive advantage for my school. Also, I started to grow an interest in economics in education, and the research on the pedagogy of poverty (Haberman, 2010) was an eye-opener in terms of the effects of poverty and economic scarcity on school environments, teachers' motivation, and improvement in schools. Studying Maslow (1943), Payne (2019), and Haberman (1991), I understood the hierarchy of needs theory that plays an important role in shaping teachers' decisions. Like many

Egyptian teachers, teachers in areas of poverty are more focused on satisfying their physiological needs (i.e., food and shelter) than working toward their self-actualization (Payne, 2019). Likewise, Egyptian teachers are more interested in private tutoring to increase their monthly income than in planning for their professional development needs (Sobhy, 2012). Teachers experience a cognitive tunnel where they are hyper-focused on one aspect of their environment and ignore other aspects. They become single-minded when managing resources, which limits their ability to be creative in the classroom. Furthermore, the stress and anxiety that characterize the school environment can lead to impulsive actions and low self-control (Haberman, 1991). Understanding the Egyptian leaders' and teachers' mentality and thinking models helped me in designing my dissertation intervention. My identity as a researcher had strengthened, and I designed a professional development program for Egyptian authentic leaders to implement an evidence-based support system for academic diversity in Egyptian schools as my Applied Dissertation intervention.

See These Children With Your Heart

At a later stage in the JHU doctoral program, my professional identity developed into that of an authentic leader for social justice. At my school, I attempted to apply improvement science, as taught in the doctoral program. I led a team of ambitious administrators who decided to make a difference. First, I led my dream team toward the big idea that we wanted to achieve, asking them questions inspired by Bryk et al. (2015), "What are we trying to accomplish as school leaders? How can we reach our target? And, how do we assess our success?" Second, we employed a four-stage problem-solving model plan-do-study-act that helped us to improve the process and reflect on our daily activities (Deming & Orsini, 2013). We collaborated to improve the internal process and communication as we were able to systematically examine the school environment through daily reflection meetings and class observation. These activities were a key strategy to develop actionable and efficient solutions to our everyday issues at school, guided by the applied research and theories I studied at JHU. I showcased how to apply improvement science at Egyptian schools. I used my courses' discussion forums to examine my context and receive feedback on my practices from my professors and colleagues. The program's readings and discussions helped me to develop knowledge and skills needed to foster academic diversity at my school. I was on a journey to build my school's capacity and apply my knowledge and skills about inclusive learning environments and authentic leadership. This was not an easy task in the Egyptian context. Thus, I decided to address this problem in my JHU dissertation intervention.

During my dissertation intervention, the participants' responses indicated that the least developed authentic leadership subskills were transparency and balanced processing, which are related to collaboration. However, all participants confirmed the importance of adopting authentic leadership styles and traits to support academic diversity in Egyptian schools. A participant confirmed that authentic leaders in an Egyptian school must "see these children with your hearts because knowing them you will know that they are worth all your efforts." After the intervention, I shared with the study participants stories about my school's dream team to explain the journey toward developing authentic leaders for social justice in our Egyptian context.

It is Just the Beginning

In December 2019, I finished my doctoral studies and said: "It is just the beginning!" I had always dreamed of making a difference on the national level. I quit my job as a school principal and aspired to a more influential leadership position. Therefore, I accepted a job in one of the publishing houses that partners with the Ministry of Education (MoE) to reform the Egyptian education system. The MoE had recently launched a reform strategy with a promise to adopt a high-quality program to integrate K–12 students with diverse learning needs (Ministry of Planning, Monitoring, and Administrative Reform, 2018). Education Reform 2.0 is intended to provide a high-quality inclusive education system for all, following international standards and new technologies. I joined this project as an Educational Content Development Manager in July 2020 with a dream and a will to make a difference and an impact at the national level.

The education department at the publishing house designs and creates four different early childhood and elementary curricula, offers training services, develops print and digital teaching resources, and provides ed-tech applications for educators and parents. I was afforded the opportunity to design and develop inclusive practices and strategies in all the curricula published by my company, which was a dream come true. In addition, I was responsible for teachers' training and professional development on the new curricula and inclusive practices on the MoE's platforms and via face-to-face training.

At this stage in my development, I saw myself as an entrepreneur for social justice, having a powerful force in changing social norms and applying efficient and positive solutions to improve my community. As a social entrepreneur, I initiate change and deliver services on a large scale to address the issue of accessibility and improve the quality of services given to Egyptian students with diverse learning needs. For example, providing access to the curriculum for my children was an unattainable goal during my professional career as a school-teacher and a school leader. Curriculum accessibility considers the variety of learners with diverse learning needs in a classroom and designs lessons and activities that will have multiple access points for them (e.g., inclusive strategies, learning tasks, and various experiences) to support students with mild to moderate disabilities on the national level.

Connecting practices to research, I am currently designing an opportunity to examine and evaluate the implementation of the curricula in public schools in one of the Egyptian governorates as I am planning a study at the American University in Cairo to explore the challenges and possibilities of implementing the new curricula in Egyptian schools. The study aims to capture public school teachers' attitudes toward a training program to support the required knowledge and skills for Education Reform 2.0. Additionally, it attempts to highlight the current training status in Egypt and its challenges considering Education Reform 2.0 and to investigate the best training model to address these challenges. At this time, I see my identity as that of a scholar-practitioner who is armed with the knowledge of practice and scholarship to rigorously examine the implementation of this curriculum.

In conclusion, reflecting on my learning journey at JHU, my personal and professional identities have changed forever. Now, I consider my life-changing experience and studies at JHU as the magic wand. This JHU wand changed me from being a teacher into an authentic school leader for social justice and a scholar-practitioner. That is, it transformed the need into opportunities and accomplishments. My mindset has evolved from being uncertain to being determined to succeed. My focus is now broader, more mature, and more inclusive to encompass all students. Currently, I am opening my own office for educational services in New Cairo to support students with diverse learning needs to reach their potential and to build their families' and schools' capacities to improve the students' home-school lives. I began my learning journey at JHU as an educator and advocate with just a dream; then I evolved into a game-changer, researcher, authentic leader, social entrepreneur, and scholar-practitioner to make an impactful and systematic change in our Egyptian community.

References

Badran, A., & Toprak, M. (2020). Sustainability of education reforms: An investigation into the professional development component of USAID/Egypt Education Reform Program (ERP, 2004–2009). *Education Policy Analysis Archives, 28*(129), 1–34. https://doi.org/10.14507/epaa.28.5010

Bryk, A. S., Gomez, L. M., Grunow, A., & LeMahieu, P. G. (2015). *Learning to improve: How America's schools can get better at getting better.* Harvard Education Press.

Crippen, C. (2012). Enhancing authentic leadership followership: Strengthening school relationships. *Management in Education, 26*(4), 192–198. https://doi.org/10.1177/08920 20612439084

DeMatthews, D. E. (2015). Clearing a path for inclusion: Distributing leadership in a high performing elementary school. *Journal of School Leadership, 25*(6), 1000–1038. https://doi.org/10.1177/105268461502500601

Deming, W. E., & Orsini, J. N. (2013). *The essential Deming: Leadership principles from the father of quality management.* McGraw-Hill.

Elzalabany, S. R. (2021). *Professional development of inclusive leadership to address academic diversity in Egyptian international schools* [Unpublished doctoral dissertation]. Johns Hopkins University.

Feng, F. (2016). School principals' authentic leadership and teachers' psychological capital: Teachers' perspectives. *International Education Studies, 9*(10), 245–255. https://doi.org/10.5539/ies.v9n10p245

Galloway, M. K., & Isimaru, A. M. (2015). Radical recentering: Equity in educational leadership standards. *Educational Administration Quarterly, 51*(3), 372–408. https://doi.org/10.1177/0013161X15590658

Haberman, M. (1991). The pedagogy of poverty versus good teaching. *Phi Delta Kappan, 73*(4), 290–294. https://www.pdkmembers.org/members_online/publications/Archive/pdf/PDK_92_2/81pdk_92_2.pdf

Haberman, M. (2010). The pedagogy of poverty versus good teaching. *Phi Delta Kappan,* 92(2), 81–87. https://doi.org/10.1177/003172171009200223

Hargreaves, E. (1997). The diploma disease in Egypt: Learning, teaching, and the monster of the secondary leaving certificate. *Assessment in Education, 4*(1), 161–176. https://doi.org/10.1080/0969594970040111.

Hargreaves, E. (2001). Assessment in Egypt. *Assessment in Education, 8*(2), 247–260. https://doi.org/10.1080/09695940124261

Maslow, A. H. (1943). A theory of human motivation. *Psychological Review, 50*(4), 370–396. https://doi.org/10.1037/h0054346

Ministry of Planning, Monitoring, and Administrative Reform. (2018). *Egypt's voluntary national review 2018.* https://sustainabledevelopment.un.org/content/documents/20269EGY_VNR_2018_final_with_Hyperlink_9720185b45d.pdf

Organization for Economic Co-operation and Development. (2015). *Schools for skills: A new learning agenda for Egypt.* OECD Publishing. https://www.oecd.org/countries/egypt/Schools-for-skills-a-new-learning-agenda-for-Egypt.pdf

Payne, R. K. (2019). *A framework for understanding poverty—A cognitive approach* (6th ed.).

Sobhy, H. (2012). The de-facto privatization of secondary education in Egypt: A study of private tutoring in technical and general schools. *Journal of Comparative and International Education, 42*(1), 47–67. https://doi.org/10.1080/03057925.2011.629042

United Nations Educational, Scientific and Cultural Organization. (1994). *Salamanca statement and framework for action on special needs education.* https://unesdoc.unesco.org/ark:/48223/pf0000098427

United Nations International Children's Emergency Fund. (2020, March 5). *Ministry of Education and Technical Education and partners celebrate key milestones for inclusive education in Egypt under Education 2.0* [Press release]. https://www.unicef.org/egypt/press-releases/ministry-education-and-technical-education-and-partners-celebrate-key-milestones

Wallace Foundation. (2013). *The school principal as leader: Guiding schools to better teaching and learning.* http://www.wallacefoundation.org/knowledge-center/Pages/The-School-Principal-as-Leader-Guiding-Schools-to-Better-Teaching-and-Learning.aspx

CHAPTER 6

Understanding Myself to Try to Better Understand You

Teresa Caswell

Introduction

I REMEMBER THE moment I realized my White privilege. I had attended a variety of trainings regarding diversity, equity, and inclusion (DEI) in my school district and believed they did not pertain to me, as I always worked to treat everyone the same. I believed if everyone was provided the same opportunities, then everyone had a choice to take advantage of those opportunities, right? Up to that point in my life and career, I would have described my identity as fair—without bias—with a belief that ideals of meritocracy, self-reliance, and determination overcame most challenges in life. I had, myself, overcome being a single mom, living on welfare, to be well educated and self-reliant. Therefore, I believed, the system must be just.

Predoctoral Identity: Cognitive Dissonance

My understanding of how blinded I was, the reality of systemic racism, and, thus, my White privilege occurred during a diversity training in my professional context. The clarity that my own experience was not that of my colleagues of color came not from the presenter or the content, but a peer participant. After a privilege walk activity, where individuals stand in order of the number of day-to-day privileges they enjoy or have enjoyed in their life so far (and most of the time individuals identifying as White are toward the front and those identifying as a person of color are ranked from the middle to end), my table group members were debriefing the experience. A colleague made the comment that, as public school administrators, we all have graduate degrees and thus do not have experience with poverty. Although this statement alone indicates a bias about who is and is not educated, it is important to note that the five individuals in that particular group discussion were also White. I indicated that my colleague was incorrect, as I lived on public assistance for several years in my early 20s, and that I would bet many in the room had also lived either below or near the poverty line at some point. I simultaneously realized that the number of White school administrators in the room vastly outnumbered those who identified as leaders of color.

That conversation (and realization) stuck with me, and I began reexamining the content of professional learning experiences I had attended. Terms I had not delved deeply into because of my own initial beliefs regarding opportunity—such as racism and implicit bias—resurfaced in my mind. I had previously been proud about being *colorblind* and was humbled to realize that I played into a narrative perpetuating oppression by adopting this approach. I had believed in the ideals of meritocracy: pull yourself up from your situation, work hard, and opportunities will come (DiAngelo, 2018)! I had done just that, and it had worked. As stated by Peterson and colleagues (2016), however, when explaining why meritocracy does not work for many marginalized groups: I was not seen as a threat, lazy, defensive, living in my ancestors' past. I had White privilege and that gave me a benefit not enjoyed by other races or ethnicities. Looking back, before the privilege walk activity, I was very individualistic and resonated with mainstream culture where, as a White individual, I did not need to think about my race. The reexamination of my beliefs moved me into what Sevig et al. (2000) referred to as a dissonance phase when I began realizing that society values, and devalues, individuals based on stereotyped norms. And I was disturbed by my part in it.

Critical Reflection of Implicit Biases and My Application to Johns Hopkins

My initial critical reflection of my predoctoral identity happened almost simultaneously to my realization, as an elementary school principal, that academic disparities occurring between race-labeled subgroups at my school, and throughout the country, were not a result of student effort or motivation, but to the biases of, and instructional methods used by, educators (Jacoby-Senghor et al., 2016). Reviewing student data and the instructional methods of the teachers I evaluated, I had been trying to understand how the same strong instruction for all students resulted in disparate achievement within a classroom. I implemented a form of inquiry-driven instruction (the Project Approach; Katz & Chard, 2000) focused on providing students various ways to access standards and demonstrate understanding. In the middle of a project a teacher approached me both excited and mortified. A student whom she had referred for intensive intervention and possible special education due to their inability to engage in grade-level reading could actually read *above* grade level! The student had been able to choose their focus within the project content and was completely enthralled with researching additional information. When seeing this student with an above-level book the teacher assumed support was needed. When the teacher tried to help, she was stunned to have the student effectively read the content and accurately answer comprehension questions! The teacher's mortification was due to her sincere belief that the child could not read and that she had, as a result, stopped holding them to the same expectations as the rest of the class.

Importantly, the student in this anecdote was a Black male and, before this chance incident, did not engage in content he either could not relate to or was not interested in. If not for the realization of his White teacher, it is very possible he would have been identified and possibly labeled as a student with a learning disability. Reflecting on this, and the school-wide data disaggregated by racial subgroup, brought clarity to my mind that implicit bias within educator expectations was an issue and one that I could not ignore as a school leader. As I began researching possible solutions and connecting with like-minded individuals, I applied to the Johns Hopkins University (JHU) Doctor of Education (EdD) program with the intent of finding more culturally responsive instructional methodologies to narrow student disparities between subgroups identified by race. What I would realize through the EdD program was a much deeper personal and professional transformation than I ever anticipated.

Contextual Immersion Through the Applied Dissertation Process

Although I entered the EdD program committed to ideals of social justice, I did not have the systems knowledge necessary to really understand why my Problem of Practice—academic disparities between racial subgroups at an affluent elementary school—was actually a problem. Upon exposure to different system frameworks in my first semester of coursework, I used Neal and Neal's (2013) networked ecological systems theory to investigate the breadth and depth of variables associated with student outcomes, and any racial disparities found therein for my Chapter 1 literature review. My increased knowledge was subsequently utilized to identify potential factors that I investigated in my research methodology courses and Chapter 2 needs assessment study. This study focused on schoolteachers and principals at three separate elementary schools with community contexts similar to mine (Caswell, 2021). I examined whether academic emphasis, educator trust in families, cultural competence, or different types of educator efficacy (i.e., personal, general, and collective) emerged as potential reasons for student data disparities within these affluent and highly diverse schools' data (similar academic disparities have been found between racial subgroups in schools across the United States for decades; Coleman et al., 1966).

Educator's cultural competency was identified in the needs assessment study as the most salient factor impacting disparate student outcomes at each of the three focal schools (Caswell, 2021). The completion of my empirical study—which included the literature synthesis and needs assessment chapters—in the summer of 2019 coincided with completion of the JHU EdD program's required multicultural education course. This course, its professor Dr. Yolanda Abel, and my advisor Dr. Ranjini JohnBull all challenged me to consider what I had captured in my first two chapters and to consider deeper connections to social justice within and beyond the classroom. It was also at this point that I came to the realization that educators cannot provide culturally responsive instruction without being culturally competent. This understanding led me to focus my dissertation intervention (and subsequent professional) work on *adult* identity development to intentionally act against forms of oppression instead of focusing on how adults can adapt their instruction, which ultimately can still be biased toward and against students. I believe at this point I was also further *immersing* (emphasis added; Sevig et al., 2000) myself in my own identity development and understanding that I possessed multiple identities to honor and accept if I were to lead and support the work of anti-racism. I was beginning to see how my White privilege could be used to do the work needed to dismantle systems built upon the oppression of others.

Using a conceptual framework of identity development (Myers et al., 1991), critical reflection (Gorski & Dalton, 2020), and transformational learning theory (Mezirow, 1997, 1998), I developed an equity- and identity-focused intervention for the full faculty of an elementary school where I served as principal (Caswell, 2021). Professional learning activities, including critical-reflection journaling, occurred over a 5-month period during eight meetings with the full faculty attending. I hypothesized that the addition of critical reflection after participating in equity-focused professional development would decrease participants' implicit bias while increasing their levels of cultural competency.

Study findings indicated that the majority of participants positively increased their cultural competency and had a deeper understanding of implicit bias after the intervention than before it (Caswell, 2021). Moreover, these results provided insight that an individual's cultural competency growth is rarely linear; rather, it twists and turns in upon itself as one engages in equity- and identity-focused professional learning and the resulting cognitive dissonance that emerges from the critical reflection process. Through this process, the frames of reference (Mezirow, 1997) that participants may have previously held changed through my intervention study that was centered on understanding oneself. Specifically, data indicated participants developed a more nuanced consideration of identities unlike their own. Interestingly, this nonlinear process was not unlike my own journey, where my understanding of racial identities and oppression outpaced my consideration of sexual orientation and gender identity. I began grappling with how to recognize the whole of an individual and identities not easily seen. I quickly realized that my dissertation study was just the start of what we all need to consider in order to recognize oppression in all its forms.

Transforming My Identity

One of the most impactful ideas imparted to me within the JHU EdD program, which ensured that I looked to understand multiple identities within an individual, was intersectionality. First termed by Crenshaw (1991), the idea that an individual may hold multiple identities and that these identities impact their beliefs and potential biases about others was something I had not yet considered in my own identity journey. Although intersectionality was introduced in my summer 2019 multicultural education course, it wasn't until I was studying for the EdD comprehensive exam the following spring that I truly internalized the power of intersectionality and how it could impact my practice. While synthesizing multiple course theories within my comprehensive exam preparation process, I often considered how they were used in my practice as a K–12 educator to be able to apply my scholarship to practice. With intersectionality, and considering myself at the time as a White, female, public school principal, I could see how individuals' lived experiences have multifaceted realities. This reflection resulted in my better seeing how being White affords me privileges in our society. However, being female, I also recognized that I am typically not the first to be acknowledged as a person of authority, especially when standing in a group of men, and thus I often need to repeatedly prove my worth as a school leader. Any gender bias is mitigated by my race, a privilege itself that a Black female public school principal would not experience. While an unexpected outcome within the process of studying for a major component of my doctoral degree, the nuance of intersectionality's impact on my identity was profound. I could more effectively empathize with others by realizing that there were likely aspects of their identity that were not visible (gender identity, for example). Moreover, I wanted to develop a greater awareness of the oppression plaguing any classifying aspect of an individual's lived experience. Thus, my own identity awareness as measured by the self-identity survey (Sevig et al., 2000) increased during my JHU EdD tenure by my intentional exposure to and subsequent research on intersectionality.

My identity as a school and district leader at the time I defended my dissertation and could take on the moniker of doctor was a combination of social-justice defender and scholar- practitioner. To me these coidentities signified a commitment to my own continued learning to utilize my practice in the advocacy of those experiencing oppression in any form. In the social-justice realm, I wanted more and more of my public school principal colleagues to both understand their identity and implement implicit bias and cultural competency work in their own schools. I took on the cochair role of a district-wide equity committee where we began developing leadership resources for school leaders' identity-growth development and the learning of their staff. As a scholar-practitioner, I worked to ensure that my collective school faculty was focused on eliminating academic disparities between student subgroups and *understand* why they exist, versus simply responding to a goal that I, as a principal, directed them to do. If instructional staff do not recognize the intersectionality of their own identities and how their level of cultural competency may impact student outcomes, there is a good possibility that their implicit biases will impact their expectations of students based on preconceptions and oppressive beliefs. The connection between these post JHU EdD coidentities was the need to communicate, through multiple venues, that we need to acknowledge ourselves to effectively *see* others. Only then can we hope to change any disparate outcomes based in our oppressive pasts.

Transformational learning theory (Mezirow, 1997, 1998) was another JHU EdD concept introduced in my multicultural education course and often discussed with my dissertation committee that further stretched how I believed people understood bias and the potential for change. With this theory, I had a framework I could use within my professional context to effect change by embedding opportunities for individuals to acknowledge their current beliefs and to critically reflect on whether they may be open to a shift (and why). Over time, I continue to find myself leaning on transformational learning theory within my own growth and as I support the learning of others in my school and district contexts.

Through my increased understanding that DEI work is all-encompassing, and that all forms of oppression are systemic issues that need to be disrupted, I have moved from a school principal role to a district-wide Senior Director position focused on DEI leadership, coaching, and support. While initially considering DEI roles that could result in positively increasing the cultural competence of thousands, I found myself searching for ways to balance all that is required within a principalship with my growing passion for providing equity- and identity-focused professional learning. A trusted colleague and friend asked if my doctoral studies had educated me beyond the schoolhouse, meaning could I be happy focusing on just one school, one staff, or one community? I had to admit that no, I could not as my current self. My identity was one that needed to grow as an anti-racist and actively disrupt at a systems level.

Postdoctoral Identity: Acceptance and Advocacy

At this point, I can see how an understanding of my multiple identities has not only supported my commitment to social justice and cultural competency but also allowed me to do so more authentically and strategically with others in my professional context. My application, acceptance, and matriculation through the JHU EdD program truly occurred at the most transformative time of my life. The embedding of social justice content throughout the JHU EdD coursework allowed me to engage in a level of critical reflection that otherwise would not have felt productive or—and more importantly—safe. Professionally, JHU provided me a systems-focused understanding of problems that transformed my leadership to a cyclical/iterative practice that researches, learns, implements, reflects, revises, and repeats *with* others as described by Bryk et al. (2015). Notably, this connection to improvement science was not only one of the first concepts taught in the JHU EdD program but was also a thread woven throughout every course. I then realized that the thread is not cut when students graduate but continues to create a tapestry through our use of the fibers in our professional contexts.

While changes in my professional practice have allowed me to be more impactful in the world of education, it is my personal beliefs that were deeply transformed by the JHU EdD program. I entered understanding that I benefited from my White privilege. Through coursework, research, periods of deep reflection, and consistent probing by my advisor and dissertation committee of how the internalization of my journey—academic and personal—was going, I realized that to better understand others, I needed to *accept* my White privilege, not just recognize it. This acceptance comes with a greater level of responsibility to counteract the impacts of oppression and injustice in all its forms. Moreover, I hold myself to a greater standard to bring this acceptance to others through the reflective and transformational processes I now lean on every day.

References

Bryk, A. S., Gomez, L., Grunow, A., & LeMahieu, P. (2015). *Learning to improve: How America's schools can get better at getting better*. Harvard Education Press.

Caswell, T. A. (2021). *Critically reflecting on equity- and identity-focused professional learning to increase cultural competency: A pilot study* [Unpublished dissertation]. Johns Hopkins University.

Coleman, J. S., Campbell, E. Q., Hobson, C. J., McPartland, F., Mood, A. M., Weinfeld, F. D., & York, R. L. (1966). *Equality of educational opportunity*. U.S. Government Printing Office.

Crenshaw, K. (1991). Mapping the margins: Intersectionality, identity, and violence against women of color. *Stanford Law Review, 43*(6), 1241–1300. https://doi.org/10.2307/1229039

DiAngelo, R. (2018). *White fragility: Why it's so hard for White people to talk about racism*. Beacon Press.

Gorski, P., & Dalton, K. (2020). Striving for critical reflection in multicultural and social justice teacher education: Introducing a typology of reflection approaches. *Journal of Teacher Education, 7*(3), 357–368. https://doi.org/10.1177/0022487119883545

Jacoby-Senghor, D.S., Sinclair, S., & Shelton, N.J. (2016). A lesson in bias: The relationship between implicit racial bias and performance in pedagogical contexts. *Journal of Experimental Social Psychology, 63*, 50–55. doi:10.1016/j.jesp.2015.10.010

Katz, L., & Chard, S. C. (2000). *Engaging children's minds: The project approach*. Greenwood Publishing Group.

Mezirow, J. (1997). Transformative learning: Theory to practice. *New Directions for Adult and Continuing Education,* (74), 5–12. https://doi.org/10.1002/ace.7401

Mezirow, J. (1998). On critical reflection. *Adult Education Quarterly, 48*, 185–198. https://doi.org/10.1177/074171369804800305

Myers, L. J., Speight, S. L., Highlen, P. S., Cox, C. I., Reynolds, A. L., Adam, E. M., & Hanley, P. (1991). Identity development and worldview: Toward an optimal conceptualization. *Journal of Counseling & Development, 70*, 54–63. https://doi.org/10.1002/j.1556-6676.1991.tb01561.x

Neal, J. W., & Neal, Z. P. (2013). Nested or networked? Future directions for ecological systems theory. *Social Development, 22*(4), 722–737. https://doi.org/10.1111/sode.12018

Peterson, E. R., Rubie-Davies, C., Osborne, D., & Sibley, C. (2016). Teachers' explicit expectations and implicit prejudiced attitudes to educational achievement: Relations with student achievement and the ethnic achievement gap. *Learning and Instruction, 42*, 123-140. doi:10.1016/j.learninstruc.2016.01.010

Sevig, T. D., Highlen, P. S., & Adams, E. M. (2000). Development and validation of the Self-Identity Inventory (SII): A multicultural identity development instrument. *Cultural Diversity and Ethnic Minority Psychology, 6*(2), 168–182. https://doi.org/10.1037/1099-9809.6.2.168

CHAPTER 7

An Opportunity of Practice

Darcie L. TeVault

Identity Shift 1: Acting on Curiosity

I SEE EDUCATION, not only as an equalizer, but also as a mobilizer.

I am a first-generation college graduate. I am the great-granddaughter of immigrants, raised primarily by a divorced mother and amazing grandparents in a very small town. I married young and taught part-time and then full-time as we raised two fine young men. Faced with a pending empty nest and some awesome encouragement, I pursued both a master's and doctorate. And now, I'm using what I learned at Johns Hopkins University (JHU) to strengthen the bridge from research to practice every day in my career as the Director of Professional Development for the Virginia Association of Independent Schools (VAIS). However, this did not just magically happen; multiple unanticipated shifts were necessary along the way.

I taught in public school and in a private consulting practice supporting learners with dyslexia for two decades. In the 10 years prior to my JHU Doctor of Education (EdD) experience, I supported students with dyslexia in the Academic Center of a suburban independent day school. In this role, I was a successful practitioner, an advocate for students and families, and an engaged lifelong learner about strategies to support learners through reading research, participating in professional learning, and collaborating with peers.

As I observed the outcomes of my diagnostic and prescriptive support using a structured model through the Orton-Gillingham approach to reading, I began to wonder if and how current neurocognitive science aligned with my practice. I set out to explore this curiosity by enrolling in a master's program at

JHU, where I was introduced to the Mind, Brain, and Teaching program. This program was a perfect fit, integrating the latest research from cognitive science, psychology, neurology, neuroscience, and education (aka the science of learning). Imagine my excitement as I explored how the current research aligned with Dr. Orton and Ms. Gillingham's original 1930s approach! I also started to think about how the Orton-Gillingham methodology was not just good practice for dyslexic students, but it was actually just plain good practice—making students feel emotionally secure, integrating modalities, establishing schema, reinforcing concepts, and assessing reading skills and comprehension authentically.

Before engaging in my graduate studies at JHU, I saw myself as a strong teacher who consistently refined my skills and made differences in the learning lives of my students. I saw graduate studies as a mobilizer to stimulate my career growth and build my skills. I imagined myself in a future role in instructional leadership or school leadership. It felt doable, but still distant. Enrollment in graduate studies shifted my identity from that of curious educator to an educator formally acting on that curiosity.

Identity Shift 2: From Learning to Leading Learning

Thinking about good practice and learning how to read and synthesize neuro- and cognitive science research seeded my excitement and gave me the confidence to try leading. Informed by mind, brain, teaching, and school administration studies in my JHU master's degree, I started the first community of practice group at my school with the purpose of exploring and applying the science of learning (aka neurocognitive research) in practice with my peers. The group met weekly, read, discussed the concepts, applied the concepts to practice, and discussed classroom outcomes. I liked leading professional learning and was fueled by the excitement of seeing teachers apply research to practice, changing their methods to benefit our students directly.

Around this time, I also joined a state-level group of female educational leaders who inspired and encouraged me to self-advocate, build a network of like-minded aspiring leaders, and put myself out there in the independent school context. In addition, I began learning more about the importance of addressing gaps in independent school leadership. I engaged in learning about the age gap between male and female heads of school, the pay gap for female leaders, and the diversity gap in independent school leadership.

Next, I successfully led several whole-school sessions on the science of learning at my school and presented at the state association's annual conference. I was leading learning for educators, applying the science of learning in my professional learning design, and building the bridge between research and practice, but I still wanted to learn more!

Before I facilitated the community of practice and other professional learning, I saw instructional leadership in my future, something to be done *after* I completed my studies. Engaging in this work *during* my JHU master's helped me see myself as an instructional leader, building my skills in real time. My school community saw me as a resource, and school leaders asked me to do more of this work. This experience and encouragement cemented my desire to dig more deeply into the research and follow through on my intentions to pursue the JHU EdD.

Identity Shift 3: Bold to Grappling

I boldly embarked on my doctoral journey, first thinking, "Three years, I can do that!" and "Work to build the bridge from research to practice, I can do that!" and "Applied Dissertation, I can do that!" Little did I know as I clicked Send on my application what I was about to encounter!

Fast-forward to my first summer residency and orientation in Baltimore. It was a blur of sessions on topics ranging from strict adherence to American Psychological Association guidelines, to online tools used to manage thousands of references, to oral comprehensive exams . . . all before defense? It was intense. Two classmates left at lunch and never returned. In a session where we began to define/redefine our Problem of Practice (POP), I shed my first Hopkins tears.

When pressed to articulate a problem, I looked around the table at my smart new colleagues. One was exploring the outcome gap in writing for middle school students of color, and how he might contribute to a shift in practice; another was addressing negative self-talk in mathematics and how journaling might support stronger mathematics competency. These were big problems! I was being asked to describe my contextual opportunities for growth as problems. Before this experience, I had been a big fish in a small sea, always prepared, always an A student, and always able to answer the question. Not having the answer was incredibly unsettling, and it felt terrible.

I clearly recall sitting outside the venue at a cafe table with my soon-to-be dissertation adviser batting ideas about my POP across the table. I explained to her that in the independent school context, return on investment is critical; the school is under consistent pressure to be $20,000 better than the free alternative down the road. Better opportunities, better outcomes, and ultimately better college admissions are the expectation. Our independent school had a 100% graduation rate; 100% of our students went on to 4-year colleges and universities; the teachers were a collaborative, caring team. Surely there was room for growth, but where exactly was the problem?

Before the EdD orientation, I saw myself as a confident student, bold, with a fresh JHU master's degree, experienced in using the learning management system and the library, and equipped with refreshed writing skills. I thought of myself as a budding scholar. However, the residency experience was unsettling and disorienting. It left me grappling with self-doubt. At this point, I questioned everything about my decision.

Identity Shift 4: From Instructional Leader to Scholar-Practitioner

Over the coming weeks, I continued slamming against walls in my own head. I had to figure out how to work within the boundaries, and the expectation was to have a problem. In fact, there was a prescribed process, a template, for articulating the POP. How could I come up with a problem in my context? Not to mention calling out a POP, literally identifying a problem in my independent school, could impact both enrollment (negatively) and my employment at the school! Amid my ongoing struggle, my husband reminded me of a time 20 years prior. Following a production accident in the glass factory where he was the engineer, his plant manager boldly asserted that it was not a problem, but rather an opportunity; an opportunity existed never to have this type of accident happen again. Thus, I proposed the idea of an opportunity to my adviser and my future committee members. My adviser was encouraging and suggested

I write about this idea, framing my work as an opportunity, with a focus on organizational growth. Little did I know, behind the scenes, my adviser was also advocating for me, bringing light to the unique entrepreneurial context of the independent school, and helping me become an insider in a place where I was feeling like an outsider. I pivoted from a POP to an Opportunity of Practice (OOP). My adviser's support and advocacy were powerful and enabling during this shift. I believe experiencing this level of collaborative support early on contributed significantly to my success in the program.

This was also my first major doctoral identity shift, from instructional leader to scholar-practitioner, advocating against the norm. My internal struggle was incredibly productive. The discomfort and self-doubt flashbulbs became dimmer. At the same time, I was successfully navigating coursework and academic writing, and making connections with my academic peers. The sense of community, especially in the early semesters of the program, was an important ingredient in my identity shift as well. Reaching out and being reached out to by others helped me to see that I was not alone and was not the only graduate student struggling with imposter syndrome.

I initially embarked on graduate education to grow my skill set to better understand the science of learning and apply this knowledge to my individual practice. However, I quickly identified the breadth of opportunity for the application of this knowledge as a conduit for whole school improvement. Thankfully, my organization was flexible enough to provide opportunities for me to apply my learning. Throughout my EdD studies, I leveraged my contextual knowledge as an organizational insider and helped implement cycles of improvement science (Bryk et al., 2015) bridging research to practice. These improvement efforts included the creation and implementation of a Pedagogical Master Plan (PMP) girded by knowledge of the learning sciences; the development and implementation of a robust teacher evaluation process; and the design and implementation of a pivot to online and hybrid learning in the wake of the COVID-19 pandemic, which became a significant piece of my dissertation study.

During each step along this path, my work was informed and challenged by my experience in the EdD program as I became a more discerning consumer of research, a more interdisciplinary synthesizer of knowledge, and a more confident educational leader. Coursework and professors in the program exposed me to ecological systems theory (Bronfenbrenner, 1979) in *Contemporary Approaches to Education Problems*; multidisciplinary thinking through the lenses of anthropology, history, sociology, and economics (Krishnan, 1990) in *Disciplinary Approaches to Education*; and the social and racial injustices and inequalities from desegregation to the current sociopolitical climate (Coleman et al., 1966; Tyack & Cuban, 1997) in *Multicultural Education*. Coursework also supported a deeper understanding of educational theory (Ertmer & Newby, 2013).

In the early part of the JHU EdD, academic reading and writing was another area of intense growth and transformation. My professor in *Contemporary Approaches to Education Problems* pushed me to deeply understand the importance of research skills, to be discerning about my own reading choices by asking questions such as, "Am I reading the articles that counter my instincts?" or "Am I drawn to authors who think the way I think?" and to commit to growth in my academic writing at this level (cf. Granello, 2001). Equipped with my developing JHU tool kit, I was eager to serve my organization and embraced the work through a lens of pedagogical best practices informed by neurocognitive science.

As I grew, I partnered with my school community, sharing what I was learning and advocating for infusing neurocognitive research into our daily practice. Under thoughtful and reflective leadership, the school community grew and blossomed. As the school embarked on a journey to articulate and implement a schoolwide pedagogical approach, I was asked to serve on the multidisciplinary team to apply the skills I was building at JHU, especially those related to pedagogy informed by neurocognitive research. This team created a PMP, a living document that would adapt as needed to meet the needs of individual learners. The PMP was developed over a 3-day workshop with a design thinking approach under the leadership of an outside consultant who later joined the faculty. My budding expertise was noted by the consultant and school leaders. Following the development of the PMP, the school created a new team and invited me to serve as a Division Director for Teaching and Learning. This role was created for me and included opportunities to design professional learning for implementation, to scaffold support for faculty, and to evaluate the progress. Thus, my move from single contributor to independent school administrator during the EdD and in tandem with my comprehensive exams preparation!

Becoming a designer of professional learning for implementation of the PMP was a perfect opportunity for me to start implementing some of my ideas and to experiment with using the neuroeducation concepts I was studying in adult learning situations. I discovered a newfound confidence in presenting to faculty, and I excitingly modeled many of the pedagogical strategies in my sessions (concept mapping, retrieval practice, arts integration).

During this time, I was also deeply engaged with the dissertation. Through my dissertation study, *The Interrelatedness of Self-Efficacy, Collective Teacher Efficacy, and Pedagogical Knowledge in an Independent School* (TeVault, 2021), I sought to deeply understand the phenomenon of the interrelatedness of pedagogical practices and teacher beliefs through a multiple methods case study. Teacher self-efficacy (TSE) is the set of beliefs one has about one's ability to succeed as a teacher (Bandura & Watts, 1996). Teacher collective efficacy (CTE) describes the shared beliefs of a group concerning their power to effect change or produce results (Bandura, 2001; Tschannen-Moran & Barr, 2004). I chose to explore both TSE and CTE because of the unique dynamics and highly experienced faculty at the school. Teacher beliefs manifest themselves in a variety of ways, including instructional practices, classroom management practices, and student-teacher relationship practices. Pedagogy is the knowledge base for teaching, the art and science of the craft. TSE was measured using the Teacher Efficacy Scale (Gibson & Dembo, 1984); CTE was measured using the Teacher Collective Efficacy Scale (Tschannen-Moran & Barr, 2004), and general pedagogical knowledge (GPK), as informed by the learning sciences (aka neurocognitive research) was measured using a pilot instrument (JohnBull et al., 2023). (The option to pilot the GPK instrument is a clear example of the adviser-student collaborative mindset in the JHU EdD program.) Prior to this study, there was a gap in the literature related to understanding these factors and their interrelatedness. It was also my hope that the study might serve to encourage and support future research in independent schools and strengthen the bridge between research and practice in these unique educational environments.

In the midst of my Applied Dissertation work, there were several additional obstacles to navigate, including a global pandemic (COVID-19), racial atrocities (summer 2020+), and distasteful political unrest. Resilience and flexibility were vital across all areas of life. Flexibility became the societal buzzword, especially in education. Given the world events of 2020, my study timeline shifted to include an exploration of the phenomena of TSE, CTE, and GPK before and during the COVID-19 pandemic.

My study findings suggested that teachers made important adaptations to practice, such as addressing the emotional climate for learning, designating more teachers' time for the design and implementation of learning, increased frequency and duration of one-on-one appointments with students, modifications to the curriculum, and adapted assessments. Findings also suggested that general teaching efficacy, a subconstruct of TSE, and instructional strategies, a subconstruct of CTE, are related. Implications of this study included (a) the importance of a better understanding of the interrelatedness of TSE beliefs, CTE beliefs, and GPK; (b) the importance of pedagogical support for teacher adaptations (i.e., the iterative work of instructional leadership during this time); (c) the potential impact of social and cognitive factors for educators during a disaster (i.e., COVID-19 shutdowns); (d) the pilot of a GPK instrument; and (e) the independent school context as an opportunity for more research (TeVault, 2021).

As suggested by my adviser early in the process, I utilized appreciative inquiry, which is a positive approach in which the researcher more deeply understands by exploring and amplifying strengths (Tschannen-Moran, 2014). Leveraging appreciative inquiry techniques through a multiple methods case study and adapting the POP mindset to an OOP approach opened the door to change on a personal level and on an organizational level. Before this transformation from instructional leader to scholar-practitioner, I saw myself as a student of education and an instructional leader at my school. As I progressed through the EdD and my study, especially when faced with the challenges of the contextual time, I began to see myself more clearly and confidently as a scholar-practitioner and as a conduit between research and practice for teachers and other leaders at my school.

Identity Shift 5: Scholar-Practitioner and Association Leader

My endeavor to explore the relationships between TSE and CTE through knowledge of the learning sciences led me to design and implement professional learning anchored by these factors and driven by best practices for professional learning in one independent school subsequent to completing my Applied Dissertation. As I grew in that organization and through my studies, I gained confidence. I looked for ways to apply my learning to an even broader context. Now, I am effecting change rooted in the same pillars in a larger context as the Director of Professional Development for VAIS. In this role, my contextual reach has grown to 95 member schools, 6500-plus educators, and more than 40,000 students.

Equipped with confidence, a robust skill set from my JHU learning, and association support, I revised the organizational approach to professional learning to be better aligned with research.

> Before revision: We strive to be the lead learner for our schools, sharing the most up-to-date information and trends in education.

> After revision: We provide the building blocks for professional learning at all levels of your organization. VAIS professional development is strengthened and informed by the Standards for Professional Learning and neuroeducation pedagogical best practices. We are committed to supporting high-quality professional learning to sustain and advance equitable educational practices that support student learning.

Now, on a daily basis, I am able to evaluate decisions through the lens of improvement science (Bryk et al., 2015) and pedagogical best practices and to support other educators in doing the same. I am abandoning once-and-done and stand-and-deliver professional development in favor of ongoing contextualized, rigorous, and transformational work. I have embedded and threaded diversity, equity, inclusion, justice, and belonging and legal issues work in every event I plan to reach the system level, threading this work through efforts at all levels of our schools and advocating for those doing this work in our schools each day.

Before the shift from leading at the school level to leading at the association level, I saw myself as a competent and confident school leader. I made a difference in one school by applying research to practice and supporting faculty in doing the same. After the shift to association leadership, my confidence for designing and facilitating professional learning has grown. I proudly see myself leading professional learning for 95 schools as they strive to support their missions.

Reflections on Identity Shifts

The EdD is a process. You embark knowing you will learn but not yet know-ing what you do not know. For example, throughout my career, I advocated for inclusion. I did not realize how very much I would learn about and apply critical perspectives on multicultural education and belonging. As I entered the JHU master's program and later the EdD program, I never imagined my-self understanding and advocating for education policy on a significant level or analyzing and interpreting quantitative and qualitative data. It is not easy! In this process, raw clay is stacked and shaped, only to be broken down and crafted into more than the original vision. Throughout my studies, more consistently in the beginning, I made statements of self-doubt such as, "I don't belong here" and "Everyone else is so smart." My adviser was a mechanism for change; she combatted my doubt with reassurances such as, "Trust the process" and "It will all come together." And she filled my tank with declarations of, "That was an amazing comps!" and "Wow, this is a beautiful dissertation!" These moments kept me going, pushed the imposter syndrome aside, and replaced the negative self-talk in my head. As my relationship with my adviser deepened, her con-structive critique blended with genuine encouragement pushed me beyond my own imagined boundaries to contribute to the field.

In the independent school world, we use the term "lifer" to describe a stu-dent who has been contiguously enrolled from kindergarten through Grade 12. I am certain, I am a lifer in education, committed to this field. I am not the same person who wept in Baltimore a few short years ago. I am confident and knowledgeable. I know that I do not have all the answers, but I know what good answers look like. I know how to read research with a discerning lens, question policy, analyze data, articulate implications, formulate new questions, and advocate for change. I have developed a broad and deep network of highly qualified colleagues with whom I partner to do this work. I'm using what I learned in the JHU EdD program to strengthen the bridge from research to practice every day in my career as a statewide leader. Despite what we read to-day in the news and on Twitter, as an educator, I find joy in being a lifer in this noble field. Education is not an equalizer; it is a mobilizer. The opportunities we can create for ourselves and others through formal and informal learning are simply limitless. I am a grateful scholar-practitioner and a Doctor of Education.

References

Bandura, A. (2001). Social cognitive theory: An agentic perspective. *Annual Review of Psychology, 52*(1), 1–26. https://doi.org/10.1146/annurev.psych.52.1.1

Bandura, A., & Watts, R. E. (1996). Self-efficacy in changing societies. *Journal of Cognitive Psychotherapy, 10*(4), 313–315. https://doi.org/10.1891/0889-8391.10.4.313

Bronfenbrenner, U. (1979). *The ecology of human development: Experiments by nature and design.* Cambridge, MA: Harvard University Press.

Bryk, A. S., Gomez, L. M., Grunow, A., & LeMahieu, P. G. (2015). *Learning to improve: How America's schools can get better at getting better.* Harvard Education Press.

Coleman, J. S., Campbell, E., Hobson, C., McPartland, J., Mood, A., Weinfeld, F., & York, R. (1966). *Equality of educational opportunity.* U.S. Department of Education.

Ertmer, P., & Newby, T. (2013). Behaviorism, cognitivism, constructivism: Comparing critical features from an instructional design perspective. *Performance Improvement Quarterly, 26*(2), 43–71. https://doi.org/10.1002/piq.21143

Gibson, S., & Dembo, M. H. (1984). Teacher efficacy: A construct validation. *Journal of Educational Psychology, 76*(4), 569–582. https://doi.org/10.1037/0022-0663.76.4.569

Granello, D. H. (2001). Promoting cognitive complexity in graduate written work: Using Bloom's taxonomy as a pedagogical tool to improve literature reviews. *Counselor Education and Supervision, 40*(4), 292–307. https://doi.org/10.1002/j.1556-6978.2001.tb01261.x

JohnBull, R. M., Eith, C., & TeVault, D. (2023). *NeuroEducation General Pedagogical Practices and Beliefs Survey: Results from cognitive interviews and pilot testing of a new instrument* [Manuscript in preparation]. Department of Education, Johns Hopkins University.

Krishnan, S. (2009). *What are academic disciplines? Some observations on the disciplinarity vs. interdisciplinarity debate.* Economic & Social Research Council National Centre for Research Methods. http://eprints.ncrm.ac.uk/783/1/what_are_academic_disciplines.pdf

TeVault, D. (2021). *The interrelatedness of self-efficacy, collective efficacy, and pedagogical knowledge in an independent school: A multiple methods case study* [Doctoral dissertation, Johns Hopkins University]. JScholarship.

Tschannen-Moran, M. (2014). *Trust matters: Leadership for successful schools.* John Wiley & Sons.

Tschannen-Moran, M., & Barr, M. (2004). Fostering student learning: The relationship of collective teacher efficacy and student achievement. *Leadership and Policy in Schools, 3*(3), 189–209. https://doi.org/10.1080/15700760490503706

Tyack, D. B., & Cuban, L. (1997). *Tinkering toward Utopia: A century of public school reform.* Harvard University Press.

CHAPTER 8

An Unexpected Transformation Journey

Kristin H. Barbour

Introduction

I BELIEVE IT is important that leaders within any context, but especially within education, understand the importance of learning. Learning can help us interpret our experiences and increase our knowledge and skills (Mezirow, 2000). However, after more than 20 years as an education leader, I am coming to realize that the learning process in and of itself is not the endgame. Further, learning and change are not synonymous. Learning is not without merit but learning that does not lead to change falls short of its potential to transform beliefs, thinking, and actions. Great leaders understand and promote the relationship between learning and changing behavior. Both take effort and require personal, mental, and emotional investments. Educational leaders who envision change and champion the mechanisms that promote change, such as learning, are more necessary than ever before as we attempt to respond effectively to the challenges and opportunities facing 21st-century educators and students. Albert Einstein, an influential scholar and changemaker, often reflected on the process of thinking and believed that when thinking changed, the world could change. Socrates, a founder of modern education, taught his students how to learn, question, and pursue truth and justice. The story that follows traces my professional identity transformation grounded in the learning associated with earning a doctorate from Johns Hopkins University (JHU) and the resulting personal and organizational changes.

Predoctoral Identity: Expert Practitioner

I am the Chief Executive Officer (CEO) of a 501(c)(3) national educator professional development organization. Although this role has many facets, the programmatic components of my job were the catalyst for my doctoral journey at JHU. Over the past two decades, I have developed curricula, taught graduate courses, and provided professional learning for private school educational therapists working with students with learning differences in reading and mathematics. Working as special educators in private schools, educational therapists provide students with learning disabilities individualized and small-group mathematics and structured literacy reading interventions. Regular engagement in the work of equipping educational therapists to work effectively with students who learn differently built and strengthened my professional identity as an expert practitioner. My career highlights include contributing to successful learning experiences in which educational therapists have increased their knowledge and developed research-informed practices to enhance students' literacy skills.

In recent years, however, I have grown increasingly concerned about the persistent reading achievement gap of K–12 private school students with learning disabilities as compared to students without learning disabilities, as highlighted by the National Assessment of Educational Progress report (NCES, 2022). The assumptions I carried associated with my expert-practitioner identity led me to believe that students' literacy skills would improve if educational therapists learned to implement research-informed cognitive reading strategies. Unfortunately, approaching improved literacy with a practitioner's lens grounded in my underlying assumptions about improving literacy instructional practices proved insufficient in my context. Analysis of student data ($n = 190$) from the 2015–2016 school year indicated improved educational therapist instruction and improved student reading outcomes that were not meaningful enough to close the reading gap (Gollery, 2017). An analysis of the effectiveness of educational therapists providing reading intervention for third- through ninth-grade private school students with learning disabilities indicated a small effect size ($d = .39$), which is not robust enough to close the reading achievement gap.

Social Justice: Civil Rights and Power of Literacy

Literacy is a student's civil right, and America has made a pledge for all K–12 students to be successful (Every Student Succeeds Act, 2015). The historical trend of reading underachievement of students with learning disabilities is problematic, creating barriers to academic achievement and success not only in school but beyond school in careers and in solving real-world problems (Cortiella & Horowitz, 2014). Education and educational reforms are long-standing social justice issues as education affords individuals with rights and opportunities. Embedded within social justice is the construct of power. From a social justice perspective, there is inherent power in being literate. The association between power and literacy is strong, as reading comprehension is connected to social class and upward mobility (Elmborg, 2012).

In my professional context, we were not effectively fulfilling our social justice mission to improve the reading ability of students with learning disabilities. I was no longer satisfied with the reading achievement status quo for students with learning disabilities. Maintaining my expert-practitioner identity was not conducive to facilitating the change needed professionally and organizationally. I recognized a need to understand better the reading achievement gap and factors affecting the Problem of Practice (POP), which is the low reading achievement of private school students with learning disabilities. This disorienting dilemma that Mezirow (2000) described as initiating a transformative learning experience challenged my assumptions and motivating me to seek multiple perspectives to help me understand how to effect meaningful change. Pursuing a doctorate at JHU's School of Education was a way to access scholarly knowledge with the intention of bridging research to practice in my context, and in the process, I had a personal identity transformation.

Mechanisms for Identity Changes

Targeted, effortful work that leads to personal learning and change requires time. Yet every day, educational leaders face the tyranny of the urgent need to respond to a myriad of evolving stakeholder needs whether they work in K–12 schools, higher education, or educational organizations. Time to self-reflect and deliberately practice new thinking habits and actions are luxury commodities difficult to acquire. However, doctoral work required me to engage in self-reflection and deliberate practice over an extended period, which in hindsight proved to be two mechanisms supporting my identity change. In addition to these mechanisms for my identity transformation, I will highlight the importance of my need to confront imposter syndrome, the literature review and needs assessment study as part of my dissertation, and the community of practice that evolved within my cohort of doctoral students to my identity transformation.

Self-Reflection

One mechanism for my identity change was self-reflection. Doctoral work promoted self-reflection practices and increased my awareness that personal and organizational change were necessary and desired. In hindsight, before starting my doctoral work, I engaged in cycles of thinking habits and practices centered on *solutionitis* as discussed by Bryk and colleagues (2015). The practices I implemented and the policies I created reflected my expert-practitioner identity. My focus was on solutions to address the low reading achievement of students with learning disabilities through direct work with those who taught them. Through the courses and writing that focused on my literature review, I reflected on and became aware of the need to fully understand the factors affecting the problem and include multidisciplinary perspectives to understand these factors and how to effect change.

Deliberate Practice

New awareness and deeper learning about my POP were imperative, but not enough to induce change. So, what would ignite internal and external transitions? As CEO of an educator professional development organization, the never-ending pressure of the tyranny of the urgent seemed to provide little or no time for me to practice critical reflection and self-evaluation about organizational practices and my thinking habits, biases, and assumptions. To understand my POP, it was imperative that I become more intentional. My studies at JHU introduced me to the concept of deliberate practice. In their book *Make It Stick*, authors Brown et al. (2014) described deliberate practice as an effortful, targeted focus on work that leads to new learning. To embed new learning in my habits of thinking and acting, I needed to engage in deliberate practice, intentionally practicing self-reflection, metacognition, and self-evaluation. I discovered that adopting the habit of being intentional requires cognitive effort to slow down, attend to learning opportunities, and be willing to learn, unlearn, and relearn. Cultivating the habit of deliberately practicing intentionality supported my identity development transition.

Confronting Imposter Syndrome

I wish I could say it was a smooth, seamless transition from expert-practitioner to scholar-practitioner. The transition was complicated, filled with dissonance, and required me to be willing to immerse myself in its uncertainties and potential. As I critically reflect on my identity development transition, I realize that I began my doctoral journey struggling with imposter syndrome and initially lacking a sense of belonging in the program. Despite my education, experience, and accomplishments as a speech and language pathologist and literacy expert, I believed I didn't belong within a community of scholars.

The lack of a sense of belonging arose early and remained intact longer than I care to admit. The absence of belonging and the presence of imposter syndrome were evident when I wrote my first discussion board post for a course assignment. I spent more than 2 hours drafting that 250-word online reflection. The fear of making mistakes, sounding less knowledgeable than my peers, and writing a post that revealed that I didn't belong in this community of scholars loomed large. I seemed only to be able to parrot others' voices, restating their research but not able to reflect critically on their work. The struggle between what I knew, what I needed to learn, and what I thought I should know was real. Noticing, reflecting, and naming my imposter syndrome thoughts and feelings pushed me to want to become a learner again. I needed to unlearn naive concepts and relearn how to learn. Rather than just using my well-practiced habits of doing school but now in a doctoral program, I allowed myself the space and grace to develop a learner identity. The shifting identity transformation with a focus on how to learn opened new pathways in my thinking, stimulated new questions and perspectives to be explored, and enabled me to recognize my mistakes as learning opportunities. In hindsight, I see that I needed to adopt a growth mindset, a characteristic of learners who are open to changing their beliefs and practices (Dweck, 2006).

Literature Review and Needs Assessment Study

The rigor, perseverance, and scholarly work required to complete the dissertation process helped to develop my learner identity. I was widening my lens by examining the factors impacting the reading ability of students with disabilities at multiple levels of the ecological systems theory (Bronfenbrenner, 1977). Through my coursework, I learned how to examine my POP using systems thinking and other theoretical frameworks, such as social cognitive theory (SCT; Bandura, 1986). As a result, through my literature review for my dissertation, I gained a deeper understanding of the interrelatedness of personal, environmental, and systemic factors affecting the reading achievement of students with learning disabilities (Barbour, 2019). The SCT perspective highlighted the importance of human agency in the learning process. Specifically, educator and student beliefs manifested in the concepts of mindset and self-efficacy. Within SCT, the construct of triadic reciprocal determinism (Bandura, 1986) provided a framework for understanding how special educators' reading instruction practices and beliefs about students' intelligence interact with mindset and self-efficacy beliefs of students with learning disabilities. As part of my dissertation, my needs assessment study findings at my context reflected the broader literature that indicated educators expressing a growth mindset correlated with higher self-efficacy (Barbour, 2019). Additionally, my needs assessment study indicated that educational therapists desired to learn more about their students' mindset beliefs and instructional practices that could facilitate students' growth mindset related to reading.

Community of Practice

The iterative rhythms of research within the JHU doctoral program fostered my sense of connectedness with scholars and promoted exchanges of resources and knowledge. My identity transformation was propelled by learning about and experiencing communities of practice (Wenger, 1998). A community of practice is a group of individuals who intentionally engage in collective learning. Learning activities and discussions focus on a common interest and the pursuit of learning how to do something better (Wenger, 1998). Researchers Brocato and Schmidt (2014) highlighted how online communities of practice build a repertoire of resources such as knowledge, tools, and approaches to addressing problems. This is what the online learning community at JHU did for me. Embracing a learning identity enabled me to become an astute consumer of research. My memories of the cycles of learning from practice grounded in writing doctoral papers and receiving feedback from peers and professors, reading and critiquing extant research, and discourse with advisers and peers provided meaningful exchanges of ideas and diverse perspectives. Within the frameworks of improvement science (e.g., Bryk et al., 2015) and learning sciences (e.g., Brown et al., 2014), my doctoral studies facilitated scholarly exploration of how people learn and the instructional strategies that can foster authentic learning and inform pedagogical approaches. I was becoming a research-informed practitioner who could apply scholarly insights to my dissertation intervention design. Furthermore, I was learning how to position my organization as a translational bridge between knowledge from learning sciences and implications for educational therapists to apply the research in developing their students' reading abilities.

Emergence and Application of a Scholar-Practitioner Identity

Developing a learner identity helped me consider others' perspectives, become comfortable with challenging others, and critically reflect on my own and others' research work. According to Reeves (2014), seeking and integrating diverse inputs enhances a person's ability to generate new ideas and make connections not previously made.

Dissertation Intervention

In social science research, a scholar-practitioner intentionally considers the role and implications of theory, research, and practice. Developing and conducting my dissertation intervention helped me to connect research knowledge with plan-do-study-act (PDSA) cycles of an improvement science approach (Bryk et al., 2015; Perla et al., 2013) to addressing the problem of underachievement in reading for students with learning disabilities. I implemented a mixed methods study to explore the effect of a revised educational therapist certification professional learning program (Barbour, 2019). The purpose of the study was to address the educational therapists' ($n = 30$) need to become knowledgeable in students' mindset beliefs and examine the corresponding educational impact on instructional practices and self-efficacy beliefs for implementing growth mindset instructional practices.

Dissertation Findings

With my newly formed scholar-practitioner identity, I was able to analyze and evaluate the study's outcomes, which revealed statistically significant differences in educational therapists' content knowledge, efficacy beliefs, and instructional practices after participating in the professional learning experience (Barbour, 2019). Qualitative data also suggested that the revised educational therapist course positively affected educational therapists' self-efficacy beliefs and instructional practices related to developing students' growth mindsets. The PDSA cycles associated with the dissertation intervention did not end with the doctoral work. Importantly, the improvement science PDSA cycles reflected in the dissertation process became an essential part of the translational bridge from research to practice in my professional context. Grounded in the SCT (Bandura, 1986), my research study indicated that engaging in mastery learning experiences can positively impact educational therapists' capacity to incorporate growth mindset instructional practices during reading instruction with students with learning disabilities. Subsequently, mastery learning experience insights that have led to changed knowledge, beliefs, and practices are now embedded in educational therapist courses. Another example of sustainable change in my organization because of my transition to the role of scholar-practitioner is the organization's use of additional PDSA cycles as a framework for developing new educational therapist courses teaching how to implement growth mindset instructional practices while teaching mathematics to students with learning disabilities.

Next Steps: Learning Journey Trajectory

Learning that leads to changed behavior provides a firm basis for personal and organizational transformation. Through my doctoral studies, my identity transformed from an expert practitioner to a scholar-practitioner by way of embracing a learner identity. Self-reflection, deliberate practice, dissertation writing, and communities of practice were the doctoral studies mechanisms for change. The ripple effect of a scholar-practitioner identity propels me to model inquiry and innovation, active engagement, reflective practices, and social justice with educational therapists and students. Social justice emerged in my dissertation study with the educational therapists as we learned new ways of working effectively with students with learning disabilities. Educational therapists enhanced their knowledge, skills, and beliefs about literacy intervention grounded in theory and research. Organizationally, our learning journey continues. As we expand our work with both regular and special education teachers in reading and mathematics, we are strengthening our role as a translational bridge between research and practice, focusing on improving how we develop the thinking and learning of all learners. Choosing to collaborate with diverse organizations and people, exploring new perspectives, and engaging in improvement science practices have set the personal and organizational trajectory for ongoing learning and changed behavior.

References

Bandura, A. (1986). Models of human nature and causality. In *Social foundations of thought and action: A social cognitive theory* (pp. 1–46). Prentice-Hall.

Barbour, K. H. (2019). *Improving educational therapists' knowledge, efficacy, and practices related to developing students' growth mindsets* [Doctoral dissertation, Johns Hopkins University].

Brocato, B. R., & Schmidt, T. (2014). Social innovation: Post-Fordist globalization and new horizons. In P. Gupta & B. E. Trusko (Eds.), *Global innovation science handbook* (pp. 539–548). McGraw-Hill Education.

Bronfenbrenner, U. (1977). Toward an experimental ecology of human development. *American Psychologist, 32*(7), 513–531. https://doi.org/10.1037/0003-066X.32.7.513

Brown, P., Roediger, H., & McDaniel, M. (2014). *Make it stick*. Belknap Press.

Bryk, A. S., Gomez, L., Grunow, A., & LeMahieu, P. (2015). *Learning to improve: How America's schools can get better at getting better.* Harvard Education Press.

Cortiella, C., & Horowitz, S. H. (2014). *The state of learning disabilities: Facts, trends and emerging issues.* National Center for Learning Disabilities. http://www.ncld.org/wp-content/uploads/2014/11/2014-State-of-LD.pdf

Dweck, C. S. (2006). *Mindset: The new psychology of success.* Random House Digital.

Elmborg, J. (2012). Critical information literacy: Definitions and challenges. In C. W. Wilkinson & C. Bruch (Eds.), *Transforming information literacy programs: Intersecting frontiers of self, library culture, and campus community* (pp. 75–95). Association of College and Research Libraries.

Every Student Succeeds Act, 20 U.S.C. § 6301 (2015). https://www.congress.gov/114/plaws/publ95/PLAW-114publ95.pdf

Gollery, T. (2017). *Phase II student achievement analysis/findings from the Woodcock-Johnson-IV* [Unpublished raw data].

Mezirow, J. (2000). Learning to think like an adult: Core concepts of transformation theory. In J. Mezirow & Associates (Eds.), *Learning as transformation: Critical perspectives on a theory in progress* (pp. 3–33). Jossey-Bass.

National Center for Education Statistics. (2022). *NAEP report card: 2022 NAEP reading assessment highlighted results at Grades 4 and 8.* U.S. Department of Education. https://nces.ed.gov/nationsreportcard/reading/

Perla, R., Provost, L., & Parry, G. (2013). Seven propositions of the science of improvement: Exploring foundations. *Quality Management in Health Care, 22*(3), 170–186. https://doi.org/10.1097/QMH.0b013e31829a6a15

Reeves, A. N. (2014). Creating creativity: Personal creativity for personal productivity. In P. Gupta & B. E. Trusko (Eds.), *Global innovation science handbook* (pp. 73–82). McGraw-Hill Education.

Wenger, E. (1998). *Communities of practice: Learning, meaning, and identity.* Cambridge University Press.

CHAPTER 9

Discovery and Reflections of a Multilingual Learner and Scholar-Practitioner

Lara Ohanian

My Armenian American Experience

I WAS BORN in White Plains, a suburb just north of New York City, in 1976, and before my first birthday we relocated to Iran, where my father and mother were born. My parents were Armenian and were born and raised in Iran. We fled Iran in 1980 during the revolution, relocating to upstate New York. I spent my school years in upstate New York and moved around the United States for over 10 years until I settled in Maryland, where I live now with my husband and young son.

After high school, I earned a BA in biology and philosophy, immediately followed by an MA in bioethics. Following the attainment of my master's, I spent 13 years as a Science Educator and the last 12 years as a District Administrator in a large mid-Atlantic public school district. Over the past 6 years, my work has focused on supporting English for speakers of other languages (ESOL) and gifted and advanced learning programming. Along the way, I earned an advanced Education Specialist (EdS) degree in educational leadership and policy and a Doctor of Education (EdD) in education with a focus in Mind, Brain, and Teaching.

Armenian American Educator (and Leader)

I often respond that I am Armenian if asked how I identify myself. My first two languages were Armenian and Farsi, and I learned English when I returned to the United States in 1980. My parents spoke English, which may have afforded me advantages that some other multilingual learners (MLs) may not have experienced whose families do not speak English. However, my school did not offer English language development or classroom scaffolds for MLs. Due to my parents' fluency in English, the school assumed I did not need help. In addition, the area of upstate New York where I grew up was not ethnically or socioeconomically diverse; it was a White, affluent suburb. At this time, I identified as a multilingual first-generation Armenian American; I did not connect my identity to my educational experience.

At 22 years old, while working on my master's in bioethics, I worked as a teaching assistant (TA) in applied ethics and logic. Both were courses for undergraduate students and could serve as a core class or an elective. The role required me to teach classes, grade assignments, and provide office hours for students. This was my first experience evaluating other students' work and analytical skills. I was astounded by the students' lack of experience with academic critical thinking activities and developing comprehensive arguments. These students wrote disjointed arguments for ethical stances and needed help to complete logic proofs. It became clear that many of these students had these challenges because they had limited exposure to activities promoting academic higher level thinking skills. Working as a TA significantly changed my beliefs about elementary and secondary education quality in the United States. Before this experience, I assumed that most students had equitable educational experiences that prepared them for postsecondary study. This experience changed the trajectory of my life. Before working as a TA, I had planned to complete my master's degree in bioethics, then continue to get my doctorate in that area of study and focus on applied ethics through academia or working directly in hospital administration. I saw myself as an academic rather than as an educator. Upon completing my master's in bioethics, I changed my pathway and instead focused on secondary science education. I completed an alternative certification in education and spent the next 10 years instructing highly intelligent students from low socioeconomic backgrounds in struggling schools. It is essential to recognize that throughout this time and into the present, the one belief that has remained the same for me is that all students can succeed with the proper support and strategic instructional programming. Thus, I began my journey to becoming an Armenian American educator.

Professionally, I have spent almost my entire educational career in public schools and districts supporting the continuum of learners, especially socially or linguistically diverse ones. My goal has always been to provide my students with the most effective instruction possible. I would attend professional learning opportunities, read educational texts, and collaborate with peers. As an administrator, I focused on supporting the continuum of learners and promoted research-based practices. I identified myself as an Armenian American educator (and leader) who did my best to support all learners and embrace learning myself. I did not focus on the leadership component of my identity and role because I have and always will identify as an educator. I see my leadership as an opportunity to share my learning and continue to educate different stakeholders—rather than directly instructing students. I have the privilege of educating other educators and learning from them. I understood that I connected with MLs and their families because of our shared immigration experiences; at this time, I did not see my shared instructional experience with MLs.

Armenian American (Lifelong) Learner and Educator

While transitioning to my role of leading the English language development (ELD) department in my district, I wanted to ensure I had a foundational understanding of how individuals develop language and the practices educators use when working with MLs. During my 20 years of working with MLs, I questioned some practices I had encountered, including teachers giving tasks well below grade level and using practices with families that often lacked the necessary linguistic and cultural considerations. As a lifelong learner, I have focused on continuing to learn and grow as an educator.

I have always been a critical thinker and passionate learner. Living in Baltimore City, I had heard about Hardiman's (2012) neuroeducation research. As a previous science instructor, I was fascinated with the developing neuroeducation field. I had a goal of being a district leader who could understand neuroscience research and effectively develop classroom practices to support successful, research-based teaching practices, especially those that positively impact MLs. In addition, Hardiman et al. (2012) recommended that a neuroeducation program can enhance the communication between neuroscientists and educators. Thus, I wanted to pursue a degree within the mind, brain, and teaching specialization. To better support MLs using practices grounded in the science of learning, I applied and was accepted to the EdD program at Johns Hopkins University (JHU) and pursued a specialization in Mind, Brain, and Teaching. At this time, I identified as an Armenian American (lifelong) learner and educator.

Researching the Impact of an Educator's Expectations of MLs on Their Practices

My dissertation research focused on educators' beliefs and expectations about MLs and how those impact classroom practices (Ohanian, 2020). I utilized the Public Education Leadership Project Coherence Framework to conduct the foundational literature review of my dissertation research (Childress et al., 2007). This framework was designed to support leaders in identifying the interconnectedness of essential components of their district when implementing reform initiatives. Through this literature review, I could better understand the impact of political decisions and subsequent policies on the progression of ML instruction for MLs. For example, in one foundational article I reviewed, "Laboratories for Inequality: State Experimentation and Education Access for English-Language Learners," O'Sullivan (2015) did an interesting analysis of some decisions and legal cases of the U.S. Supreme Court that have resulted in insufficient methods for supporting MLs. The review of the legal and political history of instruction for MLs and the shifts in deficient practices directly correlated to changes in immigration practices. This started with our earliest schools that, during colonial times, embraced multilingualism, providing language instruction in English and the languages of the earliest settlers. As immigration policies were implemented in the early 1900s, schools shifted to English-only instruction. Understanding this correlation helped me to understand some of the sociopolitical causes of the inadequate practices we see with MLs today.

To better understand the practices in my context, I conducted a needs assessment study of 110 educators; 59 were ESOL teachers (Ohanian, 2020). The results indicated that educators, even ESOL-identified educators, have preconceived notions and beliefs about how MLs learn English, and sometimes those understandings directly contradict neurological research on language development. Therefore, I designed a professional development series for educators focused on addressing misconceptions about language acquisition, developing strategies to support MLs, and improving knowledge regarding the development of the bilingual brain. For example, it is common practice for educators to ask parents of MLs to practice English at home to continue to grow their language. This is a misconception; in the learning series, I discussed the transference of language skills from a native language to English (Collier & Auerbach, 2011; Cummins, 1981). The results indicated that participants improved their knowledge of appropriate scaffolds for supporting MLs and decreased misconceptions about language development. I found these results interesting and reflected on myself as an educator and a student. I remembered my parents and their focus on ensuring I had a strong grasp of English based on advice from my teachers.

Mezirow, Understanding a Transformational Learning Experience

As part of my EdD coursework, I studied best professional learning practices, including a review of theoretical frameworks related to acquiring knowledge. One that was particularly relevant to addressing teachers' misconceptions was developed by Jack Mezirow (1997, 1998). This framework identified a transformative learning experience as reorganizing an individual's self-identity or examining their preestablished schema. Mezirow explained that a *frame of reference* is a structure of preconceived notions and beliefs; this viewpoint informed how an individual experiences the world, gains new knowledge, and sometimes rejects new information that does not align with their current frame of reference. These frames of reference can result in *habits of mind*, preconceptions or general leanings that filter how a person understands experiences and makes meaning. A transformational learning experience results in a *critical self-reflection of assumptions* that requires a person to engage in self-reflection that analyzes their beliefs or questions their preestablished schema. The goal of the professional learning series I designed was to do just this, allow participants the opportunity to reflect on their views of MLs and their language development.

I Was a Multilingual Learner?

As I mentioned, we left Iran and arrived in the United States months before I began kindergarten. My mom loves to tell the story of my kindergarten screening. I did well in all areas except two. The first was walking on a straight line—I danced my way down the line—this was more about my precocious nature than a challenge in following directions. The second area I think is more interesting instructionally. The test administrator asked me to count backward from five. So, I turned around in my seat and counted to five. My mom and the test administrator laughed and decided that technically I could follow directions, but I interpreted their instructions literally. I agree with them. However, I wondered what led me to be confused, and why? I now speculate that it was because English was not my first language. Looking back, I feel this should have been a flag for the test administrator or those evaluating my results.

Over a year later—I think in second or third grade—my class was reading and discussing a picture book about a family, and the book's setting was the kitchen. About 10 minutes into the story, I realized I had no idea of the English word for *refrigerator*. I knew at home we called it a *sarnaran* but had no idea what my peers called it. Panic fell over me. Of course, because of my shyness, the teacher and my peers had no idea I was frantically searching my brain for the right word, just on the possibility that my teacher might call on me. That day I rushed home after school and burst into my house, asking my mom the question that had been running through my head all day. She told me the English term, and I practiced saying *refrigerator* all night in case we discussed the story again the next day.

This minor incident in my educational career stuck with me. However, it was only during my doctoral journey, while I was studying common misconceptions and ineffective strategies for supporting MLs, that I began to unpack and reflect on my educational experience. I realized my misconception directly resulted from my personal and instructional background. I was not identified for ELD programming or services. However, I was a multilingual learner. The incident in the classroom with the word refrigerator was a clear example that if I had access at the time to a picture dictionary, visual supports, a knowledge organizer, exposure to relevant vocabulary, or one of many other scaffolds, these supports would have been highly effective. During my doctoral studies, I focused on educators' beliefs and expectations about MLs and their impact on instruction. During that research and study, I realized that the educators in my elementary school (a highly sought-after public school in an upper-middle-class neighborhood) made some assumptions; they mistook my parents' English proficiency and ability to speak English to mean that my native language was English. I could spend paragraphs unpacking this monolinguistic perspective. However, the point is that the school assumed my language proficiency without assessing my abilities and subsequently targeting my instruction.

This incident is one of many I have reflected on during my doctoral studies. I realized that not only was I an ML but I was impacted by some of the misconceptions and beliefs that the educators around me held. I was a solid student with a relatively strong educational experience, though my abilities in English as compared to mathematics and science were shockingly lopsided. I never received ELD instruction, even though English was my third language, and I had spent my formative years (ages 1 to 3.5) in Iran. My mother recognized my needs and hired tutors and summer support to work with me in English language arts. Even when I graduated high school—as a college sophomore—all my college credits were in mathematics, science, and social studies. I was in general English classes and gifted or advanced in all other subjects.

Prior to my doctorate, I would have told you I was a strong science and mathematics student and had some struggles in English language arts—because it just was not my forte. Upon critical reflection and through my doctoral studies, I realized I was a very hardworking student who was not given the specific ELD supports early in my schooling that would have enhanced my learning. I realized I was a multilingual learner.

Armenian American Multilingual Learner and Educator

A few things have changed since I went through my doctoral journey. Most importantly, I had my son, and I could write an entire book on having a baby while doing a dissertation. If asked, I would identify myself as a mom, or more accurately, an Armenian mom trying to ensure her son is a kind, inquisitive, multilingual little person. My personal life allows me to watch the development of a learner who is learning both Armenian and English. His experience differs significantly from my early years as he was exposed to English and Armenian (and French from his amazing nanny) for his first 3 years. My doctoral experience allows me to understand his development and support him as needed, especially as he begins his school studies. Finally, I see myself as an educator, but that has always been my professional identity; through parenting my son, I now see myself as an educator in my personal life as well.

Additionally, and directly as the result of the transformative nature of my doctoral work, I identify myself as an ML. More importantly, I did not receive the academic support in my early years that would have afforded me the optimal learning experience. I still need to improve my productive language skills, especially writing, even after earning a doctorate and writing a dissertation. Just writing this chapter is giving me anxiety. I run all my work through comprehensive online grammatical checks and never release anything without a peer or colleague review. This is good practice for any writer; for me it is more about my complex writing abilities. Since my doctorate, I now realize that my unease about writing is partially due to my initial years of instruction. Even with this anxiety, I can write anything (including a dissertation or chapter).

Professionally, I am more focused on what I identified as my initial reason for entering my doctoral program journey, ensuring educators engage in strategies grounded in research and aligned to how the brain acquires and maintains new information. Educators have the tools and understand practices aligned to the area of neuroeducation. I enter work with a critical lens for identifying and promoting best practices, engaging in professional learning, and supporting the continuum of learners. As I look back at myself as an educator and leader, I realize I worked so hard without a clear understanding of how individuals acquire, categorize, and maintain new learning. I understood research but needed to understand how to evaluate research critically and thoroughly. I now see myself as a contributor to that research, a scholar-practitioner.

More importantly, I realize how crucial personal reflection and understanding your experiences and understandings are to your work. Educators need to reflect on their experiences and frames of reference to ensure they understand how they enter their classroom. Only through both personal reflection and comprehensive knowledge can you support the continuum of learners.

Recently, I taught a graduate class in mind, brain, and teaching at JHU to a classroom of multilingual learners studying education. I was able to leverage their experiences, though different from my experience, to support and enhance their learning of the key practices that support a brain-based classroom as identified in *Brain-Targeted Teaching for 21st Century Schools* (Hardiman, 2012). I shared my experiences as an ML and did my best to help them reflect on their experiences as MLs. I discussed some of the stories I shared with them and others about my extreme shyness during elementary school. I think I helped them feel comfortable, because I had many discussions with students in my small classes and even had a few speak out publicly in the large lecture hall during my guest lecture—which they had not done all semester. I identify as an Armenian American multilingual learner and educator. I hope to continue to impact current and future educators with my newly realized personal experience and scholar-practitioner knowledge of research-based practices.

References

Childress, S., Elmore, R., Grossman, A. S., & King, C. (2007). *Note on the PELP coherence framework*. Harvard Business Publishing.

Collier, S., & Auerbach, S. (2011). "It's difficult because of the language": A case study of the Families Promoting Success program in the Los Angeles Unified School District. *Multicultural Education, 18*(2), 10–15.

Cummins, J. (1981). The role of primary language development in promoting educational success for language minority students. In *Schooling and language minority students: A theoretical framework* (pp. 3–49). California State Department of Education. https://doi.org/10.13140/2.1.1334.9449

Hardiman, M. (2012). *Brain-targeted teaching for 21st century schools*. Corwin Press.

Hardiman, M., Rinne, L., Gregory, E., & Yarmolinskaya, J. (2012). Neuroethics, neuroeducation, and classroom teaching: Where brain sciences meet pedagogy. *Neuroethics, 5*, 135–143. https://doi.org/10.1007/s12152-011-9116-6

Mezirow, J. (1997). Transformative learning: Theory to practice. *New Directions for Adult and Continuing Education, (74)*, 5–12. https://doi.org/10.1002/ace.7401

Mezirow, J. (1998). On critical reflection. *Adult Education Quarterly, 48*(3), 185–198. https://doi.org/10.1177/074171369804800305

Ohanian, L. K. (2020). *Enhancing knowledge and conceptions of educators supporting a rapidly growing English learner population* [Doctoral dissertation, Johns Hopkins University]. JScholarship. http://jhir.library.jhu.edu/handle/1774.2/63472

O'Sullivan, M. P. (2015). Laboratories for inequality: State experimentation and education access for English-language learners. *Duke Law Journal, 64*(4), 671–715.

CHAPTER 10

The Courage to Change

Crystal Downs

A Multifaceted Transformation

SINCE I WAS a young girl, I personally have desired that teachers would help all students, including those of varying backgrounds, find academic success despite differences in race, gender, or income. As a student, I quickly noticed the disparities in academic performance, access to leadership opportunities, and selection of student representatives on regional platforms in my predominately White, inner-city, private grade school. The students who were granted access shared commonalities. They were males of White or Asian descent from financially affluent households. Students like me—Black, female, living in a single-parent home—were not selected by teachers for opportunities. I interpreted this to mean I was not viewed as good enough to represent the school community, that I lacked intelligence, I wasn't a valued asset, or I didn't have the potential to achieve. Students from underrepresented backgrounds, like me, weren't viewed as having "arrived" or possessing the developed awareness to achieve beyond the basic school offerings, which were viewed by some as wonderful opportunities for this marginalized group. The difference between opportunities for White and non-White groups grew glaringly obvious to me, sparking a desire to protect myself from the hurt of prejudice and discrimination. I asked my mom why I wasn't given the same opportunities to perform, speak, or compete on academic platforms for my school. And while my mom repeatedly encouraged me to believe that I was equally, if not more, capable, intelligent, and valuable, I secretly found myself questioning if my culture was offensive or off-putting to those making the selections.

Students from marginalized backgrounds face the decision to either abandon their culture by "acting White" (Goldenberg, 2014) or abandon others' educational expectations by preserving certain communication patterns, behaviors, and areas of interest (Tabron & Chambers, 2019). I chose the former, but it was physically and emotionally exhausting. I "assimilated" because I internalized the idea that these students were better, and in order for me to be better, I needed to be like them. I gravitated toward a Eurocentric approach to education by focusing on test scores and grades, with the belief that these numbers would validate who I was as an individual. Embracing the acceptable ways of social interactions within this Eurocentric context mattered. I thought I would be ignored if I didn't adapt to the social tendencies of my White counterparts, and I did not want to be dismissed based on my presentation. Eventually, the fatigue from straightening my hair, lowering my volume, and modifying my tone evoked the desire for me to be proud of me. I began building a platform that allowed me to be seen, not for the purpose of recognition, but to avoid being dismissed based on my differences in culture. I studied late at night, arrived to school early for help sessions or club meetings, and grew persistent in being seen, removing any questions about my academic abilities, creative intelligence, or capability to lead. In growing confident in my identity as a young Black female, I craved equal access to leadership and higher education opportunities. These experiences would eventually lead me to advocate for educational equity in classrooms where all students, regardless of background, had equal academic access and a sense of value and belonging.

The Foundation: Identifying a Vision for Change

My predoctoral identity was established: I was a fighter for equal academic access. The ongoing battle was draining, but I persevered, graduating at the top of my high school class and earning bachelor's and graduate degrees. The layers of my identity began to set in; in addition to being a fighter, I became an advocate for equal access not only for myself but for underrepresented students in general. As a Speech Language Pathologist, I advocated for the academic success of neurodiverse students as well as cultural dialect speakers who were misdiagnosed with language deficits. I always knew that I would eventually want to return to school for my doctorate, but I thought the pursuit would need to align with the other layers of my predoctoral identities of wife, mom, and professional. I quickly realized the challenges in neatly aligning the multiple facets of my identities with the demands of time and attention to doctoral research. I thought in order for me to embrace the identity of doctoral student, all my other identities would need to fade into the background. However, the online education doctoral program at Johns Hopkins University (JHU) provided a manageable mechanism for identity transformation, allowing me to merge my current roles and identities with a doctoral one. The alignment between my promotion into school leadership, as an Instructional Lead Teacher (ILT), and the opportunity to begin doctoral work stirred my desire to lead my colleagues in creating effective learning communities for students from diverse backgrounds. I had a platform where I could help develop teacher collaboration as it related to culturally responsive teaching.

Culturally responsive teaching requires situating teaching and learning within the experiences of students for meaningful connections and increased interest in content (Gay, 2002), a less common approach in my context. At this point in my journey of identity transformation, I identified myself as a catalyst for change. I was given the positional opportunity to guide teachers through the process of broadening their awareness and appreciation of cultural differences. That position, paired with my decision to pursue a doctoral degree, morphed my professional approach. I immediately acknowledged that I was positioned to create change. As the only Black female administrator in my professional setting, pursuing a doctorate empowered me to educate my colleagues on the deeper aspects of cultural awareness and cultural competence while developing teachers' self-efficacy in both areas. You see, up to this point my contributions consisted of joining the team's cause, working hard toward an organizational goal. This approach was natural, even applaudable to some, and did not require bringing attention to the intersectionality of my race, gender, and position. But as a doctoral student, the focus of my identified Problem of Practice—analyzing the level of cultural awareness, cultural competence, and self-efficacy of teachers—was a completely different initiative, one that I desired to delve deeply into as a means of promoting meaningful learning and academic opportunities for students of all cultural backgrounds. Such an initiative required not only rallying the troops for a common cause but also making sure the troops held interest in fighting for that cause. It was important that my ILT team, teachers participating in the cultural responsive sessions, and higher administration understood the depths of change necessary to effectively accomplish the goal, that they found value as well as necessity in the goal of change, or better yet, that they wanted to face the ugliness and complexities that accompany a goal of adjusting traditional practices for new, more inclusive systems and structures. And so, my professional identity began to transform from supporting the missions of others to leading the initiative of examining cultural awareness within a predominately White faculty, working in a traditional, Southern private school.

The Frame: Creating a Structure for Change

For my Applied Dissertation study, designing an approach for effective culturally responsive modeling and coaching for teachers required research and intentionality. For optimal acceptance and application of culturally responsive practices, the structure of my dissertation's intervention needed research-based strategies to assess and address the cultural competence of teachers within an increasingly diverse environment. Naturally, complex tasks such as these required the work of many; one person would not be able to complete this task. My situation reminded me of a story in the *Bible*, found in the book of Nehemiah. This story is one of a community needing to build a wall to establish a structure of security and protection from intruders from neighboring villages. A wall of that size, or a community safeguard, cannot be built by one person, but their inspiration may be the catalyst for all to join in. Although the task was a community undertaking, the idea to build a wall was rooted in Nehemiah's desire to address a community need. I can relate to such a desire. Building the wall, for me, was creating an environment where students know they are safe, they belong, they are valued, and they are viewed as contributors as well as capable learners.

Typically, when faced with a systemwide initiative, my role was to contribute to the mission of an organization, rallying the troops for a common goal. Being the only woman of color in the leadership room, however, I quickly realized that my background, life experiences, and role positioned me to take charge of identifying the wall or structure necessary to protect the village, our newly established population comprising 50% students of color. My experiences during primary and secondary schooling allowed me to identify the need for a wall to protect us from the distractions of achievement gaps of underrepresented students (Coleman et al., 1966; Hanushek & Rivkin, 2009; Savage et al., 2011) and to direct our focus toward the education and cultural awareness of the adults who taught the students. The work of building the protective wall recognized the need to shield students from the intrusion of deficit views regarding their academic performance, test outcomes, family involvement, and contributions. I aimed for teachers to contribute to building a structure based on our teaching practices, examining who we teach, in an effort to be more effective in how we teach. I always desired to focus on the development of teachers and how to equip them with the skills necessary for effective, culturally responsive teaching. My literature review of culturally responsive research during the first year of my doctoral studies provided evidence that the need exists for more research on teachers' application of culturally responsive practices.

The Feat: Equipping Teachers for Change

The plan was clear; my dissertation would focus on promoting and supporting teachers' use of culturally responsive teaching. However, leading a new initiative requires research, and in the biblical text, Nehemiah took time to investigate the best approach to building a structure of protection while maintaining watch over the land and the people. Likewise, I needed research on how to accomplish the feat of preparing teachers to serve marginalized students through the teaching and learning process. The design of JHU's doctoral program, starting with the development of annotated bibliographies in my first-year courses, allowed me to "see the system" (Bryk et al., 2015, p. 57) by analyzing and synthesizing research on culturally responsive teaching. As a result, I strategically identified the actual problem prior to proposing a solution. Creating and implementing a needs assessment study in my research methods classes permitted objective identification of the actual factors contributing to the problem. This initial research examined the data regarding teachers' beliefs instead of focusing on students' performance or outcomes. Identifying an opportunity to enhance current systems through an improvement science approach allowed the advocator spirit that I had neatly tucked away in order to be diplomatic as the sole Black female administrator to be released. I created a plan to examine the current instructional practices and study new ways to enhance current instructional systems in an effort to intentionally address the increasingly diverse student body. I was driven to speak for the underdog, the unseen, the students who previously had been asked to choose between their culture and academic success. I wondered how teachers prepared and analyzed their instructional practices and developed culturally responsive skills. My needs assessment study analyzed whether teachers felt prepared to teach within the newly diversified classrooms. I wanted teachers to examine their self-efficacy and cultural competence within the shift in the cultural backgrounds of their students. Results of my dissertation needs assessment study indicated variability in personal self-efficacy, low general self-efficacy, and low average cultural competence in relation to designing a learning environment that integrated cultural content, reduced prejudices, promoted equity pedagogy, and created an empowering school culture (Downs, 2022). Once equipped with data from teachers within my context, my identity grew from an inquisitive administrator to a social and educational advocate for students of diverse backgrounds. The plan was set. We needed to identify ways in which teachers could address these areas of cultural competence and teaching self-efficacy, specifically integrating cultural content, reducing prejudices, promoting equitable pedagogy, and creating an empowering school culture.

The Change: Creating Space for Personal and Professional Growth

The group of builders within my community began with my instructional leadership and administrative teams, who fortunately agreed to support my intervention for my dissertation. Although an ongoing job-embedded professional learning design already existed within my context, my JHU *Fundamentals of Cognitive Development* class served as a mechanism for change by highlighting certain aspects of teacher learning, such as modeling, observations, and feedback, that had been previously missing in our professional learning design. As noted in Darling-Hammond and colleagues' (2017) research, professional learning intentionally designed to offer collaborative adult learning will promote implementation of newly learned practices. Even though our professional learning had previously introduced culturally responsive teaching, we needed to create opportunities for increased teacher competence and self-efficacy through observing fellow teachers while continuing the work of establishing cultural awareness and appreciation. In my doctoral *Power, Policy, and Politics in*

Education class, I learned that a plan cannot be followed to completion without the agreement of higher leadership. Confirmation and approval of the decision-makers were mandatory. It was my charge to maintain the overarching vision of the school while identifying effective mechanisms for change in our instructional practices. In order for the administrative team to endorse this initiative, I needed to build upon the familiarity of our established job-embedded structure. I also knew we would need to dive deeper, providing opportunities for our teachers to closely examine their classroom practices in a supportive and authentic manner. By creating time and space for teachers to be authentically vulnerable, we could begin unpacking the heavy, previously taboo, topics of implicit bias and microaggressions.

The process of conducting intervention research within my *Neurobiology of Learning Differences* class allowed me to create a blueprint for professional learning. Similar to Nehemiah, I wanted the community to contribute to the building of the structure; therefore, I designed a professional learning system for my dissertation intervention that would promote teacher learning and growth. My intervention demonstrated the benefits of fostering appreciative inquiry by inviting teachers to identify and share culturally responsive practices they currently used (Downs, 2022). Through this asset-based approach, teachers then engaged in challenging conversations about adjustments in their lessons and previously constructed beliefs. This approach would allow teachers to establish connections with colleagues during our professional learning sessions, bringing the village together. They became comfortable asking uncomfortable questions, being vulnerable about the challenges and discomfort experienced within a diverse environment, and recognizing the mutual desire to facilitate teaching and learning where all students have opportunity for academic success. During the intervention process, I recognized that my role was shifting from a minority representative on the administrative and instructional leadership teams to being a facilitator increasing the cultural awareness and appreciation of our teachers. I am operating as a catalyst for change in our K–12 teaching practices.

The Impact: Outcomes Within My Professional Context

Nehemiah's story highlights the importance of the village joining together to foster collaborative efforts, thus producing more influential outcomes than would be possible with the work of one or a few. The individuals worked in their areas of the village and their efforts combined together for the start of a solid foundational structure. The design of my professional learning afforded me a group of teachers who self-selected, from a list of professional learning options, cultural responsiveness as their professional goal for the semester. Nehemiah recognized that the people had a mind to work, indicating the collaborative efforts also required the agreement of a group. This self-selected community expressed the desire, motivation, and mindset to do the work. Teachers engaged in ongoing professional learning and adjusted their interactions in professional learning sessions, as well as their instructional practices within the classroom, to be more culturally responsive and inclusive. They learned new approaches to teaching through modeling, observations, and appreciative feedback of colleagues—becoming more aware of the culturally responsive teaching practices that they were already using. Collaborative professional learning sessions allowed authentic inquiry and vulnerability, which proved beneficial in the development and growth of teachers' self-efficacy and cultural competence. One participant attributed his deeper understanding of culture and how to be culturally responsive to the professional learning sessions (Downs, 2022). He went on to note that because of his growth and awareness, students presented as more comfortable, confident, and proud of their ideas and contributions within the learning environment.

Our professional learning sessions provided safe spaces to learn and grow. As teachers learned about culturally responsive teaching, I encouraged them to contribute newly attempted approaches to our collaborative conversations. By sharing what they learned, teachers experienced a learning environment where they were viewed as contributors, not only consumers—a model that they could use in their own classrooms. In turn, teachers began to acknowledge their students and the students' families as contributors to the learning environment. The teachers' asset-based view of students from all cultural backgrounds promoted student engagement and excitement to learn about the experiences and perspectives of others. Additionally, teachers assessed the positionality of the text, materials, and curriculum used within the teaching process and began to incorporate varied perspectives in an effort to demonstrate both awareness of their own cultures and systemic biases regarding norms as described by Banks (2001). Although these efforts have established a foundational structure of cultural awareness within a core group of K–12 teachers, we still have work to do. This is the beginning of a transformation of not only my identity but also our instructional practices. I am now an agent of change, empowering teachers to identify opportunities for internal and professional growth in an effort to promote academic success for students of diverse backgrounds. The work I've done through my dissertation has established a core group who knows the impact of this professional learning intervention. The benefit of having a core group who experienced the positive outcomes of culturally responsive professional learning is that the school community is now equipped with champions for change. I am not the only individual building cultural appreciation and strengths-based practices within the learning environment. There are more villagers speaking positively about the impact of such an approach and, over time, the students' outcomes will provide the data necessary to identify the benefits of such an initiative. As we proceed, teachers continue to rotate through the cultural component of our responsive teaching professional learning options. All K–12 teachers, within the next year, will participate in the culturally responsive course, experiencing, and learning to apply, the collaboration, asset-based views, and appreciative inquiry firsthand. A strong foundation has been established, creating a protective space for students of color to learn because the people within the village have the mind to do the courageous work for social justice and change.

References

Banks, J. A. (2001). *Cultural diversity and education: Foundations, curriculum, and teaching.* Allyn & Bacon.

Bryk, A., Gomez, L., Grunow, A., & LaMahieu, P. G. (2015). *Learning to improve: How America's schools can get better at getting better.* Harvard Education Press.

Coleman, J. S., Campbell, E. Q., Hobson, C. J., McPartland, F., Mood, A. M., Weinfeld, F. D., & York, R. L. (1966). *Equality of educational opportunity.* U.S. Government Printing Office.

Darling-Hammond, L., Hyler, M. E., & Gardner, M. (2017). *Effective teacher professional development.* Learning Policy Institute. https://learningpolicyinstitute.org/product/teacher-prof-dev

Downs, C. (2022). *Exploring changes in teachers' self-efficacy and cultural competence through a culturally responsive professional learning model* [Unpublished doctoral dissertation]. Johns Hopkins University.

Gay, G. (2002). Preparing for culturally responsive teaching. *Journal of Teacher Education,* 53(2), 106–116. https://doi.org/10.1177/0022487102053002003

Goldenberg, B. M. (2014). White teachers in urban classrooms: Embracing non-White students' cultural capital for better teaching and learning. *Urban Education, 49*(1), 111–144. https://doi.org/10.1177/0042085912472510

Hanushek, E. A., & Rivkin, S. G. (2009). Harming the best: How schools affect the Black-White achievement gap. *Journal of Policy Analysis & Management, 28*(3), 366–393. https://doi.org/10.1002/pam.20437

Savage, C., Hindle, R., Meyer, L., Hynds, A., Penetito, W., & Sleeter, C. (2011). Culturally responsive pedagogies in the classroom: Indigenous student experiences across the curriculum. *Asia-Pacific Journal of Teacher Education, 39*(3), 183–198. https://doi.org/10.1080/1359866X.2011.588311

Tabron, L. A., & Chambers, T. T. V. (2019). What is being Black and high achieving going to cost me in your school? Students speak out about their educational experiences through a racial opportunity cost lens. *High School Journal, 102*(2), 118–138. https://doi.org/10.1353/hsj.2019.0002

CHAPTER 11

Helping People Learn to Think Differently

Stephanie Scholes

Introduction

My story is not a dramatic chronicle with a clear narrative arc. In some ways I am very much the same person I was before my doctoral journey. I continue to care deeply about young children, believe in the potential of every learner, and work professionally with preschool students. Yet in other ways completing my doctorate degree through the Johns Hopkins University (JHU) Doctor of Education (EdD) program has changed the way I relate to the children, parents and caregivers, and colleagues in my workplace and has expanded the roles I see for myself in the community.

Setting the Stage

Before becoming a doctoral student, I was a practitioner grounded in evidence-based decision-making, though due to my introverted disposition, I generally focused my time and efforts more on the child and less on the surrounding systems. My undergraduate coursework culminated in a bachelor's degree in early childhood development. I took this learning to my work in a daycare setting wherein I tracked the development of the young children in my care. Based on my knowledge, experience, and observations, I knew when children were behind developmentally and needed help. I wanted to help. Unfortunately,

I had neither the skill in special education nor the knowledge of the process to refer them to early intervention, so I kept my concerns about the children whom I worked with to myself. As an uneasy observer, I was haunted by the unmet needs of these children. I was motivated to change, so I returned to school and obtained certification as an early childhood special education teacher.

Early childhood special education provides specialized instruction and related services to prepare young children for the academic and social demands of school and life (Individuals with Disabilities Education Improvement Act, 2004). Identification of eligible children begins when an infant or toddler is observed to take longer to reach milestones or is at risk of delay. Early childhood special education comprises early intervention services for infants and toddlers from birth through age 3 and preschool special education services from a child's third birthday through age 5.

When I took my first job as a special education preschool teacher, I was a student pursuing a master's degree in special education with an endorsement in teaching young children with visual impairments. Although I knew I was a capable special educator, I kept to myself. I provided special education services to children with disabilities placed in general education preschool classes and interacted with the teachers and other staff as necessary to support these children, but being busy with both work and school, I did not cultivate relationships with other special education teachers. Even my interactions with my mentor were voluntarily kept to a minimum.

At that time, the educational agency that I worked for contracted with another agency to provide vision services for preschool children with visual impairments. These services are crucial as the lack of vision support will widen the gap between the understanding of students with visual impairments and their typically sighted peers, causing them to fall further and further behind and decreasing their likelihood of meeting age-group standards. However, these services were not consistently provided. Due to this unpredictability, I saw several email messages from the director of preschool services to special education staff asking if children were receiving their vision services. This brought out my inner champion of the underdog. Given the opportunity, I knew I could help these underserved children. When I had finished my schooling, I went to my supervisor privately and expressed my frustration at seeing these emails when I could provide these services. Within the next year the contract with the outside agency was dissolved, and I became the preschool vision specialist in the district, a position new to the district. As a pioneer in this role I had the knowledge and skills to teach children with visual impairments but no curriculum or materials with which to do so. For the next 4 years I was stretched as I designed, developed, and refined the way vision services were and are currently provided for preschool children in my school district.

One part of this refining process was the consistent analysis of data. In my organization, each preschool child is assessed using a curriculum-based assessment three times across the school year. This assessment is used to guide instruction and evaluate program effectiveness. I observed that the students with visual impairments with whom I worked seemed to be scoring below their typically sighted peers in preliteracy areas of this assessment. These differences persisted even when I compared them with age- and gender-matched typically sighted peers from their class. Once again, I wanted to help. Thus, preliteracy delays of preschool students with visual impairments became my Problem of Practice (POP) for my dissertation study (Scholes, 2019).

Metamorphosis

Although the dissertation development process was a mechanism for transformation, it was more of a supporting actor rather than the lead. The process of refining my POP by considering it through different research lenses, through the analysis of contributing factors, and by synthesizing previous research did not ultimately change the essential problem that I wanted to address. Instead, this process provided a framework and clarity, and added depth and breadth to the role of stakeholders in this problem. These refinements directly guided my needs assessment study focus and methodology.

The events leading up to the formulation of my POP; refinement of it through research; validation of contextual needs via the needs assessment study; and the creation, implementation, and analysis of an intervention contributed to my knowledge base and expertise in my chosen field. The component of the JHU EdD program most critical to transforming my identity, however, was the comprehensive oral examination. As a master's student I functioned as an information gatherer. The process of preparing for the comprehensive oral examination and experiences following this examination evolved me into an information sharer. The comprehensive oral examination required synthesis of core content in education and application of this content to real-world scenarios. Realizing that this was outside the scope of my typical studying, I prepared in a different way.

As with many students, my initial efforts focused on recitation of content with corresponding citations. I had planned to practice answers to hypothetical questions while taking walks alone in my neighborhood and in a local park. My mom volunteered to join me and listen. I asked her to pose questions, some from provided lists and some developed by fellow students and me to prepare ourselves for the exam. Initially, my responses were factually accurate but poorly articulated and failed to synthesize the content in a manner comprehensible to anyone unfamiliar with the content. Sometimes my mom would stop me and ask about terms or ideas. As I learned to deliver cohesive, comprehensible answers, I developed confidence in my ability to communicate education theory and research to audiences outside of academia. Thus, the process of preparing for and success in the delivery of my responses on the 2-hour comprehensive oral examination served as a mastery experience, like those described by Pfitzner-Eden (2016). This process imbued me with feelings of efficacy or an inherent sense that I can successfully help other people understand education theory in practical ways. Seeing myself as an integrator of information empowered me as I embarked on the intervention to address my POP which ultimately guided me in pursuits both within my organization and in the greater community. This is the crux of my transformation.

Becoming a Special Educator's Special Educator

Although the process of preparing for and delivering extemporaneous oral essays in the context of the comprehensive oral examination was a defining experience, my identity began to be shaped as I felt the desire to share my learning with colleagues early in my doctoral student experience prior to this event. Transformation occurred in varied ways with three different groups of stakeholders: colleagues within my organization, parents and guardians, and members with whom I engaged in the broader community.

Using Mind, Brain, and Teaching Coursework to Collaborate with Colleagues

One of the mechanisms of change came early in the EdD program. I was introduced to the *Brain-Targeted Teaching Model for 21st-Century Students* (Hardiman, 2012) when it was the required text for one of my classes. I could see that the content of this book was so immediately applicable to other special education teachers and speech language pathologists in my department that when my supervisor asked for possible topics for year-long professional development groups, I created a targeted learning group of my colleagues that focused on this content. As I was familiar with the book, I led these discussions. I began to see myself as someone who could effect positive changes in my colleagues by imparting what I had learned.

My experience in leading these discussions gave me the confidence to submit a proposal with a coworker for a district-wide professional development session. This proposal was accepted, and my coworker and I presented on building positive relationships with young learners at multiple sessions during our district's beginning-of-school professional development conference. I later presented alone in a department-wide conference on a different topic. These presentations served as a mechanism for change as I transitioned from seeing myself as someone who attended requisite professional development to viewing myself as someone who fostered the professional development of others. My perception of myself in this regard is so changed that despite a markedly increased workload due to teacher shortages in the current school year, I still found myself thinking of a new presentation for an upcoming departmental professional development conference.

These opportunities helped me to develop self-efficacy in sharing the knowledge I gained with colleagues in more formal settings. However, I was also increasing in my confidence in sharing information in less formal settings. Much of this level of sharing became unconscious. For instance, I was surprised when a coworker told me that she enjoyed working with me because I knew my area of professional specialization with students with visual impairment and how to use relevant mind-brain and educational research to help teams to work with students.

As I considered submitting a chapter for this book, I called a former co-worker and friend who worked closely with me before I became a doctoral student, during my time as a student, and after I had obtained my doctorate. She related ways in which she had seen me grow in my practice and as a change agent. As we talked, I remembered discussing with her a role that I felt I had taken throughout the process. I had become a special educator's special educator, or in other words I had become someone who provides specially designed instruction adapted to the needs of the special education teacher I am working with to address the unique needs of that special educator. She agreed. I was indeed a source of knowledge and its practical application for my colleagues in the department.

Engagement with Parents Through Intervention Research

My professional responsibilities necessitate interaction with parents and guardians. Another mechanism for change was the implementation of a shared storybook reading intervention with parents of preschool children with visual impairments (Scholes, 2019) as part of my dissertation. Implementing this intervention instilled in me the sense that I can affect meaningful change by communicating research and relevant theory with parents. These parents had little, if any, instruction in how to engage their preschool students with visual impairments in shared storybook reading. Prior to the intervention, their children had little patience for the activity. During baseline sessions, children attempted to close the books on their parents' fingers, slid from their grasp, and reached for any toy or item within their reach. Their parents were frustrated in their attempts and mentioned in interviews that before the shared storybook reading intervention, reading with their child was stressful.

During my study, as I helped parents understand and implement evidence-based practices, such as following the child's cues to build engagement, linking content to the child's experience, and expanding on the child's comments, their use of successful strategies increased. As parents changed the way they interacted with their children, their children became more engaged in shared storybook reading. The success of this intervention helped forge relationships with parents, improved the way parents interacted with their children and books, and changed the children's perception of what it means to read books. I learned that connecting parents with relevant research in individually meaningful ways changed how they thought about something as seemingly simple as reading with their children. The sense that I could help parents by connecting them to relevant research learned in the context of my dissertation research study extended beyond the program as well. A colleague observed that as I gained confidence in my ability to connect with parents in my study, my relationships with parents outside my study improved as well. As a result of this change I see myself as a guide who engages parents in dialogue to understand the nature of their child's disability and growth, what they can do to effect change, and the interaction between these areas.

I used knowledge gained in the EdD program to teach parents how to help their preschool children with disabilities in both in-person and virtual settings. In one instance, I was working with a parent and preschool student learning braille in virtual sessions. The parent did not know braille technique and was not receptive to encouragement to direct the child to use multiple fingers to tactilely read braille until I explained brain research indicating that use of multiple digits in tactile activities strengthened neural pathways. When the parent understood why it made a difference, they thought about the way their child used his hands differently and encouraged their child to use more fingers in reading braille letters. Most of these applications and changes were very gradual, however, and I didn't recognize the change as it happened. I noticed later, however, ways that the child had learned new content, gained new skills, or generalized knowledge or skills that they now had. I could see it. As I learned to recognize the impact of these simple, subtle changes in parents I became a more confident purveyor of information.

Building Expertise to Support the Community

I attribute my work in the broader community directly to the changes I experienced through my doctoral experience. I came to feel the desire to share the knowledge and expertise I gained through my doctoral experience with a broader audience. Seeing myself as honor-bound, to date I have discharged this responsibility in two ways: as an adjunct instructor teaching with a local university and through participating as part of a state standards development and revision committee. Both experiences required me to reach outside of myself and my primary professional context.

I expressed interest in teaching with a university consortium that develops teachers of students with visual impairments or blindness. The first available instructor position, although affiliated with this program, was as an instructor of a basic braille course for parents, community members, paraeducators, and teachers to help them support literacy for learners with visual impairments. At first, I was trepidatious about teaching this course. Among my first students were paraeducators who, under the direction of licensed teachers of students with visual impairments, provided braille instruction to family members of children with visual impairments, general education teachers of kindergarten through 12th-grade students, and the new director of an instructional materials access center. I discovered that although the students came to the course with varying levels of braille understanding, I could help all of them gain skill and confidence in basic braille and understand how to promote learning and independence for the individuals with visual impairments in their sphere of influence. Thus, I came to see myself as a bridge between community members and the understanding they need to make a meaningful difference for people with visual impairments.

A second way in which I have felt empowered to engage with the greater community is on a state standards committee work group. In my state, braille standards were last reviewed in 2011. Since that time the state core standards for all students had been revised multiple times and the braille standards were no longer correlated with the state standards. Therefore, when I learned that the state board of education was convening a work group to develop standards for young children with visual impairments and redevelop braille standards for students from kindergarten through 12th grade, I expressed interest in participating. My request to be included on this committee was accepted. I was apprehensive in joining this group as I was used to seeing myself as one of the poor stepsisters who were not "real" teachers because we just work with preschool students.

After an initial committee meeting wherein we decided to divide the task into two subgroups, I went to work developing a draft of core standards for young learners with visual impairments. I structured my draft by developing a crosswalk that paired the state's core standards for early learning with the standards separated by age group on the left and the appropriate adjustments needed for learners with visual impairments or blindness on the right. My intent was to spur discussion, so I was surprised by the extent to which this alignment of standards and the adjustments for learners with visual impairments or blindness was accepted. My expertise in the content area refined through my review of literature relevant to my dissertation in courses such as *Disciplinary Approaches to Education* and *Multiple Perspectives on Learning and Teaching*, and my experience in working collaboratively with unfamiliar adults in virtual settings, such as in group projects as part of coursework in an online program, led me to approach the project differently. The other group, working on revising the state core braille standards for students from kindergarten through 12th grade, which had been struggling with knowing how to start, then modeled their approach after the crosswalk I created. I had not realized that this community who are invested in the education of individuals with visual impairments in my state saw me as an expert in my field. As I consider my participation in this project, I realize that I would never have volunteered for such a work group prior to my doctoral program and that even the way I participated was molded by the ways my identity has changed through my doctoral journey. I am now an expert in my field able to meaningfully contribute both academic and practical depth of knowledge to related discussions.

Conclusion

I did not change in a moment but through a gradual process. Initially, I did not see myself as a change agent, except in the context of my role as the preschool vision specialist working with individual children. I did not volunteer to lead groups, participate on committees, present at conferences, or teach adults. But being a doctoral student changed me. It changed how I see myself: it changed the roles I accept, the opportunities I solicit, and the ways I share information with others. Before, I saw myself as a bit of a lone wolf—when my supervisor told us to get together with other staff members with the same position I sat alone, as there was no one else with my position. I saw my position as a related services provider as filling a niche but not as someone with something to contribute to families, to the preschool services department, and certainly not as someone with expertise to benefit the greater community and influence the state core standards. I now see myself as a special educator's special educator, a statewide expert in the education of young children with visual impairments, and as a change agent in my community in helping parents and guardians, teachers, and community members foster the growth and independence of young children with visual impairments. I now see myself as someone who can help people think differently, in beneficial ways.

References

Hardiman, M. M. (2012). *The brain-targeted teaching model for 21st-century schools.* Corwin Press.

Individuals with Disabilities Education Improvement Act (IDEA), Pub. L. No. 20 U.S.C. § 1400 (2004). http://idea.ed.gov/uploads/finalregulations.pdf

Pfitzner-Eden, F. (2016). Why do I feel more confident? Bandura's sources predict preservice teachers' latent changes in teacher self-efficacy. *Frontiers in Psychology, 7,* 1–16. https://doi.org/10.3389/fpsyg.2016.01486

Scholes, S. (2019). *Preliteracy development of preschool children with visual impairments: Shared storybook reading intervention* [Doctoral dissertation, Johns Hopkins University]. JScholarship. https://jscholarship.library.jhu.edu/handle/1774.2/62003

CHAPTER 12

Transforming My Identities: From Hustler to Scholar-Practitioner

Earl Turner III

Introduction

FOR THE MOST part, my K–12 education and my career experiences shaped my social consciousness. A little more than 22 years ago, due to tragic experiences in my community, I was thrust out of my hometown in search of answers to questions that I have committed my entire life so far to answer. I liken my maturation process to a river. We know that rivers are large bodies of water, but they are distinct from other large bodies of water because they have a current that causes them to flow from one geographical point to another. The water making up the river emerges from a source called the headwaters from which water flows downhill, energized by the terrain and gravity. Rivers often have tributaries that deposit additional water, which strengthens them and causes them to evolve and take form. Rivers end their journey when they meet an ocean or a lake, and they typically deposit sediment that they pick up along their journey to create new landforms called deltas. Throughout this chapter, I will use this dynamic process as a metaphor to describe my personal development and the defining moments of my identity shifts as I evolved into a scholar-practitioner.

Upper Tributaries: My Predoctoral Journey

Tributaries are water sources that accumulate from collecting precipitation, groundwater, or melting glaciers and pour into mainstream rivers. The upper tributaries, or headwaters, are those water sources that provide the initial waters for a river. In my life, the upper tributaries poured in during high school. During this time, I identified myself as the *little tugboat that could* because I faced many challenges that helped me realize I could accomplish the things I wanted, even though academically, my peers and I were victimized by a failed educational system. I graduated from Walter L. Cohen High School in New Orleans, once named the most dangerous school in America. Through it all, I am thankful for the people who believed in me, provided the ingredients I needed to succeed, and began pouring hope into me, just like the upper tributaries that pour the early water into rivers.

Regardless of our circumstances, many of our teachers did not give up on us. My civics teacher held us all to a high standard, and it was the one class where even the toughest kids tried to succeed academically. My physical education teacher always provided me with a haven and a place to check in when things were not going well. And my basketball coach once challenged me to perform beyond my imagination by giving me 2 weeks to learn to dunk a basketball. With my teammates in the stands cheering at the top of their lungs, I dunked the ball on the third attempt, and the team charged toward me, tackling me to the floor as if I had hit the winning shot in a championship game.

Having learned that I could accomplish anything I put my mind to, I focused on working hard in athletics, but my high school academics suffered. At that point I wrote off any chance of getting into college. While I identified myself as a survivor and the neighborhood hustle man, my peers saw something else in me. They voted me the male classmate most likely to succeed in my graduating class. I had no idea why because the female student who received the same nomination was the class valedictorian. She had a 4.0 GPA and was headed to college right after high school. We were opposites academically. Although by all accounts she had a very promising future, she was tragically murdered a few months after our high school graduation while leaving college one day. Accompanying her was my childhood best friend, who also lost his life.

My high school days were filled with violence. I recall a time in 2001 when a childhood friend and I spent much time mourning the loss of yet another high school friend. By then, we had lost at least 30 peers or neighborhood friends to violence, and numerous others were incarcerated. To make sense of this horror, we grappled with questions focused on how so many people we knew died early or were incarcerated. We assumed it had to be a combination of spirituality and education because we believed that people who attended church and did well in school generally did not succumb to tragic life outcomes. Something inside me, however, told me there was more to the story. From there, I went on a journey in search of answers. I was the neighborhood hustle man, but I wanted to change my life and the lives of others from communities like mine. Like the initial deposits of water that begin rivers flowing, my community experiences inspired me to get out of the current and seek a new direction.

Looking back, I think that my classmates observed my hustle mentality and realized that I had a scrappiness that allowed me to accomplish my goals no matter the circumstances or barriers. I have always been a flexible person, and my agile mind was a key ingredient in starting a business and completing my bachelor's, master's, and doctoral degrees. I did not realize it then, but these were the building blocks and experiences that were preparing me to endure and overcome the most challenging moments of the Johns Hopkins University (JHU) Doctor of Education program.

The Confluence

After finishing my undergraduate degree, I decided to venture into entrepreneurship. Although my motives were appropriate and I was concerned with the financial aspects of being a business owner, I learned some lessons that can be likened to a river confluence. When rivers converge, often one of the rivers is larger and prevailing, while the other is smaller and less established. The coming together of the rivers forms a new river that has more force and is more dominant than the two rivers had when they were separate. During my life's confluence phase, I was driven by a dominant, one-dimensional perspective of business success that centered on making money. What I did not understand was that there was more to success than just the financial aspects. Like the confluence of a river, during this phase of my professional journey, I gained a new understanding of success that converged with my old way of thinking as a hustler to help me develop a new mind.

At this time, I was interested in teaching high school business and, to do so, a mentor encouraged me to start a business and not to stop running it until I was "successful." He believed that a person who teaches business to others should have owned and operated a successful business before they began educating others about it. I accepted the challenge and decided to start a construction company because Hurricane Katrina had ravaged my hometown, New Orleans, creating demand for renovation services. My hustler mentality was my dominant river mindset, and my motivation needed to shift the current more toward social innovation and away from merely financial gain. I defined my leadership goals by how well I led my team to complete projects and turn a profit. The confluence was still ahead of me.

Through a situation in which a prospective client indicated the struggle she had encountered to renovate her damaged house and her belief in me to accomplish the job, my perspective on business was transformed. At this point in my river's journey, I had become an entrepreneur who identified as a servant leader. I came to understand that financial attainment was a derivative of trust when a client put her faith in me to repair her most prized possession and paid me her money because of my reputation as a contractor who could get the job done correctly.

After 7 years serving as a contractor in New Orleans, I moved to Los Angeles aspiring to continue working in the construction field, but I wanted to get my Master of Business Administration (MBA) degree and scale up my service offerings. To reach that goal, I attended a Kaplan workshop titled *How to Get a 700 GMAT Score*. While at the workshop, I stopped by a Teach For America table where staff members were recruiting for their teacher preparation program. They made a compelling argument for considering teaching before I began an MBA program. Little did the recruiters know, I wanted to teach; I just hadn't realized that it was time for me to enter the field. I joined Teach for America and was placed in a middle school with many similarities to the middle school I attended as a child. My main objective as a teacher was to ensure that my students would be prepared to navigate the systems of society. I wanted to make good on our schools' inherent promises to families and their communities that we will educate their children and prepare them academically for success. Therefore, I set out to embody all the best qualities of the teachers I encountered along my journey. I set high expectations for myself and for my students, provided them physical and emotional safety, and created opportunities for them to challenge themselves to be better than they realized they could be.

In the beginning, I thought effective teaching was about *telling* my students how to solve mathematics problems. I was sure that if I had them solve enough problems the same way I had learned to solve them, they would eventually become strong students of mathematics. I quickly learned that my theory was far from the truth. Most importantly, I had to secure students' trust by building strong relationships with them and their families. This became easier and more natural because I shared many cultural qualities with my students. Furthermore, it became evident that social-emotional learning, content knowledge, pedagogical knowledge, and a high-quality curriculum were all key ingredients for success in the classroom. With my students' academic achievement growing and their families feeling that they made the right choice in sending their children to the school where I taught, I set out to understand how I could replicate some of the success I had in the classroom and scale it to classrooms like mine across the country.

The Delta: My Doctoral Journey

Having taught middle school and high school mathematics and completed a master's degree focused on instructional technology, I knew that I loved being in the education field and wanted to follow the current by taking my educational experience one level higher. I considered a juris doctor MBA, but I did not think I would enjoy being an attorney. Searching for programs, I found the JHU doctoral program with an entrepreneurial specialty area. I applied and focused on entrepreneurial leadership in education. It was by far the best professional decision I have ever made. I started my doctoral program with so many lessons already learned, both formal and informal; those lessons and experiences filled my heart and mind with valuable thoughts and experiences, but I realized that there could be more to come.

Deltas are nutrient-rich wetlands resulting from sediment and silt build-up that benefit people and wildlife greatly. As I began my doctoral journey—what I refer to as nearing the delta—I identified as an expert teacher of mathematics. Although I did not know exactly what I would learn through the doctorate, I kept an open mind and looked forward to growing as a practitioner. During one of the first summer residency workshops, the director of the program, Dr.

Stephen Pape, asked us to please be patient in developing solutions to our Problem of Practice (POP) until we invested the time needed to understand the problem. When he mentioned that, I remember thinking that I was sure that I knew the problem—limited instructional change despite the availability of technology in the classroom—so I did not need to spend that much more time thinking about it.

Overconfident, I identified myself as the Lebron James of classroom teachers, but I didn't realize then that I was missing the bigger picture. I held misperceptions and false assumptions about the factors that contributed to failed educational systems and inadequate solutions. When I engaged with colleagues about aspects of education, the conversation often led to discussions regarding "the problems" students have. There were often points in some of those discussions when someone would say, "Do you know what the problem is?" or "I can tell you what the problem is." Then they would explain a one-dimensional scenario that described either a continuously unaddressed problem or a solution that was no longer implemented in schools or communities. Student disrespect or the need for more parental discipline were frequently proposed in relation to "students' problems." In the first statement, the problem is not addressed. In the second statement, the proposed solution is insufficient. It's not about fixing students.

This type of thinking manifested itself for me in several ways. I assumed that I understood the challenges faced by *all* students because of their success experienced in my classroom. I learned to ensure that my students were experiencing academic growth and was convinced that I had figured out what the problem was and was ready to change education. There was one big issue. I did not realize that I was utterly ignorant of the complexities inherent in systems of education. Many unseen factors have significant impacts. I knew I was missing something; however, I would have never known how uninformed I was without completing the doctoral program.

One of the awakenings I experienced came from our examination of the principles of improvement science (Bryk et al., 2015) and systems theories such as the ecological systems theory (Bronfenbrenner, 1979) and networked ecological systems theory (Neal & Neal, 2013) in the *Contemporary Approaches to Educational Problems* course during our first semester in the program. Because I focused so much on classroom-level success factors as an education practitioner, I initially only surfaced issues in my immediate purview. These initial frameworks helped begin my transformation from an expert practitioner to a scholar-practitioner by teaching me how to see the interrelationship between systems and the factors that are key aspects of solution creation and leadership development. I began to understand my POP better when I learned to map out the contributing factors through the literature synthesis I wrote for the *Multiple Perspectives on Learning and Teaching* course during my second semester and my needs assessment study for my dissertation. Within these assignments, I was pushed to examine the factors associated with my POP and discovered teachers needed technology professional learning experiences. My journey toward becoming a scholar-practitioner had begun. I was now an inspector or detective who investigated the needs and deficiencies to be addressed before advancing a solution.

The Delta: My Dissertation Study

Systems thinking led me to develop an intervention for mathematics teachers in urban schools, which I named the *Active Uses of Spreadsheets for Mathematics Instruction* (AUSMI) workshop. My dissertation research study aimed to examine the effects of this intervention on mathematics teachers' beliefs and perceptions regarding the power of organizing data on spreadsheets and their ability to incorporate them into classroom instruction. I compared participants' responses on the Instructional Technology Adoption Survey before and following the AUSMI workshop to find that participants' self-reported uses of technology increased. Interview responses provided evidence that the workshop forwarded participants' understanding of how students can use spreadsheets to explore and analyze data. Aspects of the workshop that participants noted as supporting their growth included the demonstrations, hands-on experiences, and collaboration with their colleagues.

River systems process all types of resources through a powerful, vicious, or ferocious experience to produce delta land, which has fertile soil that becomes major agricultural production centers. Likewise, vicious, powerful, rigorous, and even violent experiences in my life have made me a fertile ground and an advocate for education. When I left the classroom, I was an instructional technology coach for schools in the Los Angeles area serving hundreds of teachers who served thousands of students. Today, I work as a Senior Researcher for an education technology company serving more than 24 million students in the United States. I have become an entrepreneurial leader with a set of research skills that allow me to effectively conduct needs assessments and determine a meaningful course of action to address problems. We are all involved in complex, multilevel systems where factors at different levels must be understood, assessed, and intervened in to see a meaningful change.

Getting people to attend church or get good grades in school are important, but those two factors alone will not solve the broader problem of youth violence. Leaders must also consider the effects of other factors such as federal drug and gun policies, state or local concealed carry laws, or school socio-emotional climate. My point here is that great leaders must be able to search the literature to develop an understanding of the interconnected elements or tributaries that contribute to a present issue so that they can see the system that is causing the resulting outcome in society. To that end, a person's leadership development, much like a river system, begins as a compilation of unassuming channels of water, with each droplet representing a formative life experience or a professional encounter.

As the river gains momentum, it twists and turns through a diverse landscape, encountering obstacles and challenges that shape and refine its journey. Similarly, my leadership development grew stronger and more refined as I navigated through the landscape of both personal and professional experiences, embracing the lessons learned from successes and failures. With every tributary that joins the main channel, the river becomes a greater force to be reckoned with, just as my collective wisdom and skills amplified my leadership and gave me the ability to inspire and guide others. Eventually, my ever-evolving river of leadership, enriched by the diverse tributaries of my life and work experiences, has found its way to the vast ocean called the field of education, where I have united with other powerful currents, known as education leaders, to shape the world in profound and lasting ways.

References

Bronfenbrenner, U. (1979). *The ecology of human development: Experiments by nature and design*. Harvard University Press.

Bryk, A. S., Gomez, L. M., Grunow, A., & LeMahieu, P. G. (2015). *Learning to improve: How America's schools can get better at getting better*. Harvard Education Press.

Neal, J. W., & Neal, Z. P. (2013). Nested or networked? Future directions for ecological systems theory. *Social Development, 22*(4), 722–737. https://doi.org/10.1111/sode.12018

CHAPTER 13

Changing My Stripes

Paula L. Clark

Introduction

"THE ONLY THINGS worth learning are the things you learn after you know it all" (Harry S. Truman). This statement by Harry S. Truman encapsulates the philosophical transformation I experienced in my learning journey at the Johns Hopkins University (JHU) School of Education (SOE). I entered the JHU SOE Doctor of Education (EdD) program with the goal of helping high school students in my school who struggle to learn mathematics, and I left with a desire to reform mathematics education. The EdD program ignited in me a desire *to learn* rather than *to become learned* and changed my perception of what constitutes authentic learning. Learning is change (Alexander et al., 2009), and the change that occurred in me during my doctoral journey transformed my philosophy of education literally and figuratively.

Describing my experience in the EdD program as transformative is an understatement. From early childhood, my career aspiration was to become a K–12 teacher, and my path never wavered. However, the JHU SOE EdD program ignited a decisive shift in my identity. The shedding of my expert teacher identity allowed me to adopt a more robust identity, the identity of a learner. One of the most pronounced differences between my former identity as a teacher or practitioner and my newly constructed identity as a learner or scholar-practitioner was my focus. As a practitioner, I focused on perfecting my instructional style, crafting a flawless lesson plan, and imparting content knowledge efficiently. As a scholar-practitioner, I have realized that these foci are secondary to a focus on learning, improvement, and creating an environment ripe for conceptual understanding.

Moving From Classroom to Jungle

Trevor Ragan, content creator, workshop facilitator, and founder of The Learner Lab, posited that learning is a superior skill humans possess (The Learner Lab, 2022). Furthermore, Ragan suggested that optimal learning occurs when, like a jungle tiger, we reside in the wild. Unlike tigers in a zoo habitat, who live a comfortable, risk-free, and struggle-free existence, jungle tigers experience daily discomfort, struggle, and risk. Ironically, in this unstable environment, tigers thrive and excel at learning.

Before entering the EdD program, my practitioner identity echoed that of a tiger in a zoo. Having a tenure of 32 years, I was comfortable within the four walls of my classroom. I was secure in my environment, and the only risks I encountered involved adapting to new administrative directives or experimenting with instructional strategies. With my sights set on earning a doctorate, I initially prepared myself to temporarily venture out of my comfort zone, engage in the adventure of the EdD program, and quickly return to safety. Unbeknownst to me, the path toward achieving my degree at JHU would take me on an unexpected and transformative journey. My experiences in the EdD program prompted the shedding of my zoo-tiger skin and, in its place, created the stripes of a jungle tiger.

In hindsight, the shedding of my former identity began when I first set foot on the JHU campus for the EdD summer residency program. With my zoo-tiger mentality, I approached Levering Hall with the sole purpose of being a quiet observer and collector of information, program requirements, and dissertation logistics. I soon realized that my new environment would require much more of me. The global outreach of the EdD program transported me to environments far beyond the classroom. Inhabitants of these environments included faculty members, advisers, and cohort peers who were experts in the fields of learning differences, neuroscience, educational technology, research methodology, and leadership. I gained footing in this dynamic and ever-expanding learning environment and quickly realized I was not just an observer. The design of the EdD program required active engagement and collaboration. It required that I fully immerse myself in this new culture and become a jungle tiger.

Acclimating to New Terrain

My induction into this new environment, the EdD community of practice, began with a chance encounter in a hotel lobby. During the JHU EdD orientation and residency, I was encouraged by a friend to approach and introduce myself to a cohort peer, a seemingly simple task but one that caused me great trepidation. Although the next 3 years would present numerous challenges, this small venture outside of my comfort zone connected me to a cohort peer who proved to be an invaluable source of support during this journey and beyond. Together we entered the JHU EdD community of practice, a community that exists, as Wenger (1998) described, to engage in collective learning activities. Members of a community of practice intentionally share knowledge, exchange experiences, and work collaboratively to address problems (Wenger, 1998). Membership in a community of practice presented new ground for me, and I readily found value in shared learning. My apprehension toward engaging with members of this new community dissipated inversely to the support, encouragement, and empowerment afforded me by my cohort peers, EdD faculty, and doctoral adviser. While I expected the EdD program to bring together individuals from diverse backgrounds, I never anticipated the intensity with which those backgrounds would impact my personal environment. I was no longer a zoo tiger, a receiver of knowledge as my sustenance. I was a jungle tiger, an engaged learner in the collective experiences of my peers and mentors. The EdD community of practice became a structural mechanism as I morphed into a scholar-practitioner.

My cohort of expert practitioners embarked on that first residency program with a motivation to solve our respective Problems of Practice (POP), a cornerstone of the EdD program. This desire perpetuated *solutionitis*, the tendency to look for answers to problems that are not fully understood (Bryk et al., 2015). The EdD faculty quickly and consistently redirected our focus as they introduced us to the first few tenets of improvement science. The POP I had identified as the cornerstone of my dissertation work centered on the struggles many students experience in high school mathematics courses. Along with identifying the problem, I had already formulated a root cause: Students who experience language-based deficits or disabilities often experience struggles in mathematics. My POP transformed more quickly than my identity as I learned to examine it from an improvement science perspective, a perspective that couples disciplined inquiry with improved practice (Bryk et al., 2015).

Grounded in improvement science, the EdD program taught me to question, clarify, and deeply examine my POP. The empirical inquiry process became a catalyst for my transformation from zoo to jungle tiger. While the EdD faculty cultivated within me an appreciation for a wider perspective, the extant literature on mathematics teaching, learning, and student outcomes revealed that a host of factors impact student achievement in mathematics (Clark, 2019). A nested model of ecological systems theory (Bronfenbrenner, 1994) captured the essence of how a student's mathematical development hinges on the reciprocal interactions among the various factors within the student's immediate and distal environments. Just as I was experiencing in my transformative jungle journey, I realized that the environments students find themselves in greatly influence their learning as well.

This realization spurred me to "see the system" (Bryk et al., 2015, p. 57) by considering the role that educators, families, peers, and even preservice education programs play in a student's understanding of mathematics. Needs assessment study data for my dissertation indicated that educator factors, namely their beliefs, practices, and knowledge, impact student achievement in mathematics (Clark, 2019). I hypothesized that if I could change these factors, ultimately transforming others the way I had been transformed, I could positively impact student achievement in mathematics. I designed an intervention to engage teachers in professional development precisely in the same way students should be engaged (Clark, 2019). Encouraged by my adviser, the SOE faculty, and my committee members, I sought to bring my colleagues into the jungle.

Becoming Attuned to the Environment

The transition from practitioner to scholar-practitioner was stimulated predominately by the interactions I shared in the EdD community of practice through multiple mechanisms of change. The importance of such interactions to my developing scholar-practitioner identity became realized in my study of sociocultural theory. Vygotsky (1978), a seminal sociocultural theorist, posited that cognitive change occurs due to the activation of the physiological process during social interactions. Furthermore, the physical act of communication propels learners to higher developmental levels (Vygotsky, 1978). In retrospect, my lived experience of sociocultural theory, the foundation of my dissertation, mobilized my professional transformation.

Recall that I entered the EdD program with intentions of quietly observing, collecting knowledge, and returning rapidly to familiar surroundings. Hesitation and apprehension were commonplace for me when advisers and professors encouraged communication and conversation. At the time, I failed to recognize the importance of these interactions and conversations as tools for personal growth. As my scholar-practitioner identity solidified, I sought out conversation, debate, discussion, and engagement with peers and faculty so as to augment my cognitive development. Furthermore, I realized that belonging to a community of practice meant contributing as much as receiving support. Being a scholar-practitioner involves sometimes *leaning* on more capable peers while at other times *being* the more capable peer. I am now cognizant that my contributions, experiences, and perspectives help form the collective wisdom I share with my peers, professors, and committee members.

Welcoming Others to the Environment

As predicted by Trevor Ragan (The Learner Lab, 2022), the personal, productive struggle I experienced in becoming a member of the EdD community of practice escalated my learning and my transformation. Ironically, the same productive struggle promoted for students' mathematical development became realized through my lived experiences in the EdD program. Productive struggle in the mathematics classroom requires student engagement, perseverance, and problem-solving (Baker et al., 2020), ventures that parallel those encountered in a community of practice. My transformation toward becoming a scholar-practitioner required the normalization, rather than avoidance, of productive struggle.

The EdD program offered ample opportunities for me to normalize productive struggle. As I advanced through the topological landscape of the EdD program, including the comprehensive examination, the intervention proposal defense, and the final dissertation defense, my jungle tiger mentality faltered. I felt a similar deterioration of my scholar-practitioner identity as I prepared to enact my intervention. Just as when I entered the doors of Levering Hall 3 years earlier, implementing the intervention I devised as an EdD doctoral candidate placed me, once again, in an unfamiliar, disconcerting environment. My newly formed identity began to wane, and I questioned my ability to implement a research-based professional development program with my colleagues. After all, I was just the teacher from down the hall.

Confidence replaced nervousness as I reframed my perspective once again. I embraced my newly forming identity and sought to collaborate with and learn alongside my colleagues during our professional learning endeavor. As an extension of the community of practice I had experienced in the EdD program, my colleagues and I supported one another in collective efforts to shift from traditional to reform-minded methods of instruction (Clark, 2019). Like my transformative experience, reform-minded mathematics instruction coaxes teachers and students to move outside of their comfort zones. Teachers and students learn to take risks, engage in discourse, consider varying perspectives, and experience productive struggle. In retrospect, my intervention asked teachers to join me in the jungle, an environment that leads to growth.

Alexander et al. (2009) proposed that permanent change can exert a reciprocal effect on the learner's surroundings. The results of my research suggest that my personal transformation from practitioner to scholar-practitioner did impose a reciprocal effect on my colleagues. Dissertation study data suggested that the professional development intervention's collaborative, learner-centered, and supportive components led to personal growth for the participants (Clark, 2019). Evidence of a reciprocal effect comes from a study participant's remark that instructional transformation occurred in them as a result of "being able to . . . participate with your coworkers on meaningful, everyday things" (Clark, 2019). Additionally, evidence that participants began their own transition toward becoming scholar-practitioners lies in a colleague's desire for "a follow-up [professional development program] that is based on new research findings in order to keep [my] growth moving forward" (Clark, 2019).

Through the Jungle and Beyond

Early in the EdD program, a professor foreshadowed the result of our JHU experience: that we would no longer be satisfied with our predoctoral identities. I concurred with this premonition quite literally, envisioning that a terminal degree would allow me to seek out opportunities in the field of education that were previously unattainable. The realization that this statement could be taken figuratively did not occur to me until I embraced my scholar-practitioner identity.

My movement from practitioner to scholar-practitioner encapsulates transformative learning, learning that "move[d me] toward a frame of reference that is more inclusive, discriminating, self-reflective, and integrative of experience" (Mezirow, 1997, p. 5). I am no longer *self-contained* in my knowledge, beliefs, and practices. Furthermore, as a scholar-practitioner, I realize that I can impact and advance learning as an educator. I am the tiger in the jungle, and I am on the move. I now live outside my comfort zone, seek new opportunities and perspectives, and am willing to take risks to reform mathematics education. Transformed by my EdD experience, I am a scholar-practitioner. I contribute to developing my students' and colleagues' understanding, constructing and disseminating knowledge, advancing school improvement, and promoting social justice.

Enacting widespread reform begins with a laser-like focus on improvement. Unlike reform initiatives of the past, Tyack and Cuban (1995) favored improvement efforts that originate "from the inside out" (p. 10). My transformation from practitioner to scholar-practitioner reflects an inside-out improvement effort personified. Leaving the safety and comfort of the four walls of my classroom and venturing out to an unfamiliar environment empowered me to seek out challenges and embrace risks, tasks necessary for authentic, collective, and meaningful learning. Once a zoo tiger, I was hesitant to greet a peer on the first day of orientation. Now, metamorphosed into a jungle tiger, I collaborate professionally with that same peer at national conferences. Once a practitioner, I viewed my educationally renowned committee members as superiors. Now, as a scholar-practitioner, I embrace their support and colleagueship. Fully transformed, I embrace the responsibility of propagating a learning identity in others.

Emerging From the Jungle

In research, *impact* can be defined as "the fundamental intended or unintended change occurring in organizations, communities or systems as a result of program activities within 7 to 10 years" (W. K. Kellogg Foundation, 2004,

p. 2). As described, the EdD program profoundly impacted my personal and professional identities. The program activities and interactions with my adviser, faculty, and cohort peers fundamentally altered my instructional practices and beliefs. I returned to my classroom transformed and with a broader perspective of the true nature of learning. The jungle tiger stripes I earned include a deep appreciation for exploring new environments, a commitment to collaboration and engagement, and a perspective that constantly seeks to understand. Ultimately, I learned to embrace the risk, discomfort, and struggle involved in authentic learning, and am eager to design such learning experiences for my students. I am fully transformed and passionate about creating *classrooms* of practice where knowledge is constructed and shared.

References

Alexander, P. A., Schallert, D. L., & Reynolds, R. E. (2009). What is learning anyway? A topographical perspective considered. *Educational Psychologist, 44*(3), 176–192. https://doi.org/10.1080/00461520903029006

Baker, K., Jessup, N. A., Jacobs, V. R., Empson, S. B., & Case, J. (2020). Productive struggle in action. *Mathematics Teacher: Learning and Teaching PK-12, 113*(5), 361–367. https://doi.org/10.5951/MTLT.2019.0060

Bronfenbrenner, U. (1994). *Ecological models of human development* (2nd ed., Vol. 3). Elsevier Science.

Bryk, A. S., Gomez, L. M., Grunow, A., & LeMahieu, P. G. (2015). *Learning to improve: How America's schools can get better at getting better.* Harvard Education Press.

Clark, P. L. (2019). *The influence of a situated apprenticeship model of professional development on high school mathematics educators' knowledge, beliefs, and use of reform-minded instructional practices* [Doctoral dissertation, Johns Hopkins University]. JScholarship. http://jhir.library.jhu.edu/handle/1774.2/62286

The Learner Lab. (2022). *Train ugly/Jungle tiger hub.* https://thelearnerlab.com/train-ugly-jungle-tiger-hub/

Mezirow, J. (1997). Transformative learning: Theory to practice. *New Directions for Adult and Continuing Education, 74,* 5–12. https://doi.org/10,1002/ace.7401

Tyack, D. B., & Cuban, L. (1995). *Tinkering toward Utopia: A century of public school reform.* Harvard University Press.

Vygotsky, L. S. (1978). *Mind in society: The development of higher psychological processes.* Harvard University Press. https://doi.org/10.2307/j.ctvjf9vz4

Wenger, E. (1998). *Communities of practice: Learning, meaning, and identity.* Cambridge University Press.

W. K. Kellogg Foundation. (2004). *W. K. Kellogg Foundation logic model development guide.* https://wkkf.issuelab.org/resource/logic-model-development-guide.html

From Instructional Coach to Instructional Leader: Identity Transformation in an EdD Program

Robert Walker

Introduction—Predoctoral Identity

"It can't be done." I heard this phrase often as an Instructional Coach as I attempted to support teachers in integrating collaborative and inquiry-based projects into their instruction. In 2009, my principal encouraged me to become a coach after watching me spend 5 years transforming my U.S. history classroom into a dynamic learning environment. Students in my classes engaged in constant investigation, discussion, and debate to better understand our world today and then designed informative and engaging ways to present their findings to diverse audiences. My principal saw me as a progressive educator who excited students to attend class and engaged them in deep discussions and authentic inquiries that connected student learning to contemporary events. She wanted me to work with other teachers, both on our campus and across our district, to adopt similar practices. I saw myself as a pioneer, embracing strategies that most teachers had yet to realize, and jumped at the chance to influence other teachers and help pave a better educational experience in my district.

Meeting Resistance as a Coach

As I began to work with colleagues, however, I quickly realized that the practices I had embraced and that, to my mind, obviously promoted a better learning environment, were akin to a foreign language to some other teachers. My experience and my reading of books by Heidi Hayes Jacobs (2010) and other scholars convinced me that the collaborative and inquiry-based practices I was integrating were essential to what was being called 21st-century learning. Repeatedly, however, teachers insisted that these practices were too complex for students or that the high scores their students received on standardized tests rested on lecture and repetition. Some would, politely but firmly, inform me that they had been teaching a certain way for over 20 years and that there was no reason for them to change. Still others would passively acknowledge the suggestions I was making, but when I would observe their classes, I saw very little change.

This resistance frustrated me. It seemed to fly in the face of the calls made in the media and by policymakers for pedagogy that prepared students to engage in an interconnected social and economic world. I also had personal experiences that demonstrated that these practices could be successfully integrated and that they were effective. Perhaps most troubling to me, though, was that my inability to influence change in these teachers seemed to call into question my ambition to become a school administrator. If I couldn't lead instructional change with teachers, how could I lead a school? I decided to enroll in the Johns Hopkins University (JHU) Doctor of Education (EdD) program to examine why teachers were reluctant to change their instructional practices and, hopefully, to learn how to be an effective school leader.

Identity Challenged During the Doctoral Program

From the start, my doctoral work challenged my conception of this problem, revealed to me how little I really understood about the learning environment I had created in my classroom, and caused me to question my identity. These are three of the pivotal moments in my identity transformation.

I'm Not Much of a Pioneer! Holes in Teacher Preparation Programs

One of the most powerful mechanisms for transforming my identity were the readings and coursework my colleagues and I engaged in throughout the program. The first text we were assigned to read upon starting the doctoral program was Bransford et al.'s (2000) *How People Learn*. I was astounded and recall asking my adviser, "Why didn't I read this in my credential program?" I saw at once that the practices that I had been successfully integrating within my instruction, and that others resisted, were in fact grounded in decades of cognitive science and had a name: student-centered learning.

While ruminating on the realization that I wasn't as much of a "pioneer of education" as I had imagined, I also recognized that my training to become a teacher had barely touched upon how learning happened and teaching practices that supported that learning. As I investigated this insight further, as part of the research related to my problem of practice that framed my dissertation, I found evidence that teacher preparation programs often do not prioritize training in the cognitive aspects of learning and instead emphasize classroom management and the behavioral considerations that support student learning, especially when it comes to students with special needs (Dubinsky et al., 2013). I discerned that, lacking training in the cognitive processes of learning, teachers rationally rely on those practices that they encountered as students, including lecture and other forms of direct instruction. The resistance I had encountered as an instructional coach started to seem more understandable, but I still was clueless on how to confront that resistance.

Can I Be an Effective Leader? The Importance of Relationships

As I began my second year of doctoral work, my identity started to shift. Instead of seeing myself as an inventive educator, I now recognized that I was an effective and engaging teacher. I still needed, however, to understand how to guide teachers effectively to enact instructional change. To dig more deeply into this problem, as part of my dissertation work as well as coursework, I further examined the factors that influence learning. In a class focused on the science of learning, I read how a student's learning is situated in their unique context, and I was assigned to post a reflection on the impact that this knowledge might have for me as a teacher. Writing that assignment, I focused on how the relationships that teachers build with their students influence students' learning in the classroom. Inspired, I began to research how teacher learning was situated and found that the relationships teachers have with administrators and other educators is a significant influence related to how they respond to professional development (PD). Although I had long prioritized building relationships with my students, I now saw that I needed to apply the same relationship-building process with other teachers if I wanted to support their growth and instructional change.

I began to put this learning into practice at my school. Though I had stepped down from my role as an Instructional Coach for the district when I entered the EdD program, the teachers at my school still sought instructional guidance from me. I began to spend more time listening to them, to learn their needs and provide support for them to reach the goals they set, rather than a vision for change that someone else set. When I visited their classes at their request, rather than critique their lessons, I focused on the positive efforts I saw and suggested minor improvements without judgment. Teachers began to trust me even more, to respect that my guidance was authentic, and to see me more as an authority in instruction and as a mentor. This new focus on building relationships empowered me to provide teachers additional support and to, increasingly, feel like a leader within our school. This practice, however, conflicted with the mentorship I received from school administrators who supported my desire to move into school administration. Their training encouraged me to remain distant from teachers, as I would need to evaluate their performance, and stressed hard work, productivity, and quick changes in instruction that could generate higher test scores. My research and experience, however, suggested that I needed to prioritize building relationships, emphasizing support and being patient as I worked to encourage gradual, but effective, change. I wondered if this approach to running a school would be accepted by administrators in my district.

Enacting Change: Improvement Science

This sense of confusion over my identity as a school leader was also fostered by my coursework and readings in improvement science (Bryk et al., 2015). Incorporating improvement science as a theoretical frame for my dissertation increased my awareness that school improvement, including instructional change, required a slower and more systematic approach than the approaches to which I had previously been exposed. Learning to question the underlying factors that may contribute to problems in education, to triangulate data to examine those factors and identify those that are actionable, and to develop plan-do-study-act (PDSA) cycles to influence long-lasting changes guided my dissertation study. It also, however, caused me to look differently at how instructional change was guided in my district. Though I had often been involved in discussions related to data, especially test scores, these analyses were usually focused on validating our curriculum. Even when it came to our accreditation self-study reports, the focus of the data analysis was often on proving the accomplishments of our school and not on a serious examination of the problems that existed or the root of those problems. As I wrapped up my third year of my doctoral work and prepared to implement my dissertation study, combined with my new emphasis on building relationships and partnering with teachers to enact instructional change, I was beginning to see myself less as a teacher and instructional coach and more as an instructional leader, someone who could support and inspire change, build effective relationships, and help make decisions that supported both students and teachers to perform at their best.

Leading for Instructional Change: Dissertation in Practice

My dissertation study, an investigation into the impact of a multimedia-based PD on teacher knowledge and beliefs as they pertained to technology-enhanced learning (i.e., the application of digital technology to support student-centered practices in the classroom), cemented my emerging identity as an instructional leader. In line with the program focus on improvement science, I used surveys and interviews to deeply understand why some teachers resisted integrating technology to support student-centered practices. I found that teachers possessed limited knowledge of these practices as well as efficacy to implement them. With a firmer understanding of the problem, I developed an intervention to address this need, a technology-enhanced PD that led to teachers designing multimedia presentations for their classes. Implementing my intervention and working through the data I collected validated my skills as a researcher and left me confident that I could lead change through an investigative and data-driven process (Walker, 2020).

More significantly, while working on my dissertation study, I found that my confidence and experience combined with my emphasis on building relationships led teachers to feel more comfortable asking me questions about instruction and seeking guidance on new instructional practices. One incident that highlighted this change was with a science teacher who was excited to have me observe a lesson where their students were engaged in a digital lab project, but also expressed concern about what their role, as the teacher, was in the lesson. As students worked through their investigation, what was the role of the teacher? As this teacher spoke, I recognized the same concern that had underlain the resistance I encountered as an instructional coach—the fear that changing instructional practice would change the role, even the identity, of the teacher in the classroom. Years before, entering the doctoral program, I had not understood this fear, but now I did. I acknowledged this teacher's concerns, and we talked about some possible ways that they could support students as a guide-on-the-side while they worked on their project. After I observed the lesson, we sat for a quick debrief during which the teacher expressed their appreciation for the guidance I provided, and we talked about ways to move this from a project that students worked on by themselves to one that was constructed as a group. This experience empowered this teacher to seek additional training on project-based learning and to recruit other teachers to join them in that training. By the time I left to become an administrator at a different school, a year after I completed my doctorate, these teachers were leading a movement to transform the school into an entirely project-based institution.

This experience, and others like it, helped me to see myself in this new identity as an instructional leader. The knowledge base I gained through my EdD program, in the learning sciences and improvement sciences, prepared me to be able to lead instructional change. Further, the insights I discovered related to the importance of building relationships with all members of the school community, but especially with teachers, prepared me to partner with teachers in leading instructional changes and to empower them with the knowledge and confidence to make these changes deep and meaningful. I was ready to step out of the classroom and assume a position as a school leader.

Pandemic and Postdoctoral Identity

As I defended my dissertation in January 2020, I felt established as an instructional leader and, fortuitously, was uniquely positioned to support my school and district as the global COVID-19 pandemic shifted the terrain of education for everyone. Zhao and Frank (2003) noted that many teachers have, traditionally, seen computer technology as an invasive species in the instructional environment. I encountered many of those same concerns as I conducted my dissertation study and became well versed in how to support teachers' beliefs as they shifted toward greater inclusion of technology in instruction. As the COVID-19 pandemic forced students and teachers out of the physical classroom and into a virtual setting, therefore, I was prepared to be a support for teachers and school leaders in my district as we navigated this new terrain. I worked to help train instructional coaches in the principles of effective design for online learning and to design asynchronous trainings that teachers could complete on their own over the summer of 2020 to prepare for the 2020–2021 school year. Over the course of that school year, I worked with administrators on how to support teachers who struggled with the new technology needs, urging patience and regular informal sessions where teachers could share their ideas, voice concerns, and seek additional support as needed. As the school year ended, my colleagues shared that they saw me more as a school leader than as a teacher and voiced their sincere appreciation for my presence. The knowledge and training I received in my EdD program prepared me to serve as an instructional leader at one of the most critical moments in recent educational history.

Leading Change as a School Administrator

With my sense of identity as an instructional leader confirmed, I felt empowered to move formally into school administration. At the start of the 2021–2022 school year, I was offered a position as Administrative Director of Instruction at one of the largest charter schools in the country. In this position, my expertise in improvement science has allowed me, in a short period of time, to work with our teachers' union to implement PDSA cycles for reforming our teacher evaluation system, as well as with other teacher leaders to begin to transform our school culture based on positive relationships. Teachers value my emphasis on building relationships with them and creating a culture based on respect and transparent practices. They also value my expertise in instructional design and my patient approach to facilitating instructional change through measured, well-informed, and data-driven steps. This is especially true in my work with our social studies department, where I am slowly guiding teachers to adopt inquiry-based instructional practices. As we review data from their instruction, research that supports embedding inquiry in social studies, and discuss their needs and concerns with a new pedagogical approach, these teachers consistently tell me that this is the first time they have felt heard and respected. Feeling validated, they also are more open to trying these new practices.

When I entered the EdD program I was an effective teacher and aspiring administrator who had struggled to coach other teachers to adopt student-centered practices that supported learning. I now know that this struggle originated with how I approached my role as a coach. Then, I perceived that instructional change was something that teachers just needed to accept, and my role was to be the director of that change. Today, I am a confident scholar-practitioner, capable of supporting broad instructional change on my campus and in other school districts. I am also a compassionate and authentic leader who emphasizes building relationships and mentoring teachers so that they can create dynamic learning environments. Now, when a teacher tells me that an instructional change "just can't be done" I can tell them, "Yes, it can, and I am here to support you."

References

Bransford, J., Brown, A., & Cocking, R. (2000). *How people learn: Brain, mind, experience, and school* (Expanded ed.). National Academies Press.

Bryk, A., Gomez, L., Grunow, A., & LaMahieu, P. G. (2015). *Learning to improve: How America's schools can get better at getting better.* Harvard Education Press.

Dubinsky, J., Roehrig, G., & Varma, S. (2013). Infusing neuroscience into teacher professional development. *Educational Researcher, 42*(6), 317–329. https://doi.org/10.3102/0013189X13499403

Hayes Jacobs, H. (2010). *Curriculum 21: Essential education for a changing world.* Association for Supervision and Curriculum Development.

Walker, R. (2020). *Supporting teacher cognition toward technology-enhanced learning* [Doctoral dissertation, Johns Hopkins University]. JScholarship. https://jscholarship.library.jhu.edu/bitstream/handle/1774.2/62473/WALKER-DISSERTATION-2020.pdf?sequence=1&isAllowed=y

Zhao, Y., & Frank, K. A. (2003). Factors affecting technology uses in schools: An ecological perspective. *American Educational Research Journal, 40*, 807–840. https://doi.org/10.3102/00028312040004807

Design Thinking: An Essential Framework for Complex Problems of Practice in Education

Joshua Pinto Taylor

Introduction

I TAUGHT UNDER the supervision of three principals in my first 2 years of instruction—both years at the same school. Three principals. Two years. In those 2 years, several of my colleagues exited the teaching profession, exited the classroom, or exited the school to pursue opportunities in other schools or districts. Over the next 5 years of teaching and leading, in multiple contexts and school types, a similar pattern of "teacher churn" and "principal burnout" continued to manifest (Atteberry et al., 2017; Federici & Skaalvik, 2012). Late in college, I made a career pivot away from architecture and real estate development toward education and human development. At that time, I was working in a design and engineering firm to earn college credit and tutoring mathematics in a local public school to pay some of my bills. Through those two experiences, I realized my purpose in life was much more aligned to the work of the schoolhouse than the work of the design studio. A year later, I graduated from college with clarity about my purpose; however, I also carried with me a false sense of confidence that most of the problems of the world could be solved—because most of the problems I had been presented in college had a solution. On reflection, most of my efforts in my first couple of years of teaching were rooted in passion but lacked the sophistication required to make me a great educator.

Prior to enrolling in graduate school, I wouldn't have known how to describe the phenomenon I was experiencing or used the term "teacher churn" because I didn't realize this was a generalizable phenomenon that had already been defined and described by scholars. As a recent college graduate, I did not realize the complexity of the problems that educational institutions face. Nonetheless, this pattern of midyear departures was generating questions for me as a relatively novice educator: "Why am I still in this profession while others I went through teacher preparation with are not? What is the impact of high teacher turnover on student achievement? Does teacher turnover disproportionately affect certain subgroups within the American population? How do we build a more just and stable teacher workforce so that our young people can experience the stability, continuity, and competence they deserve?"

As I was asking these questions, I was also beginning doctoral studies in the Doctor of Education (EdD) program at Johns Hopkins University (JHU). So, naturally, in the application materials when I was prompted to identify a Problem of Practice (POP) my mind returned to the questions that continued to vex me. Similarly, when our cohort of doctoral students was asked to reflect on a POP that might require the skill of a scholar-practitioner, my mind went back to questions on teacher retention. My decision to enroll in the JHU EdD program was confirmed the moment I found myself surrounded by a community of researchers, professors, educators, and practitioners from all over the world who were hungry to contemplate big questions while pursuing pragmatic, research-driven solutions in the context of their work. In that moment, I realized that I was embarking upon a journey of rich conversation, in a diverse community, about how to continuously improve my chosen professional context.

At this juncture in my career, I needed this cohort of people, in addition to my amazing colleagues in our school community, to deepen my understanding about how to solve problems. I was beginning my first school-level administrative role as an Academic Dean at a high school with 7 years of experience and the responsibility of directly coaching and supervising a portfolio of 10 to 20 teachers per year (among other responsibilities, of course). I had an intuition that too many of our students were feeling unmoored or disconnected at school as they experienced relational instability in community spaces like schools and classrooms due to high teacher turnover. In fact, several of the students I advised were expressing a form of loss after their favorite teacher left unexpectedly. I wondered if their negative experiences as students might reflect a broader pattern.

One thing was clear to me: There is a teacher retention problem in too many of our schools, and this problem was wreaking havoc on my colleagues, my students, and the departments I was leading. I also realized that I did not have the knowledge, skills, or methods to solve complex problems such as teacher retention. An applied EdD program, like the one designed for students at JHU, was exactly what I needed to begin the transformation that was needed in me, so that I could become the kind of leader that my students and teachers deserved.

Becoming a Scholar-Practitioner—Returning to Design Thinking

In my earliest encounters with the EdD program, there was a consistent use of the term *scholar-practitioner* to describe the profile of a graduate from JHU. Whether the context was promotional materials, orientation sessions, lectures, or advising sessions, this term was used widely and with internal consistency. In truth, I liked the sound of the calling, and that terminology drew me toward pursuing an EdD over a full-time PhD or another master's degree program. I had no interest in leaving my professional context. I found my work to be too central to my identity to remove myself from the classroom and the schoolhouse entirely. That said, I had a sense that my identity needed to evolve and expand to serve my students and their families to the best of my ability. Alas, I was drawn to the idea of becoming a scholar-practitioner. I was looking for a vocational approach anchored in sound theory, promising practices, and research methods. In retrospect, it is clear to me that the programming of the JHU EdD program was intentionally designed to have such an effect. Recalling my own humble circumstance as a new school leader in a context experiencing low teacher retention, I remember that I was in a place, both personally and professionally, where I was beginning to feel a bit disoriented and unsure about how to make an impact on such a complex problem.

When I say complex problem, I am referring to a term that designers (as stated previously, I was briefly a student of architecture) use to describe a phenomenon that is extremely difficult to solve either because of the degree of ambiguity in the context or because of the multifactorial nature of the phenomenon. Other scholars have used the phrase "wicked problems" to describe a similar phenomenon in social science and urban planning (Kolko, 2012; Rittel & Webber, 1973). Design thinking practices encourage designers to spend considerable time to expand both their understanding of the problem and the potential root causes prior to moving into solution space (Thienen et al., 2014). Design thinking is a framework that was, in some ways, replicated through our doctoral studies at JHU. My own background in design helped me see how JHU was using a process, through POPs, akin to a design thinking model to cultivate my own identity as a scholar-practitioner who was equipped to solve complex problems in the field of education.

A "universally accepted depiction" of the design thinking process that emerged right around the time I entered college was the Double Diamond Model (Ball, 2019). According to this model, in the beginning of designing a solution to a complex problem, the designer starts with a narrow definition of a problem. That definition expands until a degree of thematic saturation has been achieved and the universe of potential problem definitions (or factors contributing to the problem) has been explored or discovered. After careful and thorough contemplation of the range of problem factors and definitions, the designer can begin converging in on a narrow problem statement that has been informed and defined by a comprehensive exploration of the problem. Once the problem has been clearly and narrowly defined, the designer can then begin to develop, ideate, and iterate on potential solutions that could deliver specific outcomes to address the defined problem. The process of ideating creates another expansion of possibility for the designer, which is represented through the expansion of the second diamond. At some point in the process, the designer begins to narrow their focus on a specific design solution to deliver a specific outcome, which is represented by the final convergence of the second diamond. In a way, this concept from my previous architectural studies reemerged for me through my dissertation work.

Phase 1—Research: Problem Discovery and Definition

"What do you notice in your context? What is going well? What could be improved? How do you know what is going well and what could be improved?" This was the first set of questions I grappled with during my doctoral studies—specifically my early research methods courses. My earliest attempts to answer these questions were insufficient, but my adviser and professors patiently and expertly offered me the support I needed to improve my investigative approach. I distinctly remember feeling like we were dwelling in defining the problem in a way that I had never experienced in my life. Einstein famously said that if he had an hour to save the world, he would spend the first 55 minutes defining the problem. The first semester of the EdD program allowed me to steep myself in my context and to examine my circumstances from multiple perspectives and through multiple data sources. It also exposed me to frameworks, such as improvement science (Bryk et al., 2015), that can be used to address complex problems. As I look back on these earliest questions now, I can see how my professors were inviting me into a conversation between myself, my students, my colleagues, and a community of other scholars asking similar questions all around the world. The EdD program was forcing me to expand my understanding of the problem to include the full universe of related factors before narrowing in on a set of precise factors that might contribute to my POP. This was my first takeaway from the program: Problems in education are complex; there are usually more factors than one initially thinks.

While I was beginning to explore those questions related to my Applied Dissertation, I was also enrolled in a rigorous course of study that was always related to my dissertation work. The courses I was taking and the work I was producing during the first semester of the program made me feel like I was part of a conversation that had been happening for hundreds of years and would continue deep into the future. I was being exposed to theoretical frameworks, interdisciplinary dialogues, and various perspectives about teaching and learning that helped ground my thinking, my questions, and my understanding of teacher attrition in a larger dialogue.

In the introductory courses, I was challenged to consider how titans in our field such as Bandura, Piaget, Skinner, Vygotsky, Dewey, Bronfenbrenner, Freud, Freire, and Bloom might speak with one another if they were all in the same seminar discussion. Professors also encouraged me to consider how these researchers might speak to me if we were in the same room, answering the questions I was asking. What if they were considering factors of, and solutions for, teacher retention? Before my doctoral program, I would have considered myself either a student (person on the receiving end of the education process) or a teacher (person on the delivering end of the education process). It never occurred to me before this program that I might be worthy of being in conversation with these individuals as a student—that my ideas might be able to build upon their work. Being exposed to theoretical frameworks, interdisciplinary dialogues, and various perspectives about teaching and learning helped ground me in the context of a larger discussion happening over a hundred years. That was my second takeaway from the program: There is a grand conversation happening about teaching and learning, and I have something to contribute to it.

In the first year of the program, I quickly realized that the transformation I needed was not likely to come through coursework or conversations alone. I knew I was growing in knowledge and confidence, yet the problem of teacher turnover continued. Although instructor and adviser support along with rigorous coursework were necessary, they would have been insufficient without the research methods strand. In my first semester, the assignment to synthesize the literature related to factors contributing to the POP served at least two purposes: to provide an analytical research tool to systematically review a topic of interest and to explore in the discovery phase, as outlined in the design thinking framework above.

By conducting a literature review of the factors potentially contributing to the POP in the *Disciplinary Approaches to Education* course, I was able to more clearly see the broader conversation that was already occurring. I was able to zoom out and see the universe of potential problems and to zoom back in and arrive at a clearly defined POP. At the end of the first year, I had a clearly defined POP that precisely addressed my unique interest in teacher retention. After experiencing the breadth of courses in the EdD program, I arrived at a third important takeaway: I needed to become grounded in theory, practice, and research before any noteworthy intervention could be designed within my own professional context.

Phase 2—Design: Development and Delivery

"What is the problem you are trying to address in your context? What factors influence the problem? What proximate, intermediate, and distal outcomes are you trying to accomplish in your context? What research-based interventions have demonstrated your desired outcomes?" In the second year of studies, I went through the second part of the double diamond design thinking framework described earlier. As I continued my professional practice, I worked with my adviser on my dissertation topic and conducted the second literature review as I enrolled in rigorous academic courses where I thought about how brilliant theorists and researchers might be able to inform my own thinking. Using the language of the design thinking framework, I developed an intervention through the second literature review. I refined and revised the intervention through research methods courses, which helped me determine a mixed methods approach to conduct research. I engaged with teachers and administrators in my context to understand the pushes and pulls they were experiencing in our organization. Collaborating with instructors and advisers deepened my sense that I was becoming a scholar-practitioner who could make an impact in my professional context. At the end of the dissertation study, there was evidence to support the notion that distributed leadership structures can positively impact factors that are associated with teacher retention (Taylor, 2020). Both novice and experienced teachers who participated in the distributed leadership intervention reported higher rates of self-efficacy and a stronger future orientation toward the school. That brings us to a fourth takeaway: I can lead learning, growth, and improvement in contexts experiencing complex problems.

My doctoral studies transformed me in a very specific way. Through the EdD program at JHU, I was transformed into a scholar-practitioner with the knowledge, skills, and attitudes I needed to lead continuous improvement efforts as described by Bryk et al. (2015) in the field of education. This happened through an intentional process. Through the first year of the program, I was challenged to expand my definition of the problem until I had a very broad sense of the issue at hand. In the second year of the program, I was challenged to expand my sense of possible interventions. I was then supported to narrow my approach to address the issue in my context and to measure a very specific set of proximal, intermediate, and distal outcomes. I was being transformed into a scholar-practitioner through a familiar design thinking process as a former student of architecture. By the time I graduated from the program, I was asking a new question: What might happen in a school if the students, parents, and teachers were regularly designing continuous improvement efforts through a process like the one I experienced through my doctoral studies at JHU?

Codesigning in Complexity

Understanding the value of the approach JHU took to build me up as a scholar-practitioner came at an important time in my career because immediately after graduating from JHU I started a 2-year school design process for a new public school. I brought the insights I have outlined in this chapter into this work. Education problems are complex. There are usually more factors than are initially apparent. There is a grand conversation happening about education. We can contribute to it. We need to ground our contributions in theory, practice, and research. Complex problems can be improved in schools. Using design thinking principles, we designed a new public charter school with the belief that students, educators, and families have forms of expertise required to solve complex problems in education. We embedded improvement science methods into our professional learning structures with the belief that there would always be a need for quality improvement at every level of the school. Even in the first year of the school, when we knew we would not yet be able to articulate what our own POPs might be, we knew they would exist and would need our urgent attention. What if we designed a learning experience like the JHU doctoral program into our learning community? What if that experience was intended for our students, their families, and our educators? How might that, at an institutional level, positively impact outcomes for our students and families? Being part of a global cohort and seeing how a framework supported dozens of doctoral students through complex problems as varied as decreasing enrollment in a private school or reduced student engagement in literature classes in a public school served as a proof point. As educators, we can improve outcomes despite the complexity of the problems we face. We can codify and institutionalize quality-improvement mechanisms for our schools and our students.

We are currently building the school we designed. Embedded within the school model is a commitment to codesign the continuous improvement efforts of the school with a cohort of students, educators, and families. Simply put, every year our school will identify an equity issue within our school and then build a codesign team who will work together to go through an abbreviated journey of the JHU applied dissertation. First, the team will start with a vague sense of a problem that needs to be addressed. Then the team will broaden their understanding of the problem by examining the existing literature. All this work will result in, eventually, a narrowly defined set of factors under consideration for a POP in our community. After defining the POP, the codesign team will look for a broad range of potential interventions. Through collaborative effort and consensus building, the codesign team will develop a solution and make a set of recommendations for how to deliver a specific outcome for our community.

The more measured approach, designed through improvement science methodology (Bryk et al., 2015), is a model that I will carry with me for the rest of my career as an educator. Over the course of my doctoral studies at JHU, I internalized the importance of designing intentional moments to pause, benchmark, assess, reflect, and evaluate. I solidified my understanding of the importance of design thinking models that expand possible problem definitions and possible solutions before attempting to solve complex problems. I can now attest to the importance of a carefully crafted problem statement. As a scholar-practitioner, I am now more likely to conduct a review of extant literature prior to articulating a problem or solution. As an educator, I understand the importance of program design, monitoring, and evaluation. As a leader, I have more tools at my disposal to analyze data. Through my studies at JHU, I became familiar with a very specific model of continuous improvement and know how to go through that cycle to improve student outcomes. This more measured approach is one of the key differentiators between my work before and after the EdD program. I look forward to using this method in the school that we are opening next fall.

Leader as Learner (and Leader of Learning)

It's worth noting that what I was hoping to get out of the program at JHU is not what I got out of it. I came into the program hoping to arrive at a level of expertise that would equip me with "the answers" to the big questions I was asking and the complex problems I was not solving. I graduated from the program with answers to some questions, but also a new list of deeper questions. For most of my elementary, secondary, and postsecondary studies I thought that the mark of a good student was knowing the right answer to the questions posed by the teacher. When I assumed my first educational leadership role, I was confronted with questions to which I did not know the answer. Given my mindset as a learner at that point in my career, I felt an overwhelming sense of failure for the first year or two that I was leading. I had no idea why our teachers were leaving the field of education. I had no idea why I experienced three principals in my first 2 years of teaching.

My time at JHU helped shift my paradigm as a learner and as a leader. I learned that most of the time the problem or the question being posed should be explored, expanded, and clarified prior to being defined. I learned that a range of possible solutions should also be explored and interrogated prior to determining the path forward for this process. I learned that the mark of a great leader is not to have the answer to the question but to make sure the right question is being asked. Great education leaders galvanize their team to chart a course of action to answer the question collaboratively. In this way, leadership and learning in schools are inextricably linked. I entered the JHU program hoping to become an expert. I left the JHU program realizing that I had gained expertise but that my expertise was now in defining and addressing complex problems. I left JHU equipped to be a leader with the disposition of a learner.

References

Atteberry, A., Loeb, S., & Wyckoff, J. (2017). Teacher churning: Reassignment rates and implications for student achievement. *Educational Evaluation and Policy Analysis, 39*(1), 3–30. https://doi.org/10.3102/0162373716659929

Ball, J. (2019, October 1). *The Double Diamond: A universally accepted depiction of the design process.* Design Council. https://www.designcouncil.org.uk/our-work/news-opinion/double-diamond-universally-accepted-depiction-design-process/

Bryk, A. S., Gomez, L. M., Grunow, A., & LeMahieu, P. G. (2015). *Learning to improve: How America's schools can get better at getting better.* Harvard Education Press.

Federici, R. A., & Skaalvik, E. M. (2012). Principal self-efficacy: Relations with burnout, job satisfaction and motivation to quit. *Social Psychology of Education, 15*, 295–320. https://doi.org/10.1007/s11218-012-9183-5

Kolko, J. (2012). *Wicked problems: Problems worth solving.* Austin Center for Design.

Rittel, H. W., & Webber, M. M. (1973). Dilemmas in a general theory of planning. *Policy Sciences, 4*(2), 155–169. https://doi.org/10.1007/BF01405730

Taylor, J. P. (2020). *Teacher mentoring and distributed leadership in an urban charter high school* [Doctoral dissertation, Johns Hopkins University]. JScholarship.

Thienen, J. V., Meinel, C., & Nicolai, C. (2014). How design thinking tools help to solve wicked problems. In C. Meinel & L. Leifer (Eds.), *Design thinking research* (pp. 97–102). Springer, Cham. https://doi.org/10.1007/978-3-319-01303-9_7

CHAPTER 16

Leadership for Educational Justice— Awake, Align, Arise, and Act

Razia F. Kosi

Being the Change

THE JOURNEY OF earning a doctorate was set in motion the day I was born, when my grandfather named me Razia because he thought it best suited the prefix "Dr." Even though cultural barriers restricted my mother from receiving a formal education, my grandfather dared to imagine a future for me greater than one he could provide for his daughter. Education is highly valued in my family. My father was awarded a scholarship to earn a master's degree in the United States, which changed the trajectory of all our lives. My story shares some of the challenges and triumphs I faced while in the JHU doctoral program, but more importantly, I share how I transformed to be the leader I needed to be for educational equity, and thus, perhaps fulfilling my destiny.

Social Worker Working in K–12 Education

Walking into the Glass Pavilion at Johns Hopkins University (JHU) on a sunny August day in 2016, I was both excited and scared about embarking on one of my lifetime goals of attaining a doctorate. Being a Clinical Social Worker, I had imagined I would go back to get my Doctor of Philosophy (PhD) in psychology or even social work. Being a daughter of Indian immigrants, the value of education was instilled in me at an early age. My parents envisioned that I would become a doctor or lawyer but accepted my earning a PhD. For 2 decades the master's degree offered me the opportunity to attain my career goals, but earning the highest degree possible was still a goal to fulfill my family's dream of success in the United States.

Working in a pre-K–12 public school setting for close to 20 years exposed me to different doctoral options, including the burgeoning Doctor of Education (EdD) programs. I knew two people who were in the JHU School of Education EdD program and was drawn by the innovative approach with online classes and working with instructors who would support us in our own context of research rather than the professor's research interests. The JHU EdD would best fit my work schedule and career goals. I applied within a week of the deadline for the 2016 cohort and was speechless when I received my acceptance email. Earning a doctorate was a large investment of time, finances, and emotions. Yet, I also knew earning a doctorate was important to my professional growth. Deep down, I was lacking what I needed to feel more confident in the field of education.

My predoctoral identity, a social worker employed in the field of education, had been fraught with teachers challenging my knowledge of teaching pedagogy or viewing my suggestions as better suited for school counselors than for teachers. I recognized my social work degree offered a valuable skill set for public education. I was able to lead professional learning opportunities on cultural competence in education influenced by Cross et al.'s (1989) cultural proficiency work. I also knew that if I wanted to lead system-wide initiatives it would be valuable for me to become a scholar-practitioner so I would be valued and seen beyond a niche contributor to our district's work. Early in my career, having a social work degree, rather than an education degree, made me a target of people challenging my expertise. Working outside of mental health settings, I was no longer in the midst of clinical practice. The feelings of imposter syndrome were present both in the mental health field, as I worked among people with doctorates, and in the public school system because I was not trained as a teacher. Even with those challenges, I remained confident in my ability to deliver professional learning in a manner that engaged adult learners, and I continued to hone my clinical skills to be a culturally competent therapist in my private practice.

The application to the EdD program required that I write a central focus for my dissertation, or a Problem of Practice (POP). I found myself at a crossroads because there were two directions I could go with my research. One direction, focusing on trauma-informed practices in education, would bridge my previous academic training and solidify my expertise with mental health. The second direction could expand the current cultural proficiency work and focus more on school administrators. I debated between the Mind, Brain, and Teaching specialization and the Entrepreneurial Leadership in Education (ELE) specialization, with each offering different paths for my learning. In the end, I decided ELE would stretch my own personal growth, which would prepare me to influence leadership in our district.

Awakening as Scholar Amidst the Woke Cultural Movement

Becoming a scholar was a challenge at first. I was overwhelmed with the coursework, the discussion posts, and the lack of personal connection in an online program. I was angry with the results of the 2016 election in the United States and the immediate executive orders that targeted my identity as a woman, a Muslim, and an immigrant. My personal anger was further fueled by the rising instances of racist comments and racist acts in our public schools. Teachers were feeling unprepared to talk with their students about racism, but woke culture was expected and demanded by students. I felt anxious as a Brown Muslim woman and knew I still had to do my own work to delve into the history of systemic racism, specifically in education.

Foundational course readings within my doctoral coursework, such as *Tinkering Towards Utopia: A Century of Public School Reform* (Tyack & Cuban, 1995), offered a history into school reform in this country. These readings offered a mechanism for me to unpack how education over the centuries had shifted from educating only the sons of wealthy English landowners to a vision of free education for all children. The innovative process in the JHU EdD program of providing dissertation advisers to students, but not matching students based solely on the research interests of the professors, allowed me to focus my research to further understand the roots of the inequity and the need for cultural competence from an asset-based lens and challenge deficit framing that had influenced education. I was fortunate to have four people on my dissertation committee—two women of color, one Black and one South Asian and both from immigrant families, and two White women—who were experienced in both advising doctoral students and methodology. This support was valuable to my growth as a scholar and to my identity as a scholar of color.

Attending JHU at the time of the 50-year anniversary of the Coleman Report, the groundbreaking report requested by the U.S. Congress in response to the 1964 Civil Rights Act, heightened my understanding of the outcomes of the report and the impact today of de facto segregation and resegregation within schools. Engaging in the course discussion posts about sociological perspectives and connecting various perspectives to the current state of inequity in education influenced my own identity as a consumer of research to a critical analyzer of research and reflector of its impact. Further into my doctoral program, the ELE course *Power, Policy, and Politics* helped me to understand the unseen barriers hidden in policy that result in the inequities we see between student groups today. Understanding the politics behind school boards and the larger macrosystem were also mechanisms that were important to both my doctoral journey and my burgeoning leadership in the school system.

Aligning the Learning to My Beliefs and Actions

Becoming a scholar-practitioner meant I had to move from just managing my emotions about injustices to learning and understanding why current outcomes result from a system designed to unfairly favor White and Asian middle-class students while othering and harming Black and Hispanic/Latino/a/x/e students. Structures in the EdD program helped me become better informed about understanding nuances with reading and interpreting data; seeking recent, relevant research; and learning from scholars with greater expertise. While I can't say I enjoyed the weekly required written discussion posts, I will say this process helped me quickly learn how to summarize the important points from the articles, synthesize the information, and make connections to my work or POP. The discussion posts helped me learn from my peers by engaging in perspective-taking from their synthesis and application to their POP. While I would have much preferred verbal discussions, the discussion posts taught me to be more focused and to develop my scholar-practitioner lens.

It was important to me to share the concepts I learned from the readings with my colleagues so we could engage in conversations about our own practices in relation to recent research on leadership, adult learning, and bias. I started having these conversations with my team, by posing questions at our team meetings and with our director. Building on the trust of relationships with district-level leaders, I then continued to have informal discussions with leaders and shared articles that I thought could influence their work. This built both my credibility and my trust as I attended meetings to bring an equity perspective to these contexts. District leaders became more willing to discuss personal and systemic barriers to change more openly and honestly. They were provided a context in which they could share how they had felt shamed and blamed for current inequities in the school system. I felt it was important to stay focused on the data in our school system and mindset shifts. I articulated to the school administrators the rationale for our work by framing the inequities between student groups with questions related to why we believe those inequities exist. I invited us to question our own beliefs and current practices and policies. Although our district was familiar with the plan-do-study-act (PDSA) model for school improvement, I found myself asking questions focused on the six improvement principles, specifically "seeing the system that produces current outcomes" (Bryk et al., 2015, p. 57). This approach, which I learned in the first semester of my doctoral course in *Contemporary Approaches to Educational Problems* (CAE), helped me support leaders to see their blind spots and be willing to examine practices at all levels.

As I continued in this work, I noticed people sought me out as a scholar-practitioner. I became the go-to person when our office needed research on topics or when administrators requested talking points to enhance their ability to advocate for equity or speak out against racial bias. Other departments in our district asked to collaborate on professional learning to enhance their facilitation skills, transformative learning, and racial equity lens. Somewhere along this journey, not only had I become the change I wished to see, but my colleagues also started to view me as a leader in this work.

Centering My Leadership From Theory to Action

The ELE specialization coursework helped me understand different leadership styles and helped me identify whom I aspired to be. Transformational leaders are influential in bringing people together to attain the goals of a common vision, ultimately in service of organizational goals and effectiveness (Bass & Avolio, 1994). As a part of my doctorate, I conducted a needs assessment study with school administrators in 2017. The results illuminated that while school administrators were trained to support the goals of the organization, they were not taught how to examine the system more deeply to surface inequities (Kosi, 2020). I embraced transformational leadership when I was asked to chair our district's committee to develop the new policy for educational equity. The committee was composed of over 20 different community groups, with each group invested in protecting the needs of their own community. I worked with the committee to build a common vision for the policy and made space for committee members to develop positive relationships. I believe those transformational leadership traits contributed to the successful development of the policy. The policy was an important step, but as a leader, I still had to challenge the status quo because the district data showed many current practices at both the district and school level were contributing to the inequitable outcomes for Black and Brown students.

Having the foundational understanding on educational leadership from the ELE coursework, I continued my own research on leadership for equity, social justice, and cultural competence, which led me to Shields's (2010) work on transformative leaders. Shields's research illuminated differences between transformational and transformative leaders. One key difference between transformational and transformative leadership is that while transformational leaders work in service of the organizational goal and effectiveness, transformative leaders are committed to deep and equitable change by examining, deconstructing, and reconstructing the cultural knowledge, practices, and frameworks that generate the inequities. This difference resonated with me, because I often became frustrated with people blaming the "system" but not being willing to take the time to collectively examine, question, understand different perspectives, and deeply analyze additional information to collectively make new meaning and take action.

The needs assessment study for my dissertation also surfaced many gaps in the school administrators' leadership preparation. Sixty-three percent of current principals and assistant principals had not had any coursework on equity, social justice, or cultural competence. Most did not understand how social justice was related to educational equity (Kosi, 2020). Based on these findings, I embarked on my second literature review focused on intervention related to my POP. This review of the literature informed the development of an intervention in which school leaders could become culturally proficient leaders, including the elements of cultural self-awareness, deep understanding of societal inequities, and changing personal and institutional practices that were not serving all students (Terrell & Lindsey, 2009). The intervention for my Applied Dissertation was a new professional learning opportunity offered online during the summer of 2020 as our entire school system shifted to online learning. The new professional learning focused on transformative learning experiences, self-reflective practices, racial identity development, and increasing opportunities for principals' collective learning to increase their collective efficacy to lead for equity and social justice (Kosi, 2020).

Influencing Change Among Leaders

Organizational change in our school district started with the top tier of leadership. Elements of the professional learning I developed for the intervention in my dissertation were offered to the superintendent's cabinet and school board members, which I co-led with my director. The willingness of top leadership to discuss racial identity and how it affected their leadership was at a critical juncture in a time of national reckoning with the murder of George Floyd and the national uprising in support of the Black Lives Matter movement. I helped to create the norms for leaders to cocreate brave and courageous spaces to openly talk about racial identity, race, and racism. The knowledge I gained in the doctoral program helped me lead with confidence because I had a deep understanding of the issues and could go beyond the talking points within the woke movement.

The professional learning with the district leadership inspired the superintendent and his cabinet to set a precedent and mandate that all employees engage in professional learning focused on racial equity during the fall of 2020. My expertise was valued; I was no longer an outsider in education, but a leader in educational equity. I worked collaboratively across different departments, such as curriculum and instruction, teacher and paraprofessional development, instructional technology, and student services to create several online self-paced modules. Our team's expertise was called on to support the school-based leaders facilitating the dialogic conversations in our school. The depth of the conversations varied. Discussion facilitators who were more adept at discussing these issues and creating a brave space, and who were professionally prepared in facilitation skills were more successful. As a result, district leaders understood the importance of our office as change leaders and secured funding for three new positions to integrate the diversity, equity, and inclusion work across the district.

Leading Policy Change

Ensuring that educational equity was institutionalized through policy at both the state and district levels became a priority and I was poised to lead this work. I had already been a part of the leadership team for a statewide committee focused on multicultural education. The state superintendent charged our committee to draft new regulations guiding a statewide policy on educational equity. I used my research skills to find policies across the country that addressed equity. Learning about systems theory in my CAE class, I gained a new understanding of the barriers in the macro systems within the different counties in our state, and we were able to draft a regulation that offered multiple on-ramps for this work. This policy has given the backbone for organizational change in curriculum and instruction, allocation of resources, measuring school climate and culture, hiring and retention of teachers of color, and amplifying student voices.

Because I coauthored the statewide policy and led the work with the educational equity policy in our district I was viewed as an expert on policy pertaining to educational equity. I never viewed myself as a policy expert, but through case studies reviewed in ELE leadership courses and the coinciding professional leadership experiences, I became a person who valued policy and leading policy change from an equity perspective. Years from now, no one will remember the authors of statewide regulation and district policy, but the results of all educators in the district working cohesively to ensure equitable outcomes for students will have been my leadership contribution. I feel gratified knowing my role in the policy changes has the potential to make real changes in the lives of marginalized students, but also humbled that many leaders before me paved the way for this small, but important, policy. I fully recognize the work does not stop here, and my leadership must continue to grow and evolve.

Embracing My Leadership and Growing as a Changemaker for Educational Justice

I began the doctoral program as a social worker facilitating professional learning in the district and ended the doctoral program as district leader in a new role as the Coordinator of Culturally Responsive Practices and Anti-Racism Development. My social identity as an immigrant woman of color leading this work has not changed, but I realize the impact of someone who looks like me leading this work is important. I recognize my internal identity as a scholar, a thought-leader, and a changemaker are influenced by my social identities. My new role offers me more opportunities to work collaboratively with other departments and influence district curriculum and instruction; student services; human resources; leadership, teacher, and paraprofessional development; and community advisory groups. Although this role has a broader scope, I still lead the development of systemic transformative learning experiences. My expertise was recently sought to lead a LGBTQIA+ community advisory on professional learning recommendations. Although I worked collaboratively with the committee on the elements and content for the professional learning, I ultimately designed the four-part series to prepare other educators in how to affirm and support our LGBTQIA+ staff and students. The new educational equity policy in our district included this underserved and often invisible group, and as a result we were able to offer this professional learning opportunity to all 4000-plus employees. I was later asked to be on the search committee when our district hired our first LGBTQIA+ specialist and then I advocated for an interview question that addressed racial equity and intersectionality. After interviewing the candidates sent by human resources to the search committee, I asked why none of the interviewees were people of color. This again brought a deep examination of the current barriers in human resources practices. I share this example because I have reflected on how I can increase belonging and honor the dignity of people who remain voiceless or continue to be marginalized in the educational system. My journey as a transformative leader and changemaker is ongoing, and I strive to balance my knowledge with the experiences of those I lead toward an equitable and just educational system.

After earning my doctorate, I have found that both my confidence in the field of education and my credibility in the field of mental health have increased. I was invited to contribute a chapter to the first book on South Asian counseling and psychotherapy. This book is now published, and I continue to expand my contributions formally in the fields of both mental health and education. A piece of a new state law mandates trauma-informed professional learning for all school educators. Because of my expertise in this field, I was asked to be on the district's mental health leadership team. On this new interdisciplinary team, I advocated to include information on racial and historical trauma in our district's new professional learning on trauma-informed practices in schools. As an adjunct professor at JHU, I teach first-year students in the same doctoral program from which I matriculated. In teaching and guiding the students, I expose my vulnerability as I share my own challenges and triumphs in the program. I am committed to my ongoing growth as scholar-practitioner and developing others engaging in this journey.

References

Bass, B. M., & Avolio, B. J. (1994). Transformational leadership and organizational culture. *The International Journal of Public Administration, 17*(3–4), 541–554. https://doi.org/10.1080/01900699408524907

Bryk, A. S., Gomez, L. M., Grunow, A., & LeMahieu, P. G. (2015). *Learning to improve: How America's schools can get better at getting better.* Harvard Education Press.

Cross, T. L., Bazron, B. J., Dennis, K. W., & Isaacs, M. R. (1989). *Towards a culturally competent system of care.* Georgetown University Child Development Program, Child and Adolescent Service System Program.

Kosi, R. F. (2020). *Examining school administrators' culturally proficient practices: From self awareness to collective efficacy.* [Unpublished doctoral dissertation]. Johns Hopkins University.

Shields, C. M. (2010). Transformative leadership: Working for equity in diverse contexts. *Educational Administration Quarterly, 46*(4), 558–589. https://doi:10.1177/0013161X10375609

Terrell, R. D., & Lindsey, R. B. (2009). *Culturally proficient leadership: The personal journey begins within.* Corwin Press.

Tyack, D. B., & Cuban, L. (1995). *Tinkering toward utopia.* Harvard University Press.

CHAPTER 17

Winter Always Turns to Spring

Rachna Shah

A Journey Through the Seasons

MY DOCTORAL JOURNEY can be described as the natural seasons of the Earth—fall, winter, spring, and summer. Although the seasons are impermanent and out of our control, the challenges and joys accompanying each season through the doctoral program compelled me to embark on a continual process of unlearning and relearning. Each season was a pathway for the next, playing out like a symphony, reminding me to trust in the eternity of the cycle.

Traditional Teaching and Learning Approach

Prior to joining the doctoral program at Johns Hopkins University (JHU), I was a novice practitioner; naive and unsophisticated as a teacher, holding onto a fragmented approach to learning and teaching. Yet, this phase was akin to thriving in summer, as I believed that I was competent, and my methods were effective. I regarded learning as the degree to which one could remember and retain information and use it at will. My teacher-centered approach to education was very traditional. I assumed that the role of a teacher could be likened to that of a sage on a stage, and direct instruction was pivotal to the process of education. I failed to consider the mode of instruction or pedagogy with respect to student learning. I was a victim of more traditional approaches to learning and teaching in my own educational history, and hence had limited opportunities to challenge my existing beliefs, resulting in my own classroom practices mirroring the same.

As the English Language Coordinator in a special needs private school in urban Mumbai, India, I placed heavy emphasis on teacher professional development (PD) to improve student performance. Yet, I conceived PD as limited to mastering and implementing innovative strategies to enhance learning and teaching. This led me to constantly seek fresh perspectives from other educators in the field and transmit them to my team in the form of workshops. In this space, teachers were passively involved in memorizing concepts, rather than engaging in higher thinking skills, like reasoning, analyzing, and reflecting collaboratively. In an attempt to maximize the quantity of information delivered, I disregarded the quality of transference into the classrooms. The training sessions were planned as one-time events without any follow-up, feedback, reflection, mentoring, or coaching practices. This fractured model of PD was rooted in my teacher identity as a trainer or tutor and resulted in the delivery of information in a piecemeal manner. Moreover, I was also a compliant follower, as I attempted to replicate the behaviors, rules, tools, and techniques of other educators I held in high esteem. As such, I did not dispute this approach within my context or confront its pertinence, I merely played my part without altering the content or knowledge to suit the existing frame of reference. I failed to challenge the relevance of the one-size-fits-all approach, was unable to integrate the myriad dimensions into a coherent whole, stuck rigidly to plans and procedures, and never questioned the applicability of the knowledge.

I was forced to reevaluate my approach toward learning and teaching when the students' English comprehension achievement at the school remained unchanged over 3 years, despite the rigorous workshop sessions designed to equip teachers with enhanced pedagogical practices in the classroom. I felt that earning a Doctor of Education (EdD) degree would help me determine why this problem existed and how I might address it. The online format of the doctoral program at JHU was revolutionary and aligned with the demands of the 21st century, as it provided me with the opportunity to evaluate, examine, and study the problem within my context.

Journeying With the Seasons

Students' English comprehension achievement was a Problem of Practice (POP) at the focal special needs private school in which I was the Language Program Coordinator in urban Mumbai, India. Students in the school demonstrated poor comprehension outcomes that remained primarily unchanged in the 3 years prior to my enrollment in the JHU EdD program. I conducted a mixed methods needs assessment study in 2016 as part of my dissertation with 53 students between the ages of 6 and 16 years to help me understand the context of the POP—as Bryk and colleagues (2015) described, to "see the system that produces the current outcome" (p. 57). The students' profiles ranged from mild to moderate disabilities, including learning disabilities, autism spectrum disorder, cerebral palsy, attention deficit hyperactivity disorder, Down syndrome, fragile X syndrome, and others. The review of literature that informed the needs assessment study and the results of this study indicated that teachers' traditional instructional practices and teacher-centered beliefs about the roles of the learner and the teacher hindered students' English comprehension achievement (Shah, 2018). During this stage my identity was still rooted in a traditional framework of instruction. I identified at this time as a sage on a stage.

The intervention was implemented in 2018 with nine teachers who had worked at the school for 6 or more months. The intervention included modifying the current traditional workshop-oriented PD model (i.e., insufficient teachers' active participation, fixed schedules, and lack of follow-up support structures) to embed it in constructivist principles, which emphasized the active involvement of participants as advocated by Desimone (2009) and Guskey (2002). In addition, opportunities for reflection, which research supports (Farrell & Ives, 2015; Schön, 1984), were offered to the English language teachers at the school using three different platforms, namely, participant-driven workshops, professional learning communities (PLCs), and coaching sessions. The teachers' responses during PD sessions and teacher interviews showed that teachers regarded the PD sessions as positively impacting their reflective practices, increasing their awareness of discrepancies between their beliefs and classroom practices, and enhancing their perceptions of knowledge and skills related to constructivist teaching and learning. Participants also reported meaningful changes in their beliefs, from traditional to more constructivist approaches, from the needs assessment study to postintervention (Shah, 2018). Subsequently, the teachers' classroom practices showed improvement following the implementation of the PD program.

Mechanisms for Identity Change

Within this time period, I experienced the seasons of fall, winter, and spring as I engaged in the first years of the EdD program. Mechanisms for the transformation of my identity included learning and unlearning how to learn, working with my mentor, and exposure to the area of neuroeducation in a specialization course.

The Evolving Landscape of Learning

The fall season signals both endings and beginnings. It is a time of letting go and shedding. Simultaneously, even though mostly unseen, seeds are being sown in nature that will blossom the following spring. My doctoral journey began in the fall semester both literally and metaphorically. I was comfortable in my ability to learn while staying within my comfort zone, as I had done my entire life. The beginning of fall feels a lot like summer in India. The weather is warm and the skies are still blue, but change is happening. This was also true for me. Unlike my earlier experiences as a student, where I molded to fit the given structure with fixed routines, tasks, and skills, I began my journey at JHU with copious questions. I had to become comfortable with getting out of my comfort zone of being acknowledged and having answers, as I engaged in a continual process of discarding, confronting, and refining my POP. The summer-like fall weather was starting to feel less warm and more cold. The air was crisp. Winter was coming. The restlessness and discomfort accompanying this process of learning to learn differently propelled me into a state of helplessness and unease. Winter had come. Discussions with my peers and adviser over the following weeks impelled me to alter and develop new schemas as a reaction to the cognitive dissonance I experienced. To restore balance through the incessant revision of my POP, I was compelled to be supple in my approach and adopt cognitive flexibility as the norm rather than the exception. This process of exploration was empowering yet confusing as I struggled to consider new approaches that might be more effective in my learning journey.

The persistent battle with the inner demons of doubt, despair, and frustration continued. As an active participant engaged in the continual process of action and research, I discharged the mounting pressure of performance bounded by the need for recognition. Just like the plants and trees store energy during winter months to prepare for spring, I engaged in practices of reflection and introspection during this time. I eventually became comfortable with being held in a state of disequilibrium, where the frames of reference were fluid, rather than feeling consumed by the need to assimilate all new information into my existing schemas, as described by McLeod (2022). My notions about education were challenged and I reformulated my definition of learning from that of memorization to a means of inquiry and creative exploration. Learning and growth are continually unfolding processes. I learned that knowledge could never be fixed but steadily evolved. In Carol Dweck's (2016) terms, I made the transition from a "fixed" to a "growth" mindset, and this shifted the spotlight from arriving at a destination to enjoying the journey. So, rather than using the winter season solely as a period of preparation for the spring, I began to accept the cold, icy, and uncomfortable weather conditions of winter. Embracing the challenges of winter proved to be a great opportunity to develop my inner strength and resourcefulness. It had a significant impact on my identity, particularly in terms of resilience and adaptability.

My Adviser and Mentor

The winter season, characterized by shorter days and longer nights, are harsh and difficult to endure as temperatures drop and the climate is cold. As the program progressed, I had to balance the demands of the program with my job, family engagements, and social commitments. The trying conditions of winter continued to sting as I grappled for survival, weighed down by multiple responsibilities. As I navigated my way around the online portal, while drowning in heaps of research articles and books and simultaneously engaging in weekly discussions with peers, I began to realize qualities in myself that I wanted to improve. I often measured myself against my peers, which only accentuated the feelings of inadequacy and disbelief in my abilities. I found it increasingly difficult to sustain as my energy felt completely sapped! The winter storms continued to buffet me as the load of assignments and deadlines piled up and I was tossed around mercilessly, enveloped by feelings of self-loathing and cynicism. According to Shelley (1820/2020), "If Winter comes, can Spring be far behind?" (p. 24). While winter is characterized by stillness and dormancy, it is also a time of deep work and preparation to harness the growth potential within life.

Our lives are interwoven in a complex and intricate web of connections, as nothing exists in isolation. The process of unraveling our hidden potential to actualize our highest purpose and create value in our lives as well as those of others is not a natural occurrence, like reaching significant developmental milestones. Rather, unlocking this treasure is a labor of love by another who has boundless faith and committedly reminds one of their deep potential. Just as Rita Pierson says in her famous TED (2013) talk, "Every kid needs a champion," I was fortunate to have an adviser who nourished me to embrace every frosty bite of the winter while reassuring me of the arrival of spring.

Winter began to thaw. My biweekly conversations with my adviser, Dr. Camille Bryant, not only provided me with a sounding board, but also she gently nurtured me to shift my perspective and left me with opportunities for deep reflection. Further, when she saw me engaged in a fierce battle with statistics and I had reached my threshold, she provided me with valuable snippets and also modeled the methodology step by step. She stayed committed to my growth as she equipped me to navigate through every roadblock related to reading, writing, comprehension, timelines, or collaboration. Her consistent and timely feedback led me to strive and exert myself so I became more adept at skimming and scanning and my writing and comprehension skills grew exponentially. She persistently posed questions that allowed me to not only analyze content more effectively but also develop an inquiring mind as I inspected and scrutinized varying viewpoints without succumbing to mere acceptance or negligence. I repeatedly experimented with and arrived at new modes of planning, organizing, and self-regulating as she served as a proficient role model. Every dialogue with her helped me to break through some of my limited beliefs and uncover skills that lay deeply hidden.

I was physically, mentally, and emotionally exhausted as I struggled with the intervention for my dissertation in my context. My adviser repeatedly accommodated me in her schedule and her relaxed demeanor and good humor allowed me to experience a new surge of energy, dismissing the weariness of this season of winter. Furthermore, her ceaseless patience and faith in my ability allowed me to become comfortable in the midst of tension created by opposing forces. I could conquer all my self-limiting indulgences, and I could witness the boundless and infinite possibilities of my own life. While I was unable to appreciate the process of battling the winter as a prerequisite to savoring the sweetness of spring, my mentor held my hand gently and guided me through the seasons. She did not allow me to wallow in the pain of one season, winter, and destroy my hope and joy of the rest. My interactions with my adviser over the 3 years led me to become empowered, as I took the journey from knowledge to wisdom, from limitation to abundance, from victim to victor, from fragmentation to wholeness, and from fear to faith. As a result, I saw myself as a confident and capable scholar who was ready to take on new challenges and make a difference in my field.

Neuroeducation

The *Mind, Brain Science and Learning* course during Year 1 of my program was revolutionary in that it provided me with a new lens on the learning process. It was my first exposure into the world of brain sciences and their influence on educational practices, particularly the comprehensive brain-targeted teaching model (Hardiman, 2012). Hardiman's synthesis of learning science research, which revealed the intricate linkages between emotions and higher order cognition, was radically refreshing. I learned that the amygdala, the structure involved in processing emotion, is the primary structure involved in processing information even before the thinking center, the frontal lobe. This led me to not only appreciate the compelling need to create a positive emotional climate in the classroom but also take responsibility to create relationships with the students in the classroom as well as the teachers in PD so they feel trusted, accepted, and safe. I redefined my role in the classroom as I endorsed the quote, "I've come to a frightening conclusion that I am the decisive element in the classroom. It's my personal approach that creates the climate. It's my daily mood that makes the weather" (Ginott, 1993, p. 15). By embracing this idea, I began to see myself not just as a teacher but as a facilitator of learning who could create a positive, inclusive environment for my students and teachers. I started to prioritize building meaningful connections with my students and teachers, and to focus on their individual strengths and needs.

Also, understanding the effect of stress in releasing cortisol, which impacts the hippocampus and frontal lobe, thus impairing memory and information processing (Hardiman, 2012), was ground breaking. This new understanding shaped my intervention and led me to redesign the PD model at school to provide teachers with different spaces to enable a sense of community and safety, including PLCs and coaching. It was the combined learning about stress and emotions that led me to see teachers as whole beings with intellectual, emotional, and developmental facets and hence give credence to who they are rather than only what they do. Spring is pleasant as the harshness of winter has diminished and the heat of summer has not yet arrived. This course and similar experiences were the spring of my doctoral journey, as they brought the joy of renewal, growth, and accomplishments. Questioning my ability to succeed was replaced by a renewed curiosity about teaching and learning. Through the challenges I faced and the support I received, I developed a newfound confidence in my abilities and a stronger sense of purpose and direction. I began to see myself not just as a student, but as a researcher with the potential to make a meaningful contribution to my field. This shift in identity has not only transformed my doctoral journey but has also influenced my approach to life beyond academia.

Postdoctoral Identity

The program design, structure, courses, and instructors have enabled me to redefine and make several transitions in my identity. Firstly, they led me to reevaluate my definition of a learner. Today, I appreciate myself as a learner striving for wisdom that emerges from the beauty of contradictions and oppositional ideas rather than pursuing knowledge that is static and rigid. Moreover, they empowered me to exercise my muscles for endurance, perseverance, and reflection, trusting that growth is a process rather than an endeavor to arrive at an elusive destination. I now see myself as a lifelong learner excited about challenging the existing blueprints and rewriting them as I welcome new ideas, thoughts, and theories.

The program also facilitated my transition from a teacher to a mentor as I embody a more expansive perspective in relating to other teachers and students in and out of the classroom. I felt like I was in spring, growing and blossoming to unravel my potential. This has led me to espouse a more facilitative, collaborative, and nurturing stance rather than an instructional one. Additionally, the program afforded me the opportunities to evolve from a novice practitioner to a scholar-practitioner as I am now able to engage with scholarly literature to attend to POPs in the real world. I now appreciate and use the wealth of research to analyze the causes of the problem and to determine suitable interventions in my practice. This allows me to dismiss my preconceived assumptions and base my conclusions on research from the field and data. Also, I see myself as an academic researcher as I continue to apply the knowledge and skills gained through my study to create solutions for problems. It is the summer season that resulted from my doctoral journey, where I am able to enjoy and celebrate the fruits of my efforts.

Ripples of Identity Change

My research enabled me to be a change agent within my organization because the study allowed the school leaders and teachers to recognize the associated drivers of the low reading comprehension achievement of diverse students in the school. By using research findings rather than assumptions about the drivers, I developed an intervention that significantly influenced the school's approach to PD as the focus shifted from content delivery to considering teachers' beliefs about learning and teaching. The traditional workshop model of PD was replaced with a more interactive approach that encouraged active teacher participation. The metamorphosis in the PD approach within the English department influenced the coordinators in other subject areas to adopt a similar approach in their PDs. Overall, the research allowed us to use data-driven approaches and techniques to consider the various influencing factors related to the issue at hand instead of solely relying on leadership perspectives.

The approaches of the intervention had the most noteworthy impact within the organization. The success of the PLCs in building cohesion and comradeship between our team members was exemplary. Moreover, the PLCs were initiated across different subject areas and departments, leading to a collective responsibility toward the vision of the organization. The weekly meetings created a forum for teachers to engage in continual communication, learning, and reflection, which seems to have led to increased motivation and investment. Further, the coaching sessions created a safe space for teachers to be vulnerable as they accessed their hidden agendas, latent beliefs, and dominant values while discussing strategies and challenges in and beyond the classroom. Feedback from the teachers indicated the positive influence of these sessions on their pedagogical practices in the classroom as they were given the opportunity to dig deeper into their beliefs, self-efficacy, and practices and access areas that were obscure or concealed. Just like the program afforded me the opportunity to embrace the winter season by challenging my beliefs and rethinking my notions about learning and teaching, I was providing the teachers a platform for the same.

Even after my graduation, I continued with these individual coaching sessions over the next 6 months. After the end of the academic year, I left the organization. Yet, I stayed in touch with the team and the teachers who were part of the intervention. They continued to report deep insights and the effect of my dissertation intervention in their teaching and personal lives even 3 years after the coaching sessions. Finally, the intervention also inspired and prompted changes in the organizational leaders, who now sought to create data-driven meetings and introduce research to further opportunities for teacher and student growth.

Current Impact

The doctoral degree continues to influence my work as I have transitioned to leading a preservice teacher training program that is inspired by the Boston Teacher Residency program. The model is unique in that it is a residency-based model where teachers, along with a collaborating school, are mentored by experienced teachers in the school and teacher educators from the program while engaging in rigorous coursework and reflective practices. My doctoral course afforded me the opportunity to become a teacher education leader with the ability and confidence to design and implement teacher preparation courses including creating ample opportunities for active student involvement, collaboration, mentoring, and coaching. Further, my experiences in the doctoral program also influenced my new role as a mentor teacher in the organization. Additionally, they equipped me with the courage to translate and disseminate my learning as I began blogging on topics related to teaching and learning. The program has created a renewal that is irreversible. It equipped me with the stamina and tenacity to brave every whirlwind. The process of transformation through the EdD program at JHU felt messy, excruciatingly uncomfortable, and challenging at times. However, I hold the experience in high regard as the learnings are profound, life transforming, and value creating. I started my doctoral journey in the fall, and the winter months were hard. I underwent a significant transformation, moving away from my traditional role as a teacher and embracing a new identity as a scholar-practitioner and researcher who places a high value on building meaningful relationships with students and teachers. At times, it seemed as if that harsh season would never end; however, spring came, and now summer. My time as a JHU EdD student not only allowed me to awaken to the boundless, inherent potential of my life but it also nurtured me to share that treasure with others.

References

Bryk, A., Gomez, L., Grunow, A, & LaMahieu, P. G. (2015). *Learning to improve: How America's schools can get better at getting better.* Harvard Education Press.

Desimone, L. M. (2009). Improving impact studies of teachers' professional development: Toward better conceptualizations and measures. *Educational Researcher, 38*(3), 181–199. https://doi.org/10.3102/0013189x08331140

Dweck, C. (2016). What having a "growth mindset" actually means. *Harvard Business Review, 13*(2), 2–5.

Farrell, T. S., & Ives, J. (2015). Exploring teacher beliefs and classroom practices through reflective practice: A case study. *Language Teaching Research, 19*(5), 594–610. https://doi.org/10.1177/1362168814541722

Ginott, H. G. (1993). *Teacher and child: A book for parents and teachers* (Rei ed.). Scribner Paper Fiction.

Guskey, T. R. (2002). Professional development and teacher change. *Teachers and Teaching, 8*(3), 381–391. https://doi.org/10.1080/13540600210000512

Hardiman, M. (2012). *Brain-targeted teaching for 21st century schools.* Corwin Press.

McLeod, S. (2022, August 18). *Jean Piaget's theory and stages of cognitive development.* Simply Psychology. https://simplypsychology.org/piaget.html

Schön, D. A. (1984). *The reflective practitioner: How professionals think in action*. Basic Books.

Shah, R. (2018). *Fostering constructivist teaching beliefs in English language classrooms through the implementation of a professional development model* [Unpublished doctoral dissertation]. Johns Hopkins University.

Shelley, P. B. (2020). Ode to the West Wind. In R. A. Neilson (Ed.), *The Oxford handbook of Percy Bysshe Shelley* (pp. 123–124). Oxford University Press. (Original work published 1820)

TED. (2013, May 3). *Every kid needs a champion | Rita Pierson* [Video]. YouTube. https://www.youtube.com/watch?v=SFnMTHhKdkw

CHAPTER 18

Lessons Learned from Scholar-Practitioners and Suggestions for the Field

*Camille L. Bryant, Ranjini Mahinda JohnBull,
Stephen J. Pape, and Karen S. Karp*

*All of us bring light to exciting solutions never tried before; For it is our hope
that implores us, at our uncompromising core, To keep rising up for an earth
more than worth fighting for.*

—AMANDA GORMAN, "EARTHRISE"

Introduction

EARNING A DOCTORAL degree is much, much more than having a program of
study with a set of courses that are checked off semester by semester. Instead,
the doctoral program, as we define it, is a life-changing experience. The editors
of this book maintain that the difference between other graduate programs of
study and the doctoral degree comes most profoundly from the transformation of students' identities. This not-so-subtle shift in the way students modify
their frames of reference and recast themselves in a more scholarly persona is
not through a single course or reading but through a carefully orchestrated set
of experiences crafted by faculty to create spaces for identities to be tried on
and solidified. Identity transformation through the program experience is the
catalyst for educational change.

We have described some of these instructional moves that we believe have an impact on our students' identities in Chapters 1 through 3 of this volume and here again will support our premise on the centrality of transforming doctoral students' identities as the significant feature of any successful doctoral program. When we say *successful*, we are referring not to the program's financial efficiency, simplicity of faculty course delivery, or even high graduation rates, but to the most important goal of improving educational outcomes in our students' contexts. Through this intentional design, our involvement as faculty instructors and advisers gives us the pleasure of being part of that change, both in the professional contexts where our students work and in our students' lives.

So here in this final chapter we converse, practitioner to practitioner, to describe our evidence and we hope we can convince you through our data synthesis to build your Doctor of Education (EdD) program. We suggest you construct your program not merely with an eye for improving skills or ways to develop more scholarly writing but with the intention of transforming identities.

Student Profiles

Our doctoral graduate authors may not be representative of the general student population in EdD programs; rather, they were invited advisees of the editors. To make comparisons more transferable, we are providing some demographic information here to inform the reader of our group's characteristics. Our student authors came from seven U.S. states, the District of Columbia, Egypt, and India. The group included 11 females and three males; four authors of color and 10 authors of White or Euro-American ethnic and racial identities are represented. In Table 18.1, we include their professional role at the onset of the program and what they were doing at the time of writing, 1 to 4 years following graduation.

A central reason the 14 authors applied to and enrolled in the Johns Hopkins University (JHU) EdD program was their goal of equity, or the acknowledgment that inequitable opportunities to learn are often the result of structural racism and implicit bias. They expressed feelings of inadequacy to address these issues in their professional practice and wanted to engage in professional

Table 18.1

Alumni Authors' Positions Prior to and After their EdD Experience

Position Prior to the EdD Program	Position After the EdD Program
Executive Director Non-Profit	Executive Director Non-Profit; Adjunct Faculty
Elementary School Principal	Senior Director of Leadership, Coaching, and Support – Office Equity Affairs
Secondary Mathematics Teacher; Department Chair	Secondary Mathematics Teacher; Department Chair
Middle School and High School Learning Advocate	High School Academic Dean
Adjunct Faculty: Content Development Manager	Educational Consultant; Adjunct Faculty; Content Development Manager
School Social Worker	Coordinator of Culturally Responsive Practices and Anti-Racism Development
Director of Differentiated Learning	Partner, Emerging Services and Perspectives
Elementary Teacher; New Teacher Mentor; Tutor	Chair of Middle School Teaching and Learning; Owner of Tutoring Services LLC
Preschool Vision Specialist; Teacher of Students with Visual Impairments	Preschool Vision Specialist; Adjunct Instructor; Preschool 504 Coordinator
Language Program Coordinator	Language Program Coordinator; Faculty Mentor
High School Academic Dean	Executive Director
Language Development Specialist	Director of Professional Development for a State Association of Independent Schools
Professional Developer	Senior Researcher, Equity Research and Development
High School Social Studies Teacher	Administrative Director of Instruction

growth to effect change within the system by ameliorating the problems they were facing.

In the next sections we provide a synthesis of the authors' stories across the EdD program, the mechanisms for their identity transformations, shifts in their identity transformation, how they defined and embodied their scholar practitioner identity, and their new identity's influence on their professional practice. We hope to convince you that identity transformation is the most important element needed in all EdD programs. This formalization of this shift in students' sense of self should be purposefully woven into courses, assignments, and assessment milestones.

Mechanisms of Transformation

As we have described throughout this volume, we advocate for the careful curation of experiences within an EdD program to support identity transformation. Although we orchestrated these components carefully, our graduates' chapters provide evidence for what they came to see as the mechanisms for their transformation. Through analysis of the chapters, we have pinpointed through the student voices where these memorable moments truly yielded growth and change. We now have greater clarity about the mechanisms of transformation that were effectual in providing transformational learning experiences as described by Mezirow (1997). We offer these findings for all other doctoral programs to use as they navigate options for their students' life-changing academic exploration.

In Chapters 1 through 3 of this volume, we outlined the JHU EdD program components as conceived by the program faculty that form the backbone of the identity transformation process. We also hypothesized that several key programmatic components were powerful sources of support for our students, including the community of practice (CoP) afforded by our cohort model, our dissertation advisement, and the Applied Dissertation. In the following sections, we delve deeply into the students' experiences relative to several of these interconnected and intertwined components.

Communities of Practice

One overarching mechanism for transformation for our authors and a way to combat the potential for a sense of remoteness in an online format was the creation of CoPs based primarily in the program's cohort model. The students' doctoral experience typically started with a 3-day, in-person orientation (online starting with the beginning of the COVID-19 pandemic). Students reported meeting their colleagues and maintained the bonds they established during this 3-day meeting. For the most part, these communities emerged organically and often continued throughout the program and beyond graduation.

We expected that the cohort model would be supportive but had little idea how it would play out in a fully online environment with international participants. One author wrote, "While I expected the EdD program to bring together individuals from diverse backgrounds, I never anticipated the intensity with which those backgrounds would impact my personal environment." Here the author was referring to the enrichment of the community that manifested from the diverse national and international student population afforded by the online nature of the program.

We didn't immediately realize that the cohort would shield some students from the negative effect of the all-too-frequently-experienced imposter syndrome, the feeling of self-doubt about belonging in a current group. As one author indicated:

> The sense of community, especially in the early semesters of the program, was an important ingredient in my identity shift as well. Reaching out and being reached out to by others helped me to see that I was not alone and was not the only graduate student struggling with imposter syndrome.

Finally, one student indicated a similar sentiment but expanded this sense of student community to include the EdD faculty and advisers: "My apprehension toward engaging with members of this new community dissipated inversely to the support, encouragement, and empowerment afforded me by my cohort peers, EdD faculty, and doctoral adviser." The adviser, the focus of the next section, was an important person in the students' CoP.

Doctoral Adviser: Advocate and Cheerleader

The adviser in the JHU EdD program holds many roles. As described by our alumni authors, the adviser in an EdD program reaches out to their advisees to understand their context and to support them as they navigate building relationships within their context of professional practice. The alumni authors in this book were assigned a doctoral adviser during the first (or at latest, second) semester of their program. One alum commented: "The innovative process in the JHU EdD program of providing dissertation advisers to students, but not matching students based solely on the research interests of the professors, allowed me to focus [on] my [professional practice]."

The confidence built through the adviser-advisee partnership was one mechanism for the increase in practitioner self-efficacy (PSE) and scholar self-efficacy (SSE) as the authors' identities merged toward strong scholar-practitioner self-efficacy (SPSE). One author stated:

> My adviser was a mechanism for change; she combatted my doubt with reassurances. . . . And she filled my tank with declarations of "That was an amazing comps!" . . . These moments kept me going, pushed the imposter syndrome aside, and replaced the negative self-talk in my head.

For at least one of our alumni authors, the adviser served as a support when she wanted to navigate a change to the conceptualization of her Applied Dissertation. She wrote: "My adviser's support and advocacy were powerful and enabling during this shift." This aligns with the findings of Brabazon (2016) when she suggested doctoral advisers can "enable, assist, warn, frame, and improve the topic" (p. 16).

Program Coursework: Content

The alums' stories of their transformations frequently highlighted their experiences in the courses as central to their shifting identities. These course components included the development of content knowledge, multiple perspectives, social justice lenses, improvement science principles and processes, and systems thinking. These components were intertwined in many of the alums' stories, showing the relationship between knowledge growth and perspective taking, for example.

Our alums' descriptions of their change over time point out the importance of foundational learning (as defined by individual programs) as critical to identity transformation. The program had a general impact on several students' perspectives on learning. One student commented, "The EdD program offered ample opportunities for me to normalize productive struggle." Another student wrote, "The EdD program ignited in me a desire *to learn* rather than *to become learned* and changed my perception of what constitutes authentic learning." For many of our doctoral students, the initial learning experiences created dissonance as they came to realize that learning and knowledge at the doctoral level needed to be constructed differently from how they may have constructed understanding in the past.

Our students called out specific content that stimulated their thinking and broadened their perspectives. We purposefully tried to help students understand the use of theory to guide predictable next steps and tackle a variety of problems by using a sound connection to tested ideas and organized practice. As discussed in Chapter 1, the content of and experiences in the first-year courses support our students to take on multiple perspectives. During the first semester, students engaged in the course *Disciplinary Approaches to Education*, where they considered historical, sociological, anthropological, and economic perspectives on educational issues. One student wrote the following about one of the readings:

> *Tinkering Towards Utopia: A Century of Public School Reform* (Tyack & Cuban, 1995) offered a history into school reform in this country. These readings offered a mechanism for me to unpack how education over the centuries had shifted from educating only the sons of wealthy English landowners to a vision of free education for all children.

Several of our authors emphasized the content of an elective course, *Power, Policy, and Politics in Education*, as having a significant impact on them personally and professionally. One student illustrated this impact when she commented: "Further into my doctoral program, the *Power, Policy, and Politics* [course] helped me to understand the unseen barriers hidden in policy that result in the inequities we see between student groups today." This content enabled authors to understand the role of power in policy development.

Two of our alum authors wrote about the specialized knowledge they gained in their learning within the *Entrepreneurial Leadership in Education* (ELE) specialization. One of these students indicated that "from my specialization in entrepreneurial leadership in education, I saw opportunities for successful ventures and competitive advantage for my school. Also, I started to grow an interest in economics in education." The second author focused on the potential for self-reflection about one's own leadership style through this coursework: "The ELE specialization coursework helped me understand different leadership styles and helped me identify whom I aspired to be."

Social justice lens.

Across the program there is an intentional focus on social justice. In one alum's chapter, the author spoke to the difficult social circumstances during her dissertation study when there was a worldwide pandemic as well as significant social unrest within the United States, pointing to a shift from managing her emotions to coming to an understanding of systemic, structural racism. She commented: "Structures in the EdD program helped me become better informed about understanding nuances with reading and interpreting data; seeking recent, relevant research; and learning from scholars with greater expertise." These newly developed skills gave her the ability to frame issues of educational inequity. Another student stated: "The knowledge I gained in the doctoral program helped me lead with confidence because I had a deep understanding of the issues and could go beyond the talking points within the woke movement." These social justice components facilitated the authors' self-reflections and growing awareness through engagement with content and discourse with their peers.

Improvement science and systems thinking.

Several of the alumni authors depicted the ways in which they framed their dissertation from an improvement science perspective as it supported systematic examination of data and implementation of change. Although some were already using improvement science in their workplace, the exposure in the program led them to examine their practice more deeply by asking questions prior to jumping to answers. One alum wrote, "Although our district was familiar with the plan-do-study-act (PDSA) model for school improvement, I found myself asking questions focused on the six improvement principles, specifically about 'seeing the system that produces current outcomes' (Bryk et al., 2015, p. 57)."

Another doctoral author described her perspective on improvement science as "[i]dentifying an opportunity to enhance current systems through an improvement science approach [which] allowed the advocator spirit that I had neatly tucked away in order to be diplomatic as the sole Black female administrator to be released." She also suggested,

> The design of JHU's doctoral program . . . allowed me to "see the system" (Bryk et al., 2015, p. 57) by analyzing and synthesizing research on culturally responsive teaching. As a result, I strategically identified the actual problem prior to proposing a solution.

This relates to the act of holding back to sidestep initial impulses to leap to quick answers. One student summed up the utility of this systematic implementation of change when she wrote:

> Notably, this connection to improvement science was not only one of the first concepts taught in the JHU EdD program but was also a thread woven throughout every course. I then realized that the thread is not cut when students graduate but continues to create a tapestry through our use of the fibers in our professional contexts.

Program Coursework: Experiences

Several of the program experiences were mentioned in the alums' chapters as mechanisms for transformation that were orchestrated by the program faculty and developed within the program to support content learning but also important doctoral skills, such as analysis and synthesis. These program components included the (a) comprehensive examination, (b) Applied Dissertation, including the embedded components in the coursework and the program's emphasis on understanding the problem of practice [POP] during Year 1, and (c) course assignments and discussion posts.

Oral comprehensive examination: Consolidating knowledge and building self-efficacy.

The comprehensive exam was designed to encourage the synthesis of ideas from the required core courses and the application of these theories, research designs, and related findings to the dissertation research or to real-world scenarios. Although students expressed angst over them, on the other side of the experience they found empowerment. One student found that the process of studying was challenging but generated responses that applied important theories to a variety of situations. She summed up her experience by saying:

> This process imbued me with feelings of efficacy or an inherent sense
> that I can successfully help other people understand education theory
> in practical ways. Seeing myself as an integrator of information em-
> powered me as I embarked on the intervention addressing my POP
> and ultimately guided me in pursuits both within my organization
> and in the greater community. This is the crux of my transformation.

Another alum found connections on her journey as she explored multiple identities. She wrote:

> Although intersectionality was introduced in my summer 2019 mul-
> ticultural education course, it wasn't until I was studying for the EdD
> comprehensive exam the following spring that I truly internalized the
> power of intersectionality and how it could impact my practice.

The comprehensive exam melded the ideas from the various courses in a pur-
poseful and continuously useful way. Students walked away from the experience
with the skills to speak publicly and share their newfound status as a knowledgeable novice scholar-practitioner.

Applied dissertation: embedded in courses.

For most students, the Applied Dissertation consisted of an analysis of the
factors that may have contributed to their POP through a research synthesis
and empirical study, a deep analysis of interventions that align with the factors
examined, methodology for enacting an intervention, and evaluating and interpreting both the process and the outcomes of the intervention. The embedded
nature of the Applied Dissertation within courses supported this work. One
student wrote, "The process of conducting intervention research within my
Neurobiology of Learning Differences class allowed me to create a blueprint for
professional learning."

A distinctive feature of the JHU EdD Applied Dissertation is the focus
on the POP during the first year of the program. As a program requirement
students examined the factors that potentially contributed to their POP. One
student likened this process to the design thinking used in his former architectural background. He stated,

My own background in design helped me see how JHU was using a process, through POPs, akin to a design thinking model to cultivate my own identity as a scholar-practitioner who was equipped to solve complex problems in the field of education.

Part of this process was a needs assessment study that specifically asked the students to confirm the factors they expected were related to their POP within their context. This investigation was a powerful example of seeing the system with the long view of developing an intervention that would target the main factors. These incremental Applied Dissertation experiences allowed the authors to gradually build their SSE to be able to deliver a full dissertation and demonstrate their knowledge and skills in affirming their new identity.

Course assignments and discussions.

The second category of program experiences that our authors elevated to a mechanism for identity transformation was related to required course assignments and discussion board posts. For example, in the first two specialization courses, students explored potential interventions through a synthesis of the literature (Chapter 3 in their dissertation). One student wrote, "My JHU *Fundamentals of Cognitive Development* class served as a mechanism for change by highlighting certain aspects of teacher learning, such as modeling, observations, and feedback, that had been previously missing in our professional learning design."

Because the program was completely online, students were typically required to post a response in the discussion forum each week. The authors in this volume noted several times that the requirement to post their thoughts in the course discussions was an opportunity to reflect on the course content and to synthesize their reading as a public act. One student wrote:

> While I can't say I enjoyed the weekly required written discussion posts, . . . this process helped me quickly learn how to summarize the important points from the articles, synthesize the information, and make connections to my work or POP.

Another student wrote, "While I would have much preferred verbal discussions, the discussion posts taught me to be more focused and to develop my scholar-practitioner lens."

Summary

In their chapters the alumni authors underscored several aspects of the EdD course content that influenced them both personally and professionally. Overwhelmingly, these authors lauded the CoP established in our online program. This community extended to the adviser, and, for some, to the group of advisees of an individual adviser. Students were encouraged to develop these lifelong communities in subtle and not-so-subtle ways. For example, we became more explicit about the advantages of forming a community with which to study for the comprehensive examination when we realized singletons were struggling with this program milestone. Advisers provided a welcome entrée to the schol-ar-practitioner arena and supported their students' developing self-efficacy through a great deal of verbal persuasion along with other sources to support positive efficacy judgments.

Several of the authors explored the course content as a significant mech-anism for their identity transformation. Their stories tell of developing deep knowledge in education, in general, through the core and specialization course-work. These alums expressed the importance of their learning about systems thinking and the structural racism inherent within their professional contexts. The systems perspective and deep knowledge our students developed led to shifts in their professional contexts and their identity changes.

Finally, the students mentioned how program experiences were important to their identity transformation. The embeddedness of the Applied Dissertation enabled students to take up their dissertation in an orderly fashion across the coursework guided by the course instructors and dissertation adviser. The comprehensive examination afforded the students opportunities to consoli-date knowledge, to develop positive self-efficacy beliefs, and to practice their oral communication of their knowledge. Course assignments, especially the discussion posts, provided another perceptible support for identity transforma-tion. These discourse opportunities made their thinking visible, and students engaged in deep reflection and honed their skills in communicating their new learning. In the following sections, we briefly describe their professional identity stages that resulted from these transformational mechanisms.

Professional Identity Stages

Rather than the linear route from the identity of an experienced practitioner-aspiring scholar to that of a scholar-practitioner that we originally depicted in Figure 2.1 (Chapter 2), we found that the stories and reflections of the doctoral students highlighted a sometimes circuitous and wavy path. What we have learned from their stories is that this path from an experienced practitioner to a scholar-practitioner is long and winding with many dips in confidence, reflection moments, swells in self-efficacy, recurrences of self-doubt, and upsurges of confidence. Students often experienced increases and decreases in their self-efficacy, which are depicted by the wavy line between their initial PSE and SSE as they approach one another in SPSE. While students may experience lower self-efficacy at times during the program, their PSE and SSE ultimately increase. What we realized in writing this book together is that facilitating students' identity journeys is an essential part of their program experience. Furthermore, we believe that all graduate programs could likely benefit from applying a lens of intentional identity development to help adults progress through their higher education learning experiences. We illustrate this new version of the path that the doctoral graduates described in Figure 18.1. In the next sections, we describe the various stages of their identities as told in their stories in this book.

Experienced Practitioner-Aspiring Scholar

Many of our authors described their predoctoral identities as experienced practitioners, educators, and leaders seeking knowledge to help them enhance their professional practice. We call this first identity stage the *experienced practitioner-aspiring scholar.* These professionals possessed high levels of PSE, practice-based knowledge, experience, and expertise; they were already highly proficient in their professions. Several graduates used metaphors to describe themselves during this launching period, such as a zoo tiger or a seed waiting

Figure 18.1

Circuitous Scholar-Practitioner Self-Efficacy and Identity Growth Model

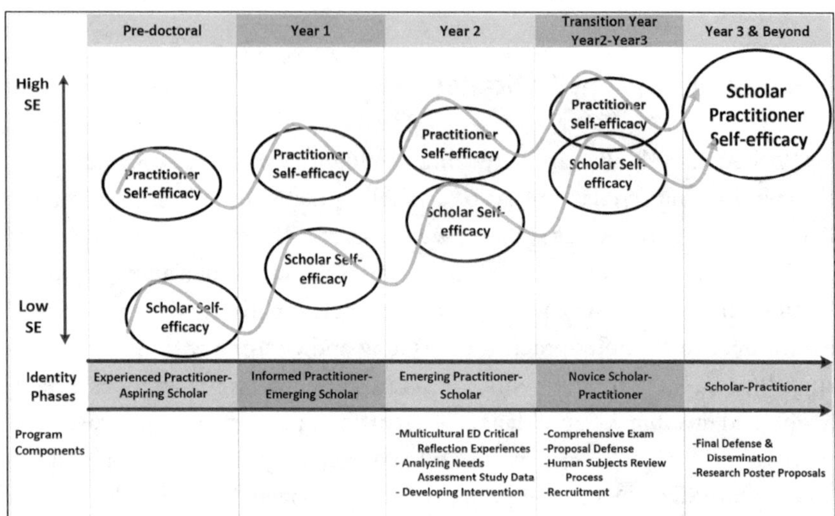

Note: This figure depicts the circuitous nature of the scholar-practitioner self-efficacy as it blends and increases across the different phases of students' identity transformation within the JHU EdD program.

for water and ready to sprout. Each of these metaphors represents the maturity of the doctoral students as practitioners who felt confident about their practice and were poised for the next stage of growth. Most of the authors described this stage in terms of advocacy for students, for teachers, or for more equitable practices. For example, one author mentioned that she was a "fighter for equal academic access" and another mentioned that her identity had evolved as "an advocate for children with diverse learning needs." These authors were working toward greater equity in their workplaces and more effective educational practices on behalf of underserved populations.

Many authors mentioned that they realized that they needed more knowledge to move their work forward even though they already identified as lifelong learners and advocates. One author illustrated this realization when he stated, "I had a sense that my identity needed to evolve and expand to serve my students and their families to the best of my ability." Another author echoed this same sentiment, saying, "My passive engagement in issues of social justice would no longer suffice; I could no longer be a seed simply waiting for some rain." These authors described a realization that they needed a formal program to grow into the practitioners that they desired to be.

Informed Practitioner-Emerging Scholar

During the first year of the doctoral program, the authors transitioned to the identity of *informed practitioner-emerging scholar* through reflections on research and theory, engaging in course activities, and better understanding their POPs through exploring a variety of factors and conducting a needs assessment study. This identity stage is characterized by the authors' recognition that they were both learner and practitioner, and that to become a scholar, they needed to adopt a deeper learning posture. Their initial decreases in self-confidence and self-efficacy were primarily related to self-doubt and an unsettling change in their confidence in their knowledge. This unsettling process occurred through exposure to many bodies of literature and new systems frameworks in the courses, which allowed them to understand their professional contexts differently. One author illustrated this shift in identity by sharing, "Instead of seeing myself as an inventive educator, I now recognized that I was an effective and engaging teacher. I still needed, however, to understand how to guide teachers effectively to enact instructional change." This author described his awareness that he did not yet possess all the knowledge needed to help others learn. Another author confirmed this same unsteadiness through her reflection,

> As I look back at myself as an educator and leader, I realized I worked so hard without a clear understanding of how individuals acquire, categorize, and maintain new learning. I understood research but needed to understand how to evaluate research critically and thoroughly.

Both these authors and many others realized that despite being experienced and informed practitioners, they needed to adopt learner postures and identities to move to the next level of professional growth.

This new awareness of their need for more knowledge was likely linked with their experiences of imposter syndrome. Several authors expressed initially feeling doubt about whether they belonged in the EdD program. This experience of dissonance often caused cognitive friction for authors, which is illustrated by the following quotation from one author:

> The absence of belonging and the presence of imposter syndrome were evident when I wrote my first discussion board post for a course assignment. I spent more than 2 hours drafting that 250-word online reflection. The fear of making mistakes, sounding less knowledgeable than my peers, and writing a post that revealed that I didn't belong in this community of scholars loomed large. I seemed only to be able to parrot others' voices, restating their research but not able to reflect critically on their work.

Like others within this book, this author's experiences of low sense of self-efficacy and self-doubt were coupled with an awareness of a need for more knowledge. We assert that understanding the limitations in their knowledge and knowing how to learn can allow scholar-practitioners to become effective change agents in their contexts. To be a scholar, one must also be a humble learner. We use the word *humble* to convey a sense of awareness about the vast worlds of knowledge available in print and in our CoPs.

Emerging Practitioner-Scholar

The *emerging practitioner-scholar* identity phase represents an empowerment period where doctoral students experience a surge in their self-efficacy as both practitioners and scholars. The synthesis of their knowledge while working in practice allowed the doctoral students to emerge in their professional contexts as leaders, catalyzers, social justice advocates, and systems disrupters. Not only did they develop these identities within the EdD program, but their colleagues from their professional contexts and organizations started interacting with them differently. They were no longer seen by their colleagues as students but as innovative leaders and contributors. The authors were perceived differently because they engaged with their professional partners in new ways, using their research-based insights and approaches to practice. For example, one author stated,

> I was beginning to see myself less as a teacher and instructional coach
> and more as an instructional leader, someone who could support and
> inspire change, build effective relationships, and help make decisions
> that supported both students and teachers to perform at their best.

Propelled by their knowledge, experiences, new roles, and ways of practicing in their organizations, the authors' new identities allowed them to partner more deeply with their colleagues and to lead and advocate better for those who needed it most. Many authors shared these sentiments of transitioning to contributors and leaders in their organizations. Their newfound identities as emerging practitioner-scholars afforded them a different level of regard and openness from their colleagues. This new openness from colleagues led one author to reflect, "I began to see myself as someone who could effect positive changes in my colleagues by imparting what I had learned." These new shifts allowed the authors not only to change their personal practices, but also to begin to positively share their new knowledge within their organizations for a greater impact.

Furthermore, these new emerging practitioner-scholars began to purposefully engage in their work of advocacy for underserved populations and nuanced problems during this phase. One author identified that she "needed to grow as an anti-racist and actively disrupt at a systems level." The authors described that this stage was one of growing awareness of problems that were caused by systems-level factors, and that they possessed the knowledge, skills, and positions to influence these systems. One author illustrated this point by saying:

> I saw myself as an entrepreneur for social justice, having a powerful
> force in changing social norms and applying efficient and positive
> solutions to improve my community. As a social entrepreneur, I initiate change and deliver services on a large scale to address the issue
> of accessibility and improve the quality of services given to Egyptian
> students with diverse learning needs.

Like many of the authors, this author used her position, knowledge, and relationships within her organization to begin to disrupt systems of injustice. Further, the authors' organizations welcomed these changes because the improvements grew out of ideas and partnerships from within the organization. The authors were change agents *and* organizational insiders who were creating the change from the inside out.

Novice Scholar-Practitioner

Later in the doctoral journey, an identity transition occurred that shifted the emerging practitioner-scholars to *novice scholar-practitioners*. This signifies the authors' embracing their identity of scholar as equal to their practitioner identity. Their self-efficacy in their abilities to consume, conduct, and communicate research had increased. We describe this identity stage as the melding and fusing of both the researcher identity and the professional identity. These authors described this last leg of their doctoral journey in two major ways: they became research-policy contributors in their fields and social justice change makers.

As research contributors and policymakers, the authors described how they could no longer see their professional problems without consulting the literature, considering multiple factors at all system levels, and exploring data to inform their understanding. One author asserted that she saw herself "as a confident and capable scholar who was ready to take on new challenges and make a difference in my field." These reflections reveal how the authors no longer limited their impact to their contexts but felt compelled to help their fields improve. Another author noted that she "became a person who valued policy and leading policy change from an equity perspective." They approached this policy work with an eye on the research and an anchor in social justice.

Additionally, by this stage, the authors placed an emphasis on elevating the needs of the most vulnerable community members through their advocacy work. One author reflected that her identity of a "social-justice defender and scholar-practitioner . . . signified a commitment to [her] own continued learning to utilize [her] practice in the advocacy of those experiencing oppression in any form." This quotation illustrates the sentiment that even as the authors grew in their self-efficacy for research-informed practice, they still strongly identified as humble learners in an ever-changing world of knowledge of self and knowledge of systems of oppression and injustice.

Understanding the research and having strong findings from their context cemented these alums' commitment to use research findings to illuminate and combat injustices for students from diverse backgrounds. This type of social justice leadership emerged from many authors as their novice scholar-practitioner identities emerged. Their chapters tell the stories of these newly integrated identities and how they used these identities to inspire and enact liberatory and emancipatory changes in their professional contexts to ensure that minoritized and underserved populations would be recognized. Further, they committed to seeing that the systems' problems be elucidated, addressed, and in some cases, dismantled. They became social justice defenders and equity change makers.

Defining a Scholar-Practitioner: In Their Own Words

In Chapter 1 we defined *scholar-practitioners* as individuals who rely on and value research at the forefront of thinking about and changing their practice in conjunction with knowledge and traditions built from years of practice. As authors within this volume described their transformation from experienced practitioner-aspiring scholar to scholar-practitioner their words provided deeper meaning of this definition. Their characterizations of scholar-practitioners were represented by three themes; they (a) were no longer stymied by "solutionitis," (b) collaborated to facilitate change, and (c) saw themselves as contributors to the body of educational research.

As scholar-practitioners, the authors in this volume reported feeling efficacious in their ability to diagnose why a problem existed within their educational context. As such, they no longer felt compelled to prematurely identify solutions to problems. Instead, they relied on research and empirical evidence to understand the underlying contributing factors. One author stated, "I am now more likely to conduct a review of extant literature prior to articulating a problem or solution." Another author who was a principal was dealing with a wicked problem, the achievement gap. She stated, "I worked to ensure that my collective school faculty was focused on eliminating academic disparities between student subgroups and understand why they exist, versus simply responding to a goal that I, as a principal, directed them to do." In this example, she was not only investigating problems using the approaches learned from the program but also leading her faculty to engage in a more productive approach to problem-solving. In another example, an author noted the importance of seeing the system in which the problem operates. He stated, "[G]reat leaders must be able to search the literature to develop an understanding of the interconnected factors that may contribute to a present issue so that they can see the system." These examples shed light on the importance of thoughtful examinations of problems through the contributing factors and the systems within which they operate to fully understand why a problem exists, its salient contributors, whom it impacts, and its instigators, to name a few. In these examples, research is central to guiding practice and addressing educational problems.

The scholar-practitioners within this volume have acknowledged the role of collaboration to facilitate change. This manifestation of the improvement science principle, networked communities (Bryk et al., 2015) within the program and among their colleagues, demonstrates an understanding that problems are not addressed in isolation. One author stated,

> I know that I do not have all the answers, but I know what good answers look like. I know how to read research with a discerning lens, question policy, analyze data, articulate implications, formulate new questions, and advocate for change. I have developed a broad and deep network of highly qualified colleagues with whom I partner to do this work.

In this example, the author has revealed the intentionality of collaboration with professional partners and the reliance on skills gained from the program to impact change.

Finally, as scholar-practitioners, the authors perceived themselves as contributors to their field within both their professional practice and the broader research community. In two examples, authors acknowledged that their identity transformation supported their desire to make an impact within their sphere of influence. One author stated, "I began to see myself not just as a student, but as a researcher with the potential to make a meaningful contribution to my field," while the other author stated, "I now see myself as someone who can help people think differently, in beneficial ways."

Further, authors stated feeling efficacious in contributing to the field. In one example an author wrote,

> As I look back at myself as an educator and leader, I realize I worked so hard without a clear understanding of how individuals acquire,

categorize, and maintain new learning. I understood research but needed to understand how to evaluate research critically and thoroughly. I now see myself as a contributor to that research, a scholar-practitioner.

These examples shed light on the important role of the program's influence on the scholar-practitioner identity as a contributor to educational practice and scholarship. The authors' words have extended the program's definition of the scholar-practitioner from one who values research prior to changing practice and uses traditions built from years of practice to one who can also contribute to research knowledge.

Identity Change and Impact on the Professional Context

The impact of students' identity transformation on their professional contexts revealed that as they shifted from expert practitioners to scholar-practitioners, they expanded their knowledge and skills by modeling and reflecting on practices and applying their learning to diverse situations. Contributing authors within this volume promoted their knowledge and skills within and beyond their contexts as scholar-practitioners. Several authors noted how their knowledge of improvement science guided their pathway to addressing problems of practice within their contexts. One author stated:

> We collaborated to improve the internal process and communication as we were able to systematically examine the school environment through daily reflection meetings and class observation. These activities were a key strategy to develop actionable and efficient solutions to our everyday issues at school, guided by the applied research and theories I studied at JHU. I showcased how to apply improvement science at Egyptian schools.

In this example, sharing and applying improvement science within their contexts stemmed from valuing its contribution to approaching, understanding, and addressing POPs. Students also transferred their knowledge to diverse situations, both personal and professional. One contributing author explained:

> My professional and personal identities are inextricably linked rings
> and branches on the same tree, sprung from the same roots. As such,
> I find myself continuing to integrate lessons learned in the program
> into my personal identity. I bring a systems-thinking understanding
> to politics, societal challenges, and misunderstandings in my own life.
> I continue to use insight gained in those early courses to maintain a
> practice of self-reflexivity, especially as it pertains to power and priv-
> ilege dynamics.

This statement effectively captures the commingling of identities, how the EdD
program influences both professional and personal identities, and how knowledge transfer influences thinking across both.

The propagation of knowledge also meant that as scholar-practitioners, authors felt the need to spread their knowledge to influence larger contexts and
to reach beyond their context. One alum stated:

> As I grew in that organization and through my studies, I gained con-
> fidence. I looked for ways to apply my learning to an even broader
> context. Now, I am effecting change rooted in the same pillars in a
> larger context as the director of professional development for VAIS
> [the Virginia Association of Independent Schools]. In this role, my
> contextual reach has grown to 95 member schools, 6500-plus educa-
> tors, and more than 40,000 students.

Another alumni author stated:

> I came to feel the desire to share the knowledge and expertise I gained
> through my doctoral experience with a broader audience. Seeing my-
> self as honor-bound, to date I have discharged this responsibility in
> two ways: as an adjunct instructor teaching with a local university and
> through participating as part of a state standards development and
> revision committee. Both experiences required me to reach outside
> of myself and my primary professional context.

As authors gained confidence in their scholar-practitioner identities, they used
opportunities to spread knowledge learned from the program. In doing so, they
reached larger audiences and transferred their learning across their identities.

Conclusion

At the time of this writing, the JHU EdD program was continuing to shift and change. This book and the stories within are a record of what happened in a specific time period. As we in higher education know, university programs adapt, morph, and, yes, even transform. But what we still hold true is that students' identity change is the game changer that comes from personal and professional transformations that we can nurture by well-thought-out and sequenced programmatic decisions.

The JHU EdD program was crafted to foster the scholar-practitioner identity. While the phases of identity transformation were not clearly delineated at the inception of the program, each alum's chapter provides a compelling story of change, the program components that facilitated that change, and the impact it had on the alum's personal and professional identities and contexts. If you are a current EdD student reading this book, it is our hope that these chapters contribute to your scholar-practitioner identity alongside your current program of study. We believe that the potential commonalities between your journey and the contributing authors of this book can be an encouragement. Further, if you are current EdD faculty designing or reconceptualizing your program or courses, we anticipate that the ideas in this book will cement the importance of students' identity transformations and possibly inform changes within your program. We leave our readers with this quote from American poet Amanda Gorman, which illustrates to us that, as scholar-practitioners, paving the path to improving educational problems will take intentional and systematic action, rooted in scholarly knowledge. To do so, we must bravely and willingly shed old identities for new ones—a process that is both comfortable and uncomfortable at times. In doing so people, communities, and systems are transformed.

> *The only way to correctly predict*
> *The future is to pave it,*
> *Is to brave it.*
>
> —AMANDA GORMAN, "AUGURY OR THE BIRDS"

References

Brabazon, T. (2016). Winter is coming: Doctoral supervision in the neoliberal university. *International Journal of Social Sciences & Educational Studies, 3*(1), 14–34. https://doaj.org/article/34fd1496d40a4d68b3981235bbe65fd1

Bryk, A. S., Gomez, L., Grunow, A., & LeMahieu, P. (2015). *Learning to improve: How America's schools can get better at getting better.* Harvard Education Press.

Gorman, A. (2021). "Augury or the birds." In *Call us what we carry: Poems* (p. 176). Viking Books.

Mezirow, J. (1997). Transformative learning: Theory to practice. *New Directions for Adult and Continuing Education, 74,* 5–12. https://doi.org/10.1002/ace.7401

Editor Biographies

Stephen J. Pape is professor of Education at Johns Hopkins University (JHU) where he was the founding Director of the Doctor of Education program (2013–2019). He earned his doctorate in Educational Psychology from the City University of New York. Previously, he taught middle school mathematics and science in New York City public schools and served as assistant and associate Professor of Mathematics Education at The Ohio State University and University of Florida. His research focuses on online learning environments, technology-enhanced classroom contexts that foster mathematical understanding, and the development of strategic behaviors. To support this research, he has provided professional development for mathematics and science teachers across elementary, secondary, and Community College levels for over 20 years. Funded projects include a national randomized control trial that examined the impact of classroom connectivity technology on Algebra I achievement and classroom interactions and *Prime* Online, an online professional development program for grades 3–5 general and special educators. He was the co-principal investigator for *Florida Promise,* a statewide professional development program for preK–12 science and mathematics teachers. He recently served on the Association of Mathematics Teacher Educators taskforce, *Re-thinking Teaching and Learning: Unpacking Mathematics Education Online* and has published over 60 peer-reviewed articles and book chapters, and conference proceedings papers.

Camille L. Bryant is an associate professor in the School of Education at Johns Hopkins University who teaches research methods courses. She is the former Research Methods Coordinator and Director of the Doctor of Education program. As an education research methodologist, she focuses on program evaluation, intervention research, mixed methodologies, instrument development, and approaches to support graduate students' research methods knowledge acquisition and self-efficacy. Her most recent research interest aims to (a) better understand the role of embodied pedagogy on mitigating students' research methods apprehension and anxiety, and (b) support students' competencies as they engage with and conduct socially responsible research.

Ranjini Mahinda JohnBull, PhD is an assistant professor at Johns Hopkins University School of Education serving as the faculty lead for the Mind, Brain, and Teaching program area and teaching in the doctoral and masters programs. Her research focuses on teacher self-efficacy, cultural competence and multicultural identity development, and arts-integration and culturally relevant neuroeducation interventions that improve teacher and student outcomes. Dr. JohnBull earned a BA from Washington University in St. Louis, an MEd and PhD in Education Leadership both from University of Virginia's School of Education and Human Development. Prior to her appointment as an assistant professor, she served as a postdoctoral research fellow at JHU SOE working on an IES-funded study of student memory in arts-integrated science classrooms. Prior to JHU, Dr. JohnBull served as a U.S. Peace Corps Volunteer in rural eastern Uganda to collaboratively support and enhance education, health, and finance projects. Before Peace Corps Uganda, she was a music teacher in two St. Louis city charter elementary and middle schools.

Karen S. Karp is a professor in the School of Education at Johns Hopkins University. Previously, she was a distinguished teaching professor of elementary mathematics education at the University of Louisville where she is now professor emeritus. Her scholarship focuses on the intersection of mathematics education and special education. She is the author or co-author of many book chapters, articles, and books, including the recent U.S. Department of Education Institute of Science's *What Works Clearinghouse Practice Guide on Assisting Students Struggling with Mathematics: Intervention in the Elementary Grades*, and other titles such as *Strengths-based Teaching and Learning in Mathematics: 5 Teaching Turnarounds for Grades K-6, The Math Pact: Achieving Instructional Coherence within and Across Grades*, and *Elementary and Middle School Mathematics: Teaching Developmentally* which has been translated into seven languages. Dr. Karp is a former member of the board of directors of the National Council of Teachers of Mathematics (NCTM) and a former president of the Association of Mathematics Teacher Educators. In 2020, she was selected for the NCTM Lifetime Achievement Award for Distinguished Service to Mathematics Education. She also is a member of the U.S. National Commission on Mathematics Instruction and holds teaching/administrative certifications in elementary education, secondary mathematics, K–12 special education, and educational administration.

Author Biographies

Kristin H. Barbour is the Executive Director of the National Institute for Learning Development, a 501(c)(3) educator training organization. Dr. Barbour completed her doctorate in the Mind, Brain, and Teaching specialization program at Johns Hopkins University. Her dissertation focused on developing educational therapists' knowledge, self-efficacy, and instructional practices related to developing a growth mindset in students with learning disabilities. Kristin has served as an educational leader in various settings including school boards, K–12 schools, and higher education. For over 20 years, Kristin has provided national and international educational workshops on research-based instructional practices to develop students' thinking and learning abilities.

Dr. Teresa Caswell is Senior Director of the Office of Equity Affairs within the Wake County Public School System and an adjunct professor in the School of Education at Johns Hopkins University (JHU). Dr. Caswell earned her doctorate from JHU (2021) with research focused on integrating critical reflection into equity- and identity-focused professional learning to decrease implicit bias. Dr. Caswell's current research-to-practice interests include integrating identity-development with teacher instructional practices to positively impact student outcomes. Dr. Caswell's professional background includes K–12 art education, post-secondary art history, and the integration of both into projects using learning-science strategies to support student achievement.

Paula L. Clark is a mathematics educator, mentor, and department chair at Eastlake North High School. She received her doctorate in education with a specialization in Mind, Brain, and Teaching from Johns Hopkins University. Her research interests include mathematics accessibility for all learners and the professional development of mathematics educators. She is a member of the National Council of Teachers of Mathematics and the Ohio Council of Teachers of Mathematics and has presented at national conferences on the topic of meaningful mathematics experiences for students who learn differently. Paula co-authored *Decimals, fractions, and percents: Student workbook* for the National Institute for Learning Development.

Crystal Downs is the Academic Dean and PK12 Instructional Lead Teacher for an Atlanta area independent Christian school and an adjunct professor at Johns Hopkins University. Her passions focus on supporting instructional process for diverse learners. Dr. Downs has over 15 years of speech language pathology experience and helped launch an elementary academic support program prior to holding several PK12 administrative roles. A graduate from Johns Hopkins University's Doctor of Education program, Crystal received the 2023 Student Excellence Award for Mind, Brain, and Teaching specialization. Her dissertation research analyzed the professional learning process for culturally responsive practices within a PK12 academic setting.

Soha R. Elzalabany is a passionate K–12 educator and school principal, instructor, and researcher in Egypt. Elzalabany has been teaching courses at the American University in Cairo (AUC) related to best practices, differentiation, and academic diversity for teachers and administrators. Also, she has been a member of the curriculum designing and reviewing committees at AUC and a member of the Teacher Education Paper Committee at the World Council for Gifted and Talented Children. Dr. Elzalabany received several local and international scholarships to support her postgraduate education and has presented cases of building the inclusive capacity of general educators and leadership at several national, regional, and international conferences. Her doctoral studies focused on developing school teachers, leadership, and organizing systems to include all students in general education settings.

Razia F. Kosi is an adjunct professor in the School of Education at Johns Hopkins University and the Coordinator of Culturally Responsive Practices and Anti-Racism Development for a diverse PreK-12 public school system. Her work focuses on cultural proficiency, equity, inclusion, and social justice and her recent scholarship includes a chapter in *Counseling and Psychotherapy for South Asian Americans*, titled *Considerations for South Asian Parenting*. Additionally, she leads policy change at the state and local level for education equity. Dr. Kosi is also a mental health professional serving on executive boards for AAPI communities. Dr. Kosi is a co-founder and current president of the Asian American Educators of Howard County. Her awards include the Society of Excellence for Doctorate of Education (2021) and The Edward F. Pajak Award (2023) from Johns Hopkins University.

Dr. Lara Ohanian is a Partner with The New Teacher Project (TNTP). In this role, she leads the development of new services and perspectives for TNTP to ensure they can develop new approaches and ideas. Before this role, she was the Director at Baltimore City Schools, supporting the continuum of learners. Her doctoral work focused on the Science of Learning, with a deep dive into practices designed to help Multilingual learners. In addition, Lara is an adjunct professor at the Johns Hopkins School of Education. Lara lives outside Baltimore with her husband and son.

Amanda L. Palmer is a special education teacher serving learners 6-21; Diversity, Equity, Inclusion, and Belonging practitioner; and Instructional Coach at the Lab School of Washington. Dr. Palmer is the founder and CEO of Palmer Educational Services, LLC, through which she supports schools, organizations, and individuals as they develop their culturally responsive and inclusive practices. She provides academic services and professional learning to students of all ages through a brain-based approach that values neurodiversity. Her scholarship focuses on increasing the use of culturally responsive teaching practices, with a focus on practitioner reflexivity.

Stephanie Scholes is the Teacher of Students with Visual Impairments (TVI) for preschool in Granite School District, a large school district in Utah. She also works as a preschool special educator, and as the preschool 504 coordinator in the same district. She is an adjunct instructor at the University of Utah. Her paper, *Building Emergent Literacy for Preschool Children with Visual Impairments Through Individualized Shared Storybook Reading*, was selected for the poster session at the American Educational Research Association Annual Meeting in 2020. She is a member of the workgroup currently rewriting the Utah Braille Core Standards.

Rachna Shah currently serves as the Program Coordinator for the Post Graduate Diploma in Learning and Teaching at *I Am a Teacher*, an organization dedicated to teacher education. In addition, she provides private counselling services to children and adults. Previously, Dr. Shah worked as an Instructional Coach at The Bombay International School, where she supported teachers in developing research-based instructional strategies to enhance teaching and learning and improve student achievement. She has also held roles as the

Language Program Coordinator and Outreach Program Manager at The Gateway School of Mumbai, a private non-profit school for children with learning difficulties. Rachna has organized parent support groups and conducted workshops for children and educators, and she shares her insights and experiences through her blog. Rachna holds an EdD in Education from Johns Hopkins University, USA, a master's degree in Clinical Psychology from S.N.D.T. University, Mumbai, and Postgraduate Diplomas in Counselling Psychology and Dyslexia and Literacy.

Joshua Pinto Taylor is the Executive Director at The Anchor School, a public middle and high school in Georgia. Previously, he was an award-winning educator and educational leader. His scholarship focuses on the intersection of school, community development, and neighborhood planning. He is interested in how strategic relationships at all levels of our social ecosystem impact human and community development. He earned a master's degree in Urban Planning and Public Policy from the University of Illinois – Chicago and a Doctor of Education from Johns Hopkins University. In his research, Dr. Pinto Taylor has explored the role of schools as anchoring institutions in neighborhoods, the impact of teacher retention on learning communities, and the impact of participatory planning practices in the school design and improvement processes on student and family experiences at school. His goal as an educator and planner is to create the conditions for inclusive and transparent planning practices in school design and improvement processes. He lives in Atlanta, GA with his wife and three children.

Darcie L. TeVault is Director of Professional Development for the Virginia Association of Independent Schools (VAIS) and adjunct faculty at Johns Hopkins University's School of Education. Previously, Dr. TeVault served as a Language Development Specialist and Assistant Director for Teaching and Learning at an independent day school. Her scholarship focuses on the interrelatedness of teacher self-efficacy, collective teacher efficacy, and pedagogy in the independent school context. Darcie has experience in successful grant writing and an understanding of sound governance practices through the lens of her multiple roles. She earned a Bachelor's degree in elementary and special-education from Salve Regina University and both a Master's and Doctor of Education from Johns Hopkins University.

Earl Turner III, Senior Researcher for Equity Research and Development at GoGuardian, has had a career dedicated to fostering equity in K–12 schools. Having climbed the ranks from an Associate Efficacy Researcher, Dr. Turner's accomplishments include the development of a research platform for real-time analysis of student digital behavior and actualizing the innovation program, Giant Steps, where he served as a founding member and associate consultant for the 12-member team. He has been a Lead Author and Principal Investigator on six large-scale research studies. Earl has dedicated his expertise to building social impact in education policy across Los Angeles. He was a key figure in the establishment of the restorative justice organization, Angelenos Organizing for Education (AO4E). Among his accomplishments, Turner holds dear his role in reconstructing New Orleans post-Hurricane Katrina.

Robert Walker is currently Administrative Director of Instruction at Granada Hills Charter High School, one of the largest charter schools in the nation. A National Board Certified Teacher, he previously spent 18 years as a social studies teacher, including 7 years as an instructional coach, and was recognized as Teacher of the Year for his school three times. In 2014, he served as a fellow in the U.S. State Department's Teachers for the Global Classroom initiative. His research focuses on the intersection between pedagogy and technology.